David & C

Cross Stitch C

Tigers

Contents

A DAVID & CHARLES BOOK

First published in the UK in 2004

Distributed in North America by F&W Publications, Inc.
4700 East Galbraith Road
Cincinnati, OH 45236
1-800-289-0963

A catalogue record for this book is available from the British Library.

ISBN 0 7153 1759 8

Printed in Singapore by KHL for David & Charles
Brunel House Newton Abbot Devon

Walking Tiger

Tiger Portrait
© Jayne Netley Mayhew

Tiger in the Lake
© Jill Gordon

Walking Tiger – chart 1

Walking Tiger

DMC STRANDED COTTON

Cross stitch

472	738
471	758
470	712
469	3033
937	3032
935	938
367	300
368	301
369	435
839	437
841	white
842	310

Long stitch whiskers: 1 strand of white

WALKING TIGER

STITCH COUNT	128 x 188
DESIGN SIZE	23.2 x 34cm (9⅛ x 13⅓in)
FABRIC USED	Aida 14-count cream, over 1 block
THREADS USED	See key: 2 strands of stranded cotton (floss) for full and three-quarter cross stitch & 1 strand of white for long stitch whiskers (shown grey on chart)

PLAN OF CHARTS

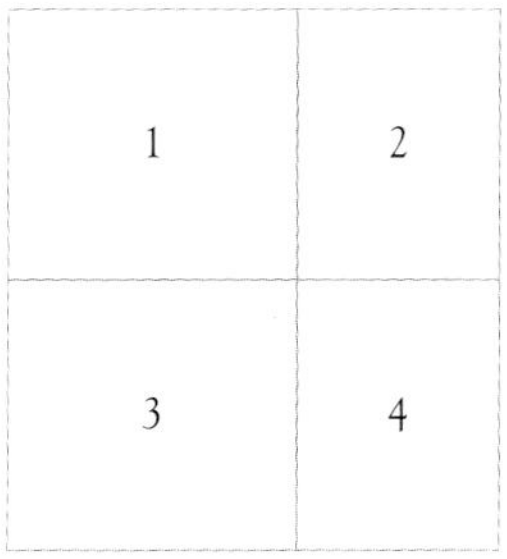

1	2
3	4

Walking Tiger – chart 2

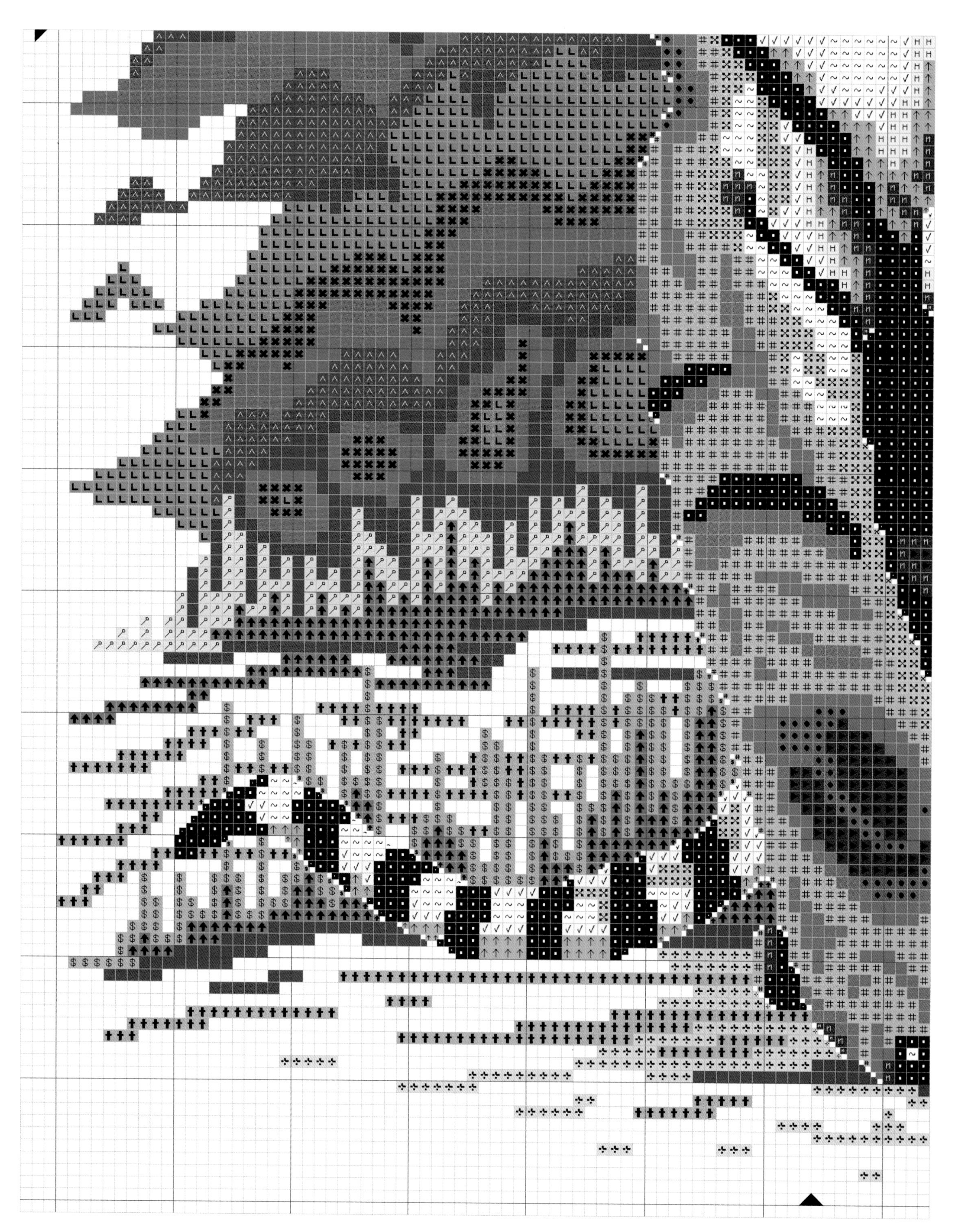

Walking Tiger – chart 3

Walking Tiger

DMC STRANDED COTTON

Cross stitch

472	738
471	758
470	712
469	3033
937	3032
935	938
367	300
368	301
369	435
839	437
841	white
842	310

Long stitch whiskers: 1 strand of white

PLAN OF CHARTS

1	2
3	4

Walking Tiger – chart 4

Tiger Portrait – chart 1

Tiger Portrait

DMC STRANDED COTTON

Cross stitch

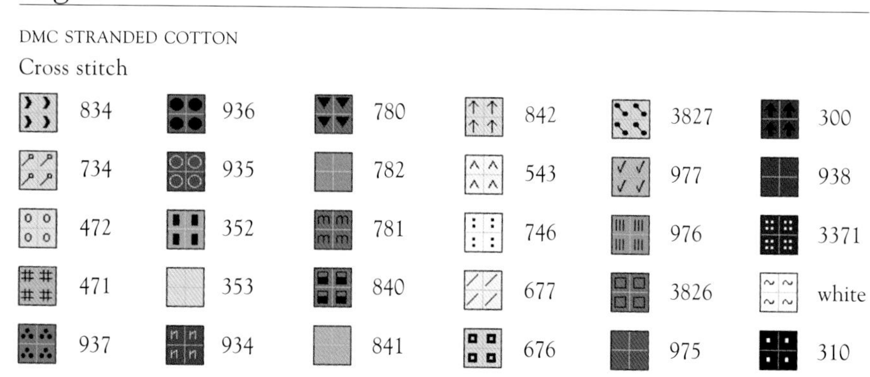

PLAN OF CHARTS

1	2
3	4

Tiger Portrait	
STITCH COUNT	190 x 178
DESIGN SIZE	34.4 x 32.3cm (13½ x 12¾in)
FABRIC USED	Aida 14-count summer khaki, over 1 block
THREADS USED	See key: 2 strands of stranded cotton (floss) for cross stitch

Tiger Portrait – chart 3

Tiger Portrait

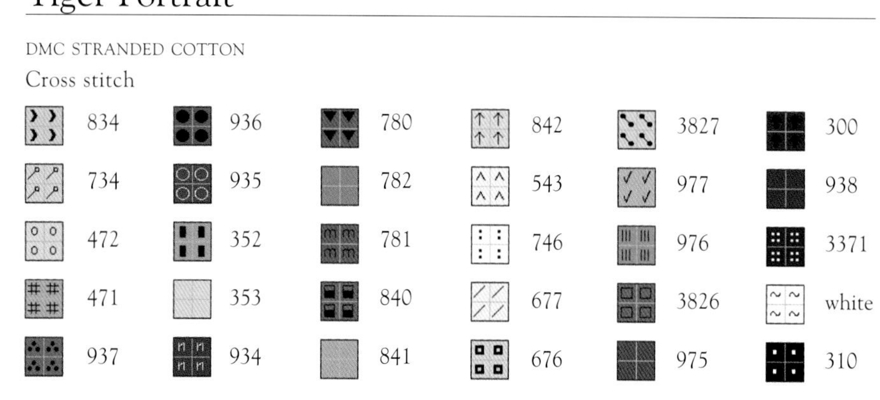

PLAN OF CHARTS

1	2
3	4

Tiger in the Lake

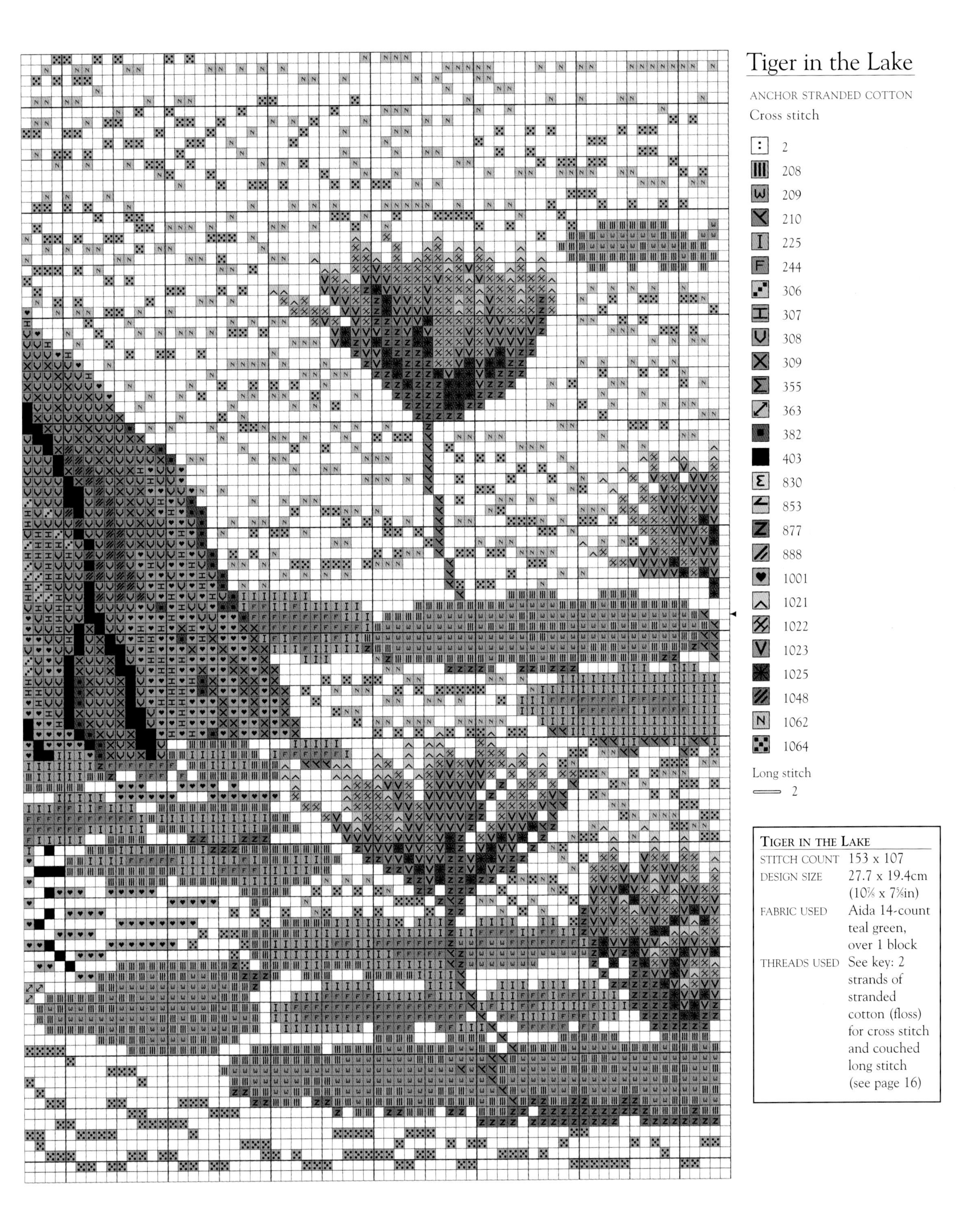

Tiger in the Lake

STITCH COUNT	153 x 107
DESIGN SIZE	27.7 x 19.4cm (10⅞ x 7⅝in)
FABRIC USED	Aida 14-count teal green, over 1 block
THREADS USED	See key: 2 strands of stranded cotton (floss) for cross stitch and couched long stitch (see page 16)

Stitching Advice

The following section is relevant throughout the David & Charles *Cross Stitch Collection* series, not just the charts in this book. It will provide you with all the information you need to stitch the designs charted.

MATERIALS

FABRICS

Fabrics used for counted cross stitch are woven so they have the same number of threads or blocks to 2.5cm (1in), both horizontally and vertically. The two main fabric types used are blockweaves such as Aida, and evenweaves such as linen. Cross stitch can also be worked on other fabrics such as waste canvas, plastic canvas and stitching (perforated) paper.

AIDAS These fabrics are woven in blocks and are available in many colours and counts – 8, 11, 14, 16, 18 and 20 blocks to 2.5cm (1in). They are made from various fibres and as different width bands. When stitching on Aida, one block on the fabric corresponds to one square on a chart and each cross stitch is worked over one block.

EVENWEAVES These fabrics are woven singly and are made from various fibres and as different width bands. They are also available in many different colours and counts. When stitching on evenweave, each cross stitch is usually worked over two threads of the fabric.

WASTE CANVAS This is designed for stitching on fabrics where cross stitching wouldn't normally be possible because the threads are uneven, such as clothing. To use, tack (baste) a piece of waste canvas large enough for the design into position on to the chosen article and cross stitch the design through both fabrics. When all stitching is complete, dampen the canvas and use tweezers to draw out the threads. You may find it easier to work backstitches after the canvas has been removed.

PLASTIC CANVAS This is a rigid but flexible mesh-like material that can be cut and assembled into three-dimensional objects. It is available in various counts and as pre-cut shapes. Cross stitches are worked over intersections of the mesh.

STITCHING PAPER Cross stitch designs can be worked on perforated paper which can then be cut, folded and glued to make a variety of items such as cards, bookmarks and notebook covers. The right side is the smoother side of the paper and cross stitch is normally worked with three strands of stranded cotton (floss) and backstitch with two.

THREADS

The most commonly used thread for counted embroidery is stranded cotton (floss) but there are many other types available, including rayons, space-dyed or variegated threads, perlé cottons and metallic threads.

STRANDED COTTON (FLOSS) This six-stranded thread can be bought by the skein in hundreds of colours with ranges made by DMC, Anchor and Madeira (see DMC/Anchor conversion chart at the front of this book). Colours can be mixed or 'tweeded' in the needle. The stitching information with the charts will tell you how many strands to use for a design.

VARIEGATED THREADS There are many lovely variegated threads available now. The chart keys give the name and code of the thread used. When stitching with variegated threads work cross stitches as complete stitches, not in two journeys or the colour sequence will be spoiled.

METALLICS AND BLENDING FILAMENTS Metallic threads are available in many gorgeous colours and finishes from various companies and they can be used in cross stitch designs to create glitter and interest. Blending filaments can be stitched with stranded cotton (floss) to create an overall sparkle to a design. Use shorter lengths of thread when working with metallics to avoid tangles and excessive wear on the thread.

TAPESTRY WOOL (YARN) Many cross stitch designs can be stitched on canvas in tapestry wool (yarn) instead of stranded cotton (floss), using half cross stitch or tent stitch instead of cross stitch. Ask at needlework shops for suppliers and colour conversions from stranded cotton (floss).

EQUIPMENT

Very little equipment is needed for cross stitch embroidery and the following basics are all you need to get you started.

NEEDLES Use blunt tapestry needles for counted cross stitch. The commonest sizes used are 24 and 26 but the size depends on your project and personal preference. Avoid leaving a needle in the fabric unless it is gold plated or it may cause marks. A beading needle (or fine 'sharp' needle), which is much thinner, will be needed to attach beads.

SCISSORS Use dressmaker's shears for cutting fabric and a small, sharp pair of pointed scissors for cutting embroidery threads.

FRAMES AND HOOPS These are not essential but if you use one, choose one large enough to hold the complete design, to avoid marking the fabric and flattening stitches.

TECHNIQUES

USING CHARTS

The designs in this series are worked from black and white charts with symbols, or colour charts with a black and/or white symbol to aid colour identification. Each square, both occupied and unoccupied, represents one block of Aida or two threads of linen, unless stated otherwise. Each occupied square equals one cross stitch. Some charts also have three-quarter cross stitches (sometimes called fractional stitches) and these usually occupy part of a square, either a triangle or a small square. French knots are indicated by circles, usually coloured in the colour charts and labelled in the key or on the chart. Backstitch (and sometimes long stitch) is shown on charts by straight lines, usually coloured in the colour charts, with the code either on the chart or in the key. Arrows at the sides of the charts allow you to find the centre easily.

CALCULATING DESIGN SIZE

Each project gives the stitch count and finished design size but if you plan to work the design on a different count you will need to be able to calculate the finished size. To do this, count the number of stitches in the design and divide this by the fabric count number, e.g., 140 stitches x 140 stitches ÷ by 14-count = a design size of 10 x 10in (25.4 x 25.4cm). Remember that working on evenweave usually means working over two threads not one, so divide the fabric count by 2 before you start. See the bottom of page 15 for a quick stitch count table.

PREPARING FABRICS

The sizes given with the charts are for the finished design size only, therefore you will need to add about 10–12.5cm (4–5in) to both measurements when cutting embroidery fabric, to allow enough fabric around the edges for working and for making up later.

Before you begin stitching, press your embroidery fabric if necessary and trim the selvage or any rough edges. Work from the middle of the fabric and middle of the chart where possible to ensure your design is centred on the fabric. Find the middle of the fabric by folding it in four and pressing lightly. Mark the folds with tailor's chalk or with lines of tacking (basting) following a fabric thread. When working with linen, prepare as described above but also sew a narrow hem around all raw edges to preserve them for finishing later.

STARTING AND FINISHING STITCHING

Unless indicated otherwise, begin stitching in the middle of a design to ensure an adequate margin for making up. Start and finish stitching neatly, avoiding knots which create a lumps.

KNOTLESS LOOP START This start can be used with an even number of strands i.e., 2, 4 or 6. To stitch with two strands, begin with one strand about 80cm (30in). Double the thread and thread the needle with the two ends. Put the needle up through the fabric from the wrong side, where you intend to begin stitching, leaving the loop at the back (see diagram top of page 15). Form a half cross stitch, put the needle back through the fabric and through the waiting loop to anchor the stitch.

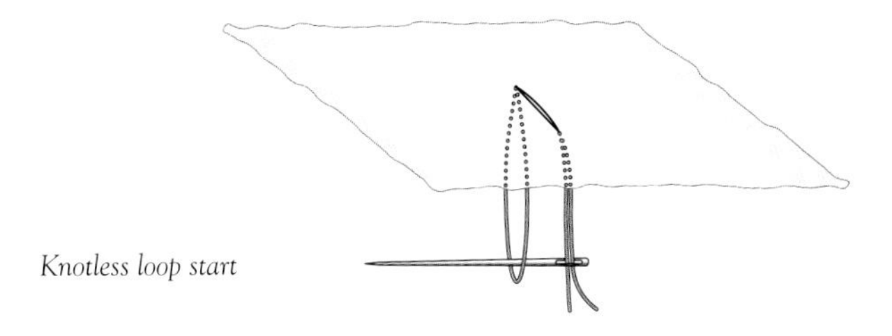

Knotless loop start

AWAY WASTE KNOT START Start this way if using an odd number of strands. Thread the needle with the number of strands required and knot the end. Insert the needle into the right side of the fabric, away from where you wish to begin stitching (see diagram below). Stitch towards the knot and cut it off when the threads are anchored. Alternatively, snip off the knot, thread a needle and work under a few stitches to anchor.

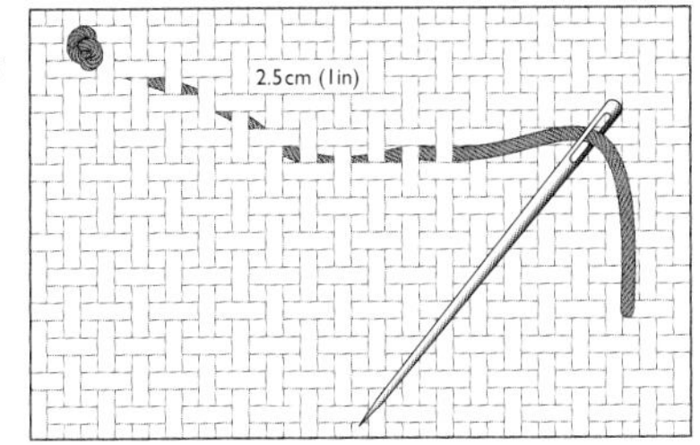

Away waste knot start

FINISHING STITCHING At the back of the work, pass the needle and thread under several stitches and snip off the loose end close to the stitching. Begin new colours by passing through stitches on the back in a similar way.

Number of Strands

Stranded cotton (floss) is available in six-stranded skeins and different numbers of strands will be needed for use on different gauges of fabric. Generally two strands are used for cross stitch and one for backstitch but the following table gives further advice.

How Many Strands?

FABRIC	NUMBER OF STRANDS OF STRANDED COTTON
6-count Aida	6 or 8 for cross stitch, 2 for backstitch
8-count Aida	6 for cross stitch, 2 for backstitch
11-count Aida & 22-count evenweave (over 2 threads)	3 for cross stitch, 1 for backstitch
14-count Aida & 28-count evenweave (over 2 threads)	2 or 3 for cross stitch, 1 for backstitch
16-count Aida & 32-count evenweave (over 2 threads)	2 for cross stitch, 1 for backstitch
18-count Aida & 36-count evenweave (over 2 threads)	1 or 2 for cross stitch, 1 for backstitch

Blending Threads

Many threads can be used together in the needle to create new colour combinations or to add the shine and glitter of metallic threads such as blending filament. Simply thread the needle with both threads, usually one strand of each, and stitch as normal.

Changing Names and Dates

Some cross stitch designs feature names and dates or other wording which you will need to alter using the alphabet provided (or one of your own favourites). Before you begin to stitch, ensure the words will fit the space by counting the squares in the space available (width and height) and marking this on square graph paper. Pencil the letters or numbers on the graph paper, remembering the spaces between letters and words.

Attaching Beads, Charms and Buttons

Bead positions are shown on the charts as circles (coloured in the colour charts), with details of the bead type in the key. You might find using a frame or hoop is helpful to keep the fabric taut as you pull the thread firmly to keep the beads in position. Attach beads using a beading needle or very fine 'sharp' needle, thread which matches the bead colour and a half cross stitch (or a full cross stitch if you prefer).

Charm and button positions are usually shown on the chart or described in the key or shown on the photograph of the model. Attach charms and buttons with matching thread.

If you cannot find the beads, charms or buttons suggested on the charts simply substitute something else – there is a wealth to choose from nowadays.

Using Ribbon

Narrow ribbon can be used to create additional interest in a cross stitch design. It may be used to form stitches, such as simple straight stitches, lazy daisy stitch or detached chain stitch. It can also be couched flat on to the fabric and held in place with cross stitches or narrow straight stitches or beads. Ribbon can also be threaded through evenweave fabric after several threads have been removed to create a channel.

Tips for Perfect Stitching

- Organize your threads before you start a project as this will help to avoid confusion later. Always include the manufacturer's name and the shade number.
- Separate the strands on a skein of stranded cotton (floss) before taking the number you need to stitch with. Realign them before threading your needle.
- If using a frame, try to avoid a hoop as it will stretch the fabric and leave a mark that may be difficult to remove.
- Plan your route around a chart, counting over short distances wherever possible to avoid mistakes.
- Work your cross stitch in two directions in a sewing movement – half cross stitch in one direction and then cover those original stitches with the second row. This forms single vertical lines on the back that are very neat and give somewhere to finish raw ends. For neat work the top stitches should all face the same direction.
- If adding a backstitch outline, always add it after the cross stitch has been completed to prevent the solid line being broken.

Quick Stitch Counts (see Calculating Design Size, page 14)

	STITCH COUNT									
FABRIC	20	30	40	50	60	70	80	90	100	110
11-count Aida & 22-count evenweave	1¾in (4.6cm)	2¾in (7cm)	3½in (9.2cm)	4½in (11.5cm)	5½in (13.8cm)	6¼in (16cm)	7¼in (18.5cm)	8⅛in (20.7cm)	9in (23cm)	10in (25.4cm)
14-count Aida & 28-count evenweave	1½in (3.6cm)	2⅛in (5.4cm)	2¾in (7.2cm)	3½in (9cm)	4¼in (10.8cm)	5in (12.7cm)	5¾in (14.5cm)	6½in (16.3cm)	7⅛in (18cm)	7⅞in (20cm)
16-count Aida & 32-count evenweave	1¼in (3cm)	1¾in (4.8cm)	2½in (6.3cm)	3⅛in (8cm)	3¾in (9.5cm)	4¼in (11cm)	5in (12.7cm)	5½in (14.3cm)	6¼in (16cm)	6¾in (17.4cm)
18-count Aida & 36-count evenweave	1⅛in (2.8cm)	1½in (4.2cm)	2¼in (5.6cm)	2¾in (7cm)	3⅜in (8.5cm)	3¾in (9.8cm)	4½in (11.3cm)	5in (12.7cm)	5½in (14cm)	6⅛in (15.5cm)

THE STITCHES

Algerian Eye

This star-shaped stitch is a pulled stitch which creates 'holes' in the fabric. It can be worked over two or four threads of evenweave and is more successful on evenweave than Aida.

Start to the left of a vertical thread and work from left to right around each stitch in an anticlockwise direction (or vice versa but keeping each stitch the same). Pass the needle down through the central hole and pull quite firmly so a small hole is formed in the centre. Take care that trailing threads do not cover the hole as you progress.

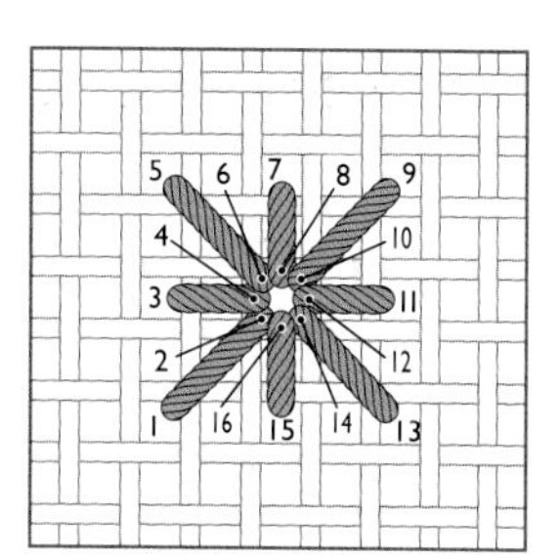

Backstitch

Backstitch is used for outlining, to add detail or emphasis and for lettering. It is added after the cross stitch to prevent the backstitch line being broken. It is usually indicated on a chart by solid lines with the suggested shade on the chart or key.

Follow the numbered sequence, right, working the stitches over one block of Aida or two threads of evenweave.

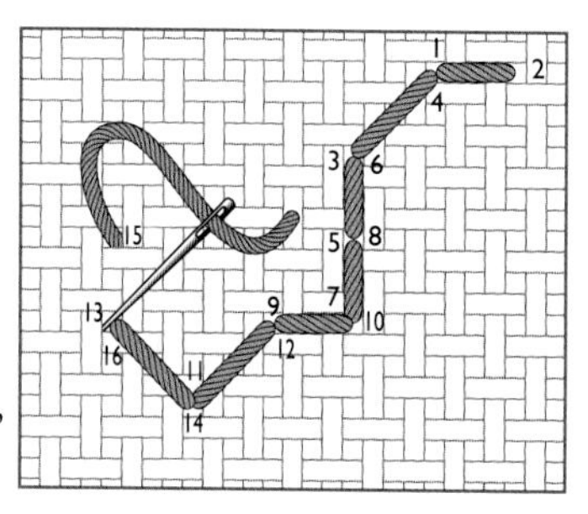

Cross Stitch

This simple little stitch is the most commonly used stitch in this book. Cross stitches can be worked singly or in two journeys but for neat stitching, keep the top stitch facing the same direction. It does not matter which way it faces but it should be the same for the whole project.

Cross stitch on Aida

Cross stitch on Aida fabric is normally worked over one block.

To work one complete cross stitch

Follow the numbered sequence in the diagram: bring the needle up through the fabric at the bottom left corner, cross one block of the fabric and insert the needle at the top right corner. Push the needle through and bring it up at the bottom right corner, ready to complete the stitch in the top left corner. To work the adjacent stitch, bring the needle up at the bottom right-hand corner of the first stitch.

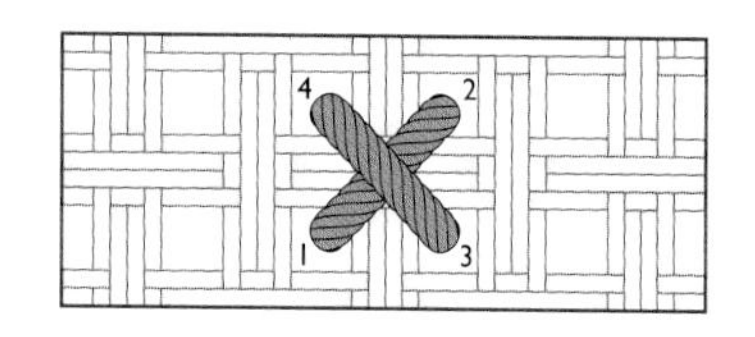

To work cross stitches in two journeys

Work the first leg of the cross stitch as above but instead of completing the stitch, work the adjacent half stitch and continue on to the end of the row. Complete all the crosses by working the other diagonals on the return journey.

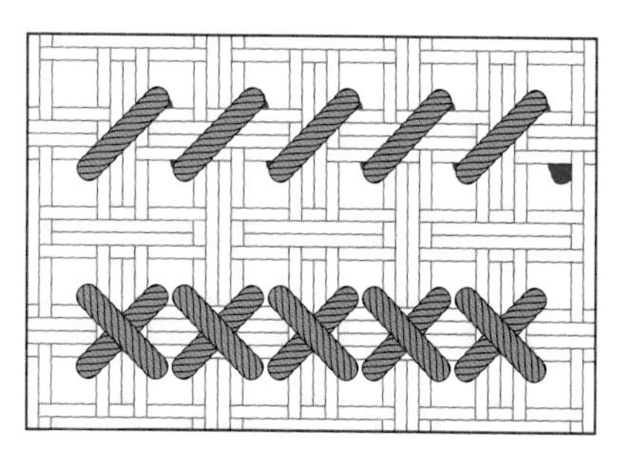

Cross stitch on Evenweave

Cross stitch on evenweave is usually worked over two threads of the fabric in each direction to even out any oddities in the thickness of the fibres. Bring the needle up to the left of a vertical thread, which will make it easier to spot counting mistakes. Work your cross stitch in two directions, as described before. This forms neat, single vertical lines on the back and gives somewhere to finish raw ends.

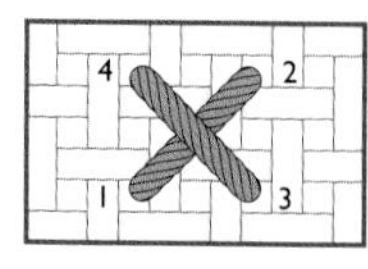

Three-quarter Cross Stitch

Three-quarter cross stitch is a fractional stitch which produces the illusion of curves when working cross stitch designs. The stitch can be formed on either Aida or evenweave but is more successful on evenweave. They are usually shown on charts as a triangle (half square).

Work the first half of a cross stitch as usual. Work the second 'quarter' stitch over the top and down into the central hole to anchor the first half of the stitch. If using Aida, you will need to push the needle through the centre of a block of the fabric. Where two three-quarter stitches lie back-to-back in the space of one full cross stitch, work both of the respective 'quarter' stitches into the central hole.

Some designs use half cross stitch and quarter cross stitch and these are, respectively, a single diagonal line and a quarter of a diagonal line.

French Knot

French knots are shown on charts as circles, coloured on colour charts. Bring the needle through to the front of the fabric and wind the thread around the needle twice. Put the needle partly through to the back, one thread or part of a block away from the entry point, to stop the stitch being pulled to the wrong side. Gently pull the thread you have wound so that it sits snugly at the point where the needle enters the fabric. Pull the needle through to the back and you should have a perfect knot in position. For bigger knots, add more thread to the needle.

Long Stitch

This is a long, straight stitch used to create animals' whiskers and so on. Bring the needle and thread up where the stitch is to start and down where the chart indicates it should finish. Occasionally long stitches are couched down – that is, held in place along their length with little stitches, as shown here.

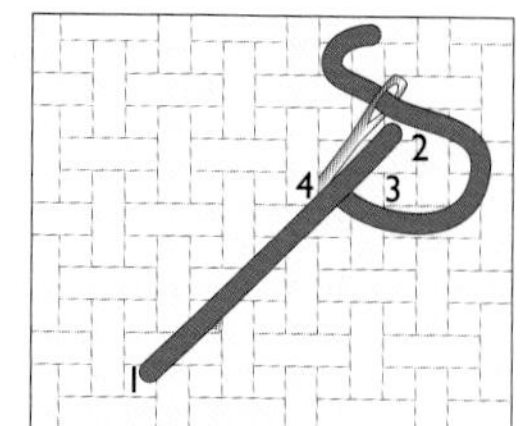

Tent Stitch

This stitch is usually used for working with wool (yarn) on canvas. It looks like half cross stitch from the front but has long, slanting stitches on the back, which means it uses more yarn and thus is harder wearing. Follow the diagram, taking the needle under the stitches from right to left.

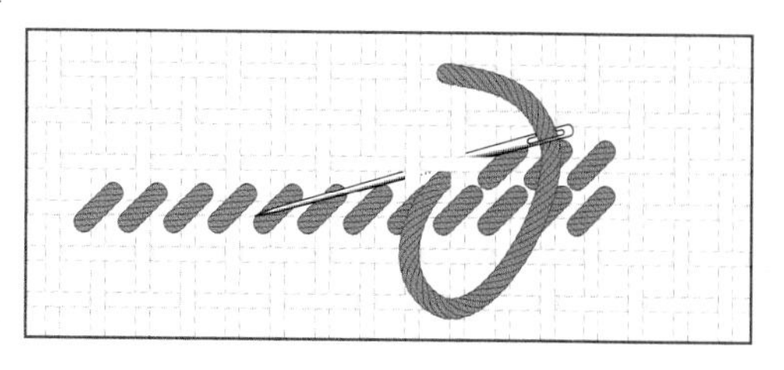

Salvador Mafé Hu

Mirage III IAI Nesher/Dagger

Mirage At War

Many people have contributed in order that this volume sees the light, among them: Juan José Fernández Martín, Rafael Treviño Martínez, Ignacio Bengoechea, Tono Fernández, Joquín Sánchez Díaz, José Miguel Quintana, Jesús García Labajo, Jorge Albalat, Jorge Portalés Alberola, Argentine Air Force Historical Branch, Horacio Clariá, Santiago Rivas, Shlomo Aloni and Javier Ruberto.

Dedicated to Mateo Mafé; thanks for being there during the last six years

Mirage III IAI Nesher/Dagger. Mirage At War • Salvador Mafé Huertas • First edition • LUBLIN 2019

• ISBN 978-83-66148-47-5

Editing: **Salvador Mafé Huertas** • Translation: **Salvador Mafé Huertas** • Cover artwork: **Anastasios Polychronis** • Color profiles: **Javier "Javo" Ruberto, Bill Dady** • Photos: **Ruben Dimeglio, Raul A. Diaz, A. Cnel Kidon via Brig (R) Luis Barreira, Jorge M. Fazio, William S. Posadas, VI Air Brigade, Horacio Viola, IAI via Brig (R) Luis Villar, Carlos N. Martinez, Collection Vladimiro Cettolo, Angel Bertogna, Horacio J. Clariá / Avialatina, Jorge R. Figari, Carlos A. Garcia, Javier A. Mosquera, FAA via Christian Amado, Juan J. Janer Com., Fighter Group 6, Hunting Group 6, Collection Mauricio Chiófalo, Santiago Cortelezzi, IAI via Vcom Erasmo Zabala, Ruben Palazzi, Juan J. Martinez, Collection Javier A. Mosquera, Manuel Vilchez, William P. Gebel, TECNODINAMICA, Gustavo Piuma Justo, Guillermo Posadas / Avialatina, Carlos Maiztegui, Roberto Janett, Shlomo Aloni** • Design: **KAGERO STUDIO**

KAGERO Publishing
Akacjowa 100, Turka, os. Borek, 20-258 Lublin 62, Poland, phone/fax: (+48) 81 501 21 05
www.kagero.pl • e-mail: kagero@kagero.pl, marketing@kagero.pl
w w w . k a g e r o . p l
Distribution: **KAGERO Publishing**

Editorial

Israel Aircraft Industries manufactured 51 single and ten two-seater Mirage 5s, the IDFAF named them Nesher; after an outstanding performance in the Yom Kippur War, most were sold to Argentina late 70s.

By the beginning of the decade, the Argentina Air Force was in the process of modernizing its fleet of combat aircraft. While that stage had begun some years earlier with the introduction of the first batch of Douglas A-4P Skyhawk, it began with the incorporation of the BAC Canberra (intended to replace veteran Avro Lincoln and Lancaster killed in 1967) bombers and the signing of the phased out contract for the first supersonic jet FAA: the Mirage III.

This contract would mean the starting point for a long tradition operating this family of fighters designed by Avions Marcel Dassault Delta - Breguet Aviation (AMD-BA).

To further complicate the picture, the fall of the constitutional regime in 1976, motivated by anarchy and disarray in the country, which had initially been supported by the United States, it led to this country to impose shortly after an arms embargo due to the pressure from the international community.

Thus, the implementation of Presidential Directive 13, known as the Humphrey-Kennedy Amendment, signed by James Carter in 1977 and prohibiting the sale of advanced weapons technology and training to governments with human rights problems, locked all negotiations for the acquisition new material, so the Air Force undertook the task of acquiring combat aircraft via alternative routes, but this search became extremely complicated by the pressure exerted on their usual combat equipment providers.

Initial contacts with France for a number of Mirage 5, the simplified version of the M-III and optimized for fighter-bomber missions were quickly discarded because the factory argued that it could not meet the deadlines that required the FAA. While this was an important limitation, the reality was that the French firm did not make much effort to pressure from international organizations to lock sale. the IAI Kfir: At that time, produced in Israel was a machine that would be the aim of the FAA for many years but could never materialize.

Developed as a much improved evolution of the Mirage 5 airframe, the product of Israel Aircraft Industries represented a marked increase on the performance of the French origin Mirage, largely due to the adoption of canard foreplanes and a more powerful US-made engine, the General Electric J79 of 8,119 kg of thrust, similar to that used by the F-4E Phantom.

However, the source of that power plant would be an insurmountable obstacle that would scuttle Argentine aspirations. However, IAI countered with an offer that at first seemed unbeatable under the established political situation. It was the Nesher, an unlicensed copy of

The eight drivers who made the flight course Eitam air base(Israel) as part of an accelerated training scheme in view of a possible border conflict with Chile. Photo taken during the solo flights 28 December 1978. Note the registration deleted in the original photo taken by IAI. [Brig (R) Ruben Dimeglio]

the French, Mirage 5 but that because of the arms embargo on Israel after the Six-Day War of June 1967 by France, most aircraft components and engine T were obtained from Dassault and Snecma, contravening the embargo.

Thus, in total the Argentine Air Force acquired a total of 92 Mirage III/5 of different models, the last being phased out in November 2015.

Additionally, this special also try to Israeli aces flew the Mirage III (Shahak in Israel) and Nesher, and as although not entering in combat, they were a key element in the modernization of the Spanish Air Force, an article is devoted to the Mirage IIIEE/DEs belonging to Ala 11 at Manises AB, and which now flies the superb Eurofighter Typhoon.

Salvador Mafé Huertas

From Nesher to Dagger, the fabulous history of the Israeli Mirage 5s

Israel Aircraft Industries manufactured more than fifty of Mirage 5, within the Israele Defence Force/Air Force were known as Nesher; after an outstanding performance in the Yom Kippur War, most were sold to Argentina in the late 70s.

By the beginning of that decade, the Argentina Air Force was in the process of modernizing its fleet of combat aircraft. While that stage had begun some years earlier with the introduction of the first batch of Douglas A-4P Skyhawks, it began with the incorporation BAC Canberra bombers (intended to replace veteran Avro Lincoln and Lancaster phased out in 1967) and the signing of the contract for Argentin's first supersonic jet the Mirage III.

This contract would mean the starting point for a long tradition in the operation of the delta winged fighter designed by Avions Marcel Dassault Delta - Breguet Aviation (AMD-BA).

In parallel, by then was culminating its career an emblematic machine, which marked the elite of the fighter pilots, the Gloster Meteor F.Mk.4. The logical frontline replacement of combat aircraft contemplated the withdrawal of North American F-86F Sabre by 1976 and its replacement by another jet that could perform the tasks of fighter-bomber and secondary functions of air defense.

This decision began to become a priority given the rapid deterioration of relations with Chile due to border issues, and was expected to trigger an armed conflict in the short term.

On the other hand, contacts for an additional batch of Skyhawk to the United States began, which was finalized successfully. However, in this case could not be contracted the complete overhaul of the airframes (as had happened with the A-4P - called by the FAA as A-4B) whereby 25 A-4C Skyhawks were received in condition "as is, where is" and put into service by the area Material Rio Cuarto in a long and difficult task, giving the first operational aircraft to his unit in 1976.

To further complicate the picture, the fall of the constitutional regime in 1976, motivated by anarchy and disarray in the country, which had initially been supported by the United States, led to this country imposing shortly afterwards an arms embargo by pressure from the international community.

1° Teniente Raul A. Diaz (right) was one of six pilots sent to Peru to train in the Cap. Quiñones González Base of the Peruvian Air Force (FAP) in Fighter Squadron 611 during October and November 1978. [Com (R) Raul A. Diaz]

The first batch of Daggers ready to leave from IAI facilities at Ben Gurion to the port of Ashdod (40 km from Tel Aviv)

Thus, the implementation of Presidential Directive 13, known as the Humphrey-Kennedy Amendment, signed by James Carter in 1977 and prohibiting the sale of advanced weapons, technology and training to governments with human rights problems, locked all negotiations for the acquisition new material, so the Air Force undertook the task of acquiring combat aircraft via alternative routes, but this search became extremely complicated by the pressure exerted on their usual combat equipment providers.

Initial contacts with France for a number of Mirage 5, the simplified version of the Mirage III and optimized for fighter-bomber missions were quickly discarded because the factory argued that it could not meet the deadlines that required the FAA. While this was an important limitation, the reality was that the French firm did not make much effort to pressure from international organizations to blockade the sale. At that time, in Israel the production of a machine that would be the aim of the FAA for many years and could never materialize: the IAI Kfir.

Developed as a much improved evolution of Mirage 5 airframe, this product of Israel Aircraft Industries represented a marked increase on

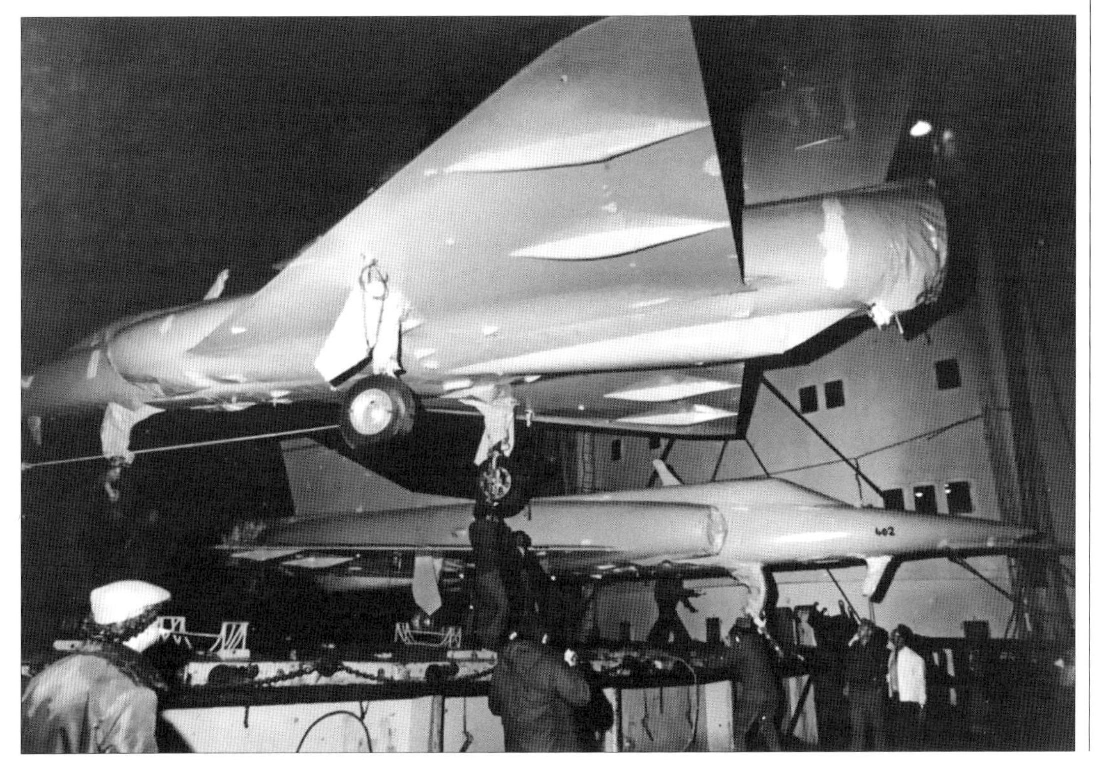

Loading C-401 and -402 on board the ship Jaspers in the early hours of 3 November 1978. The aircraft were coated with a layer of Spraylat to protect them while traveling to Argentina. The first batch of six aircraft arrived at the port of Buenos Aires on 26 November. [A. Cnel Kidon via Brig (R) Luis Barreira.]

the performances of the French Mirage, largely due to the adoption of canard foreplanes and a more powerful American-made engine, the General Electric J79 of 8,119 kg of thrust, similar to that used by the F-4E Phantom.

However, the source of that power plant would be an insurmountable obstacle that would scuttle with Argentine aspirations. However, IAI countered with an offer that at first seemed unbeatable under the established political situation.

With the addition of the Kfir, the Hey'l Ha Avir (Israel Defense Force/Air Force - IDF/ AF) was about to begin the process of withdrawal its IAI Nesher, a transition variante developed from Mirage 5 with some modifications.

These jets were available virtually immediately and the factory also offered a further development to take the Nesher to a standard similar to the Kfir, but retaining the French Snecma Atar engine.

The offer included a first batch of 24 single-seaters Nesher and two twin seaters Nesher Ts with an inspection of 600 hours and changing different items according to Argentine requirements.

The machines had on average about 600 flight hours, representing 85% of their remaining useful life and were built between 1971 and 1974.

In June 1978 a group of officers and NCOs of the VIII Brigada Aérea (home of the Mirage IIIEAs) with a high degree of confidentiality, left for Israel to contact the Air Force and the Israeli Defense Ministry in order to verify the status of the Neshers offered. This commission was headed by Commodoro Luis Barreira, plus Vicecomodoros Juan C. Luscher and Manuel Mir and and NCOs Carlos Ambros and Ferraras. Viccomodoro Mir also had the task of evaluating the operational capabilities of the aircraft, its particular conditions and limits of the flight envelope. In view of the positive analysis subsequently carried out by this committee and the similarity between the Nesher and the Mirage IIIEA, finally it was decided to purchase these jets.

The Dagger purchase

It materialized on 10 Augus 1978 with the signing of the contract DAG/I for a total amount of US $ 109.192.000 and contemplated the incorporation of 24 single-seaters at a cost of U$ 3.958.000 and two twin-seaters at a cost of U$ 7.100.000 each.

These machines, renamed Dagger and designated by the FAA as "Mirage 5" would be subject to further inspection on the premises of Israel Aircraft Industries at Ben Gurion Airport (Tel Aviv), to where they were taken in flight from its home at Eiram air base in the Sinai peninsula.

The contract included the guidelines to develop an upgrade of these jets with modern avionics was established, although the priority of the FAA was to have the aircraft as soon as possible, requessting to that effect that IAI undertake a "P" inpsection (periodic) and updating some equipment to assure at least 200 flight hours by aicraft before the first necessary inspection to be held in Argentina.

Immediately the study began to select pilots that would fly the new aircraft. This task was carried out by Commodo Nelsis Rodoni, a IIIEA Mirage experienced pilot, who was head of the Department of Training in the Air Operations Command (COA). His task was extremely

Upon arrival at the port of Buenos Aires, the Daggers were sent to Aeroparque and from there to VIII Brigada Aérea (Jose C. Paz, Buenos Aires.). where they received a brief review and finally departed for Area Material Rio Cuarto. In the picture it can be seen C-417 and -407 belonging to the second shipment arrived on 28 December 1978. [SM (R) Jorge M. Fazio]

Dagger Squadron Hangar No. 1 in front of the platform ARMACUAR in early 1979, while operating as a hosted unit in Rio Cuarto. [My (R) William S. Posadas]

important because the selection of students and instructors should be very rigorous because it was required the pilots were operating with Dagger as soon as possible. In the case of students, the selection included officers with experience in high performance jets (F-86F Sabre and A-4B Skyhawk) and had reached Phase III (suitable for combat) in their respective weapons systems, counting with at least 250 hours in single-seater fighters. While for flying the M-III were required at least 500 hours, this time it was decided to reduce this requirement, in order to incorporate more pilots to the new weapons system. In the case of instructors, he searched among officers with proven qualification with the M-III.

The formal birth of the then *Dagger Escuadrón* crystallized soon after the 28 August 1978, with sending the subpoenas to pilots assigned to the three main fighter units of (IV, V and VIII Brigadas Aéreas) and the Military Aviaction School to show up at the VIII Brigada Aérea premises at the Dr. Mariano Moreno airfield, near the town of José C. Paz, west of the city of Buenos Aires.

The Squadron, commanded by Mayor Mario E. Roman, Mirage III pioneer pilot in the FAA, would be subordinate to the Head of Operations Grupo VIII (this unit operating since 1972 the Mirage IIIEA/DA)s led by Comodoro Edgardo Cáceres, part of the VIII Brigada Aérea commanded by Comodoro Jorge A. Van Thienen. This denomination of units corresponding to the restructuring of the Air Force implemented years ago and did have a short application.

Leading the technical committee in charge of receiving the Daggers was the then Chief of the Technical Group VIII Brigada Aérea, Comodoro Barreira who would be in charge with a group of NCOs (Federico Bohm, Lucio Beraldi, Jorge Corando, Enrique Hlaczik and Jesús Robles) were responsible of the official reception and inspection of the machines from Israel. The process was completed with acceptance test flights conducted by Mayor Juan Carlos Sapolsky traveling to Israel whenever batches of jets were technically approved, except for the first batch of six aircraft.

The most important changes included the replacement of the UHF communication with Collins VHF, incorporating a Collins VOR and changes in the instruments, however the old Cossor ADF was retained.

Regarding the 600 hours airframe and engine "P" inspection cell and engine, an Inspection "P" of 600 hours, some special ítems were added: stripping of the original camouflage scheme (later it was verified not to have been completed) and repainting with the requested FAA scheme. Furthermore, new braking parachutes were fitted or at least with 80% of their available life and new brake discs.

In September 1978 a commission left for Israel to complete the mantenance course, this group was formed by Vicecomodoro Antonio Rizzo Corallo, Tenientes Roberto Mammana and William Posadas and thirty NCOs.

This course, lasting three months and included weapons (DEFA 552 cannon and Shafrir II), structure, avionics and engine, was held in the premises of IAI in Ben Gurion and on several occasions cadets moved to Eitam in a twin-engine IDF/AF IAI Arava Light transport to observe maintenance operations on the frontline.

The first pilots are trained

For flight adaptation a programme was devised through which future pilots received tra Dagger training at different places in order to accelerate this stage.

A group led by Vicecomodoro Manuel Mir was posted to Israel and was formed by twelve pilots, Mayor Sapolsky, Captains Alberto Kajihara, Hector Pergolini, Carlos Martinez, Luis Puga and Guillermo Donadille and 1st Lieutenants Carlos Arnau, Horacio Mir Gonzalez, Eduardo Almoño, Roberto Janett, Carlos Musso, and Ruben Dimeglio.

Four of these officers, Sapolsky, Pergolini, Arnau and Mir González, with previous experience in Mirage III, left for Israel in mid-October 1978, accompanied by Vicecomodor, for the air´to-aire combat and instructor courses. This course, the first one given to foreign crews would continue later in Argentina.

The remaining eight pilotoswent to Israel on 1 November1978, aboard an Aerolineas Argentinas flight destination Frankfurt, and from there boarded an El-Al Boeing 727 for the flight to Tel Aviv. Prior to their departure, they received a brief familiarization in the Mirage IIIDA two-seaters, but without flying solos. They also conducted an intensive English course, because during during the whole training stages were to be held in that language.

The arrival of the contingent was surrounded by a host of security measures organized by the Mossad (the famous Israeli intelligence service) in order to cover up the operation. As part of discretion mentioned, all Argentine personnel wore civilian clothes, and only the pilots Dresde with their flight overalls inmediatly before each flights As part of the cover-up, Israeli intelligence told them that before any question about their origin and activities should indicate that they belonged to a country called "Oswald" and were conducting the IAI Arava course, which was the airplane in which were shuttling to Eitam, and thus do not arouse greater suspicion.

The course was conducted by two experienced IAF instructors. One was Yoram Geva, a pilot that between 1972 and 1973 shot down six aircraft (four Syrians and two Egyptian), and the other was Shlomo Erez, also with active participation in the Yom Kippur war where he gota n Egyotian MiG-21 kill. The latter used to surprise with his skill each student on his first flight by a particular maneuver was to take off and stabilize the aircraft at low altitude over the runway and then over the desert to Mach 0.9 with AB (afterburner) engaged, then perform a 90° climb to reach zero speed and then fall on its tail preventing entring into a spin and recovering the the jet.

For the flight activity, only the aircraft acquired by the FAA were used, who continued to

Dagger C-403 ready to start a training flight in the exercise Ranquel (June-July 1979) operating from shelters specially built due to the border conflict with Chile in ARMACUAR. [My (R) William S. Posadas]

wear Israeli camouflage and insignias. The flying course was noticeably different from that taught by the French and after a brief adaptation stage in the two seaters (no more than four or five sorties), the first solo flight was carried out.

The Israeli school of thought contemplated the use of the aircraft to the limit of its capabilities on the basis of experiences gained in combat while French style operated the jet always within the limits set by the flight manual in a more conservative style.

The flying activities revealed as extremely demanding because communications were in English, without instrumental precision navigation and flying in the middle of the desert, with few visual references and in very small sectors whose limits should not be exceeded because the west Egypt and east were the Israelis who did not hesitate to shoot the aircraft that entered its aispace without identification or authorization.

The experience was extremely important, living the Argentine pilots in a permanent state of alert due to the tense relationship between Israel and its Arab neighbors.

In this way and completed the adaptation, it was completed the first "solo" of an Argentine pilot on a Dagger on 8 November 1978. That honor went to the senior officer, Mayor Sapolsky, while Capitán Pergolini and 1° Tenientes Mir Gonzalez and Arnau did the same on 13 November.

Upon completion of the course, these pilots immediately returned to the country, to make the reception and transfer of Dagger who were close to arrive to the Port of Buenos Aires.

On 27 November Captains Donadille, Kajihara, Puga and Martinez recorded their fist solo flights and on 28 November the 1° Tenientes Almoño, Dimeglio, Janett and Musso. After the qualification, each pilot made a total of six to eight flights until the end of the course. The contingent quickly returned to the country on 20 December 1978 at a time when military actions with Chile seemed imminent.

Moreover, training other pilots assigned to the new material, was carried out with the Fuerza Aérea del Perú, at Chiclayo AB and with VIII Brigada Aérea in Argentina.

1° Tenientes Higinio Robles, Jorge Gatti, Jorge Ratti, Roberto Benavente, Jorge Senn and Daniel Herlein began the course in the Mirage IIIEA/DA, performing solo flights on 31 October 1978 with the pilots who would make up the group travelling to Peru. However Gatti and Benavente handed down their "wings" soon after their solo flight.

The group of pilots sent to Peru conducted training at Cap Quiñones González Air Force Base of the Peruvian Air Force (FAP) within the 611 Escuadrón de Caza equipped with Mirage 5P/DP. This group was formed by 1° Tenientes Amílcar Cimatti, Raul Diaz, Carlos Maffeis, Al-

IMI (Israel Military Industries) bombs P. G. 130 kg TNT MOD.4 mounted on the C-403. The Madnap tanks supported a maximum of two bombs per tank with a total weight of 1,000 kg. [VI Air Brigade]

During the important operating Blazon I conducted in October 1981 in northern Argentina, the Dagger operated from the Jujuy Airport. [VI Air Brigade]

berto Dorado, Jorge Dellepiane and Carlos Rohde.

On 1 October 1978, aboard an Aerolineas Argentinas flight, this group of pilots arrived to Lima in civilian clothes, because as with the contingent sent to Israel, it was desired to keep the maximum reserve on the operation. Two days later, a a FAP transport flew them to Chiclayo, on the north coast of Peru.

They stayed at the Officers Mess of the unit and not in the city as not to raise any suspicion, starting immediately with advanced academic courses on Mirage 5 materials, equipment and operations.

On its completion, the flying stage started with the dual controls. Each pilot made seven thirty to forty minutes long sorties in which several subjects were fulfilled: air-to-air combat, safety margins anda ir-to-ground tactics, among others.

During such training an emergency was recorded with a lucky end. When the 1° Teniente Diaz was making his second flight in two-seater, shortly after takeoff, the aircraft suffered a bird ingestion. Feeling the blow and subsequent vibrations in the engine, the instructor declared an emergency and since the aircraft was in the vicinity of the base, landed without consequences.

On 18 October, the pilots made a single flight and then by concluded the course. They immediately moved to Lima to return and join the Escuadrón Dagger in early November.

Arrival and immediate activation of Escuadrón Dagger

In parallel, at the IAI facilities continued preparing the aircraft for transfer to Argentina by sea. Once the inspection has been completed, the aircraft were preserved by applying a layer of light brown Spraylat (a process called "cocooning"), covering them completely, except wheels to which a cover and the brake discs were placed, which were impregnated with a preservative grease.

Under the cloak of an overnight secret operation organized by the IDF/AF they were transferred to the Mediterranean port of Ashdod (40 Km from Tel Aviv) where they embarked for Argentina. The first six aircraft (C-401 to C-406) arrived on 26 November 1978 aboard the ship Jaspers.

Captains Julio Farkas July and Carlos F. Neme (Operations Grupo VIII) were responsible for receiving the aircraft in the Port of Buenos Aires and then monitor their transfer by land to a hangar of Austral airline at Jorge Newbery Airport . Normally this task unfolded at night to avoid traffic congestion by moving aircraft through the streets and as an additional measure to maintain the discretion of the operation. Once in the hangar mentioned and with the assistance of a team of Israeli technicians and FAA noncommissioned officers, they were placed airworthy, taking off a few days to VIII Brigada Aérea.

The first four aircraft then made their first flight in Argentina by Mayor Sapolsky

(C-402), Capitán Pergolini (C-401), 1° Teniente Mir Gonzalez (C-403) and 1° Tte. Arnau (C-404) that led the first four aircraft from Jorge Newbery Airport to José C. Paz on 1 December 1978, afterwards it was the turn of the remaining two machines (C-405 and C-406). Once in the Brigade, the six received a minor inspection. The first days of December, the pilots who had completed training in Peru initiated the Dagger academic course and made their solo flights between 12 and 14 of the same month t with Sapolsky, Pergolini, Arnau and Mir Gonzalez acting as instructors.

Regionally, the political situation began to deteriorate markedly in early December, so all combat units began deployment tasks according to the concept of Airmobile Squadrons in view of the impending conflict.

This doctrine of use of air assets provided for the operation of the of combat assets from forward operating airfields. All means of the Force, were in turn subordinate to two commands. These were the Southern Theatre Air Command (CATOS) with jurisdiction over the south of the country and the Northern Theatre Air Command (CATON), in charge of operations on the northern border.

In this way and according to a directive of the Strategic Air Command, on December 7, 1978 the six Dagger were deployed to the facilities of the Area Material Rio Cuarto (ARMACUAR) in the town of Las Higueras, near Rio Cuarto (south of Cordoba Province) with the mission to train with the material just received and get ready to be redeployed subordinating their operations to CATON.

The Daggers deployed ARMACUAR into three sections, the first integrated by Roman - Dorado, the second by Sapolsky - Cimatti and finally Pergolini - Arnau in the third. According to documentes filed in the FAA Historical Division, the official order for the transfer of such machines was dated 18 December, when the jets were already in Rio Cuarto, which clearly demonstrates the urgency in the deployment of the unit.

In Rio Cuarto, it also would have enough technical support to solve some problems encountered with the initial operation of the aircraft. Finally Escuadrón Dagger was formed with the following structure: Squadron Leader, Mayor Roman; Flight Leaders Mayor Sapolsky and Capitán Pergolini; Section Leaders, 1° Tenientes Mir, Arnau and Mir González and pilots 1° Tenientes Cimatti and Dorado. The position of Operations Officer initially and unofficially, was conducted by Captain Pergolini and later, officially, by Captain Kajihara.

The technical flight, was commanded by Teniente William S. Posadas, first C.O. of Dagger Maintenance Squadron, set off on a Lockheed C-130H Hercules and Fokker F-27 (TC-79) to Area Material Rio Cuarto with thirty NCOs and all the support team to its new destination. Later Antonio Rizzo Corallo would take over the Vice Commander of the Technical Squadron.

The transfer of the first aircraft to Rio Cuarto proved problematic, but was successfully completed, resulting in the start of operations from the ARMACUAR. In turn, two factors affected the development of the new unit, one unfamiliarity with the new weapon system and second, many of the pilots from other squadrons had very little experience in piloting pure delta winged jets. But the iron will of the same and the proximity of a conflict caused this to be shortly remedied.

The honour for the first landing at the then BAM Tandil, future site of the Dagger, corresponded to C-421 at the controls of Vicecomodor Horacio Viola on 11 July 1979. [Brig (R) Horacio Viola]

The Escuadrón Dagger deployment significantly altered the normal rhythm of this base, it implemented an operational unit, which required deep to allow the change of activities, from the technical/logistical field, to first line operations. Also performed were a number of works, such as building shelters at the head of runway 05.

One of the shortcomings of CATON was the lack of an interceptor for its operacional sector, therefore the Dagger had to assume that role, fulfilling day alerts equipped with Shafrir missiles and with its full ammunition for the 30 mm guns, in Air Defence Sector under the CIC (Center for Information and Control) responsabilty from the V Brigada Aérea based in Villa Reynolds, in the neighboring province of San Luis.

The moment of maximum tension reached on 23December when the units were readied for the start of offensive operations. Fortunately, the intervention of the Vatican envoy, Cardinal Antonio Samore, managed to unlock the negotiations and the situation was overcome without major incidentes. The jets started to redeploying to their units in early January 1979,

Second contract Daggers at Ben Gurion Airport in June 1981, photographed as advertising material by IAI. [IAI via Brig (R) Luis Villar]

After his first flight in a Dagger, 1st. Lieutenant William Posadas (in charge at Israel Aircraft of the batch) was "baptized" according to local tradition, although this time the tank had fuel and no water as usual! [IAI Via Brig (R) Luis Villar]

although the Daggers continued in Rio Cuarto deployed as a VIII Brigada Aérea.

It was also established that minor and intermediate inspections were conducted by the Technical Group 8 in Moreno, given its experience with M irage III, until the new Escuadrón technical staff got the swing of their new fighter. That is why, initially, the technicians and mechanics performed extraordinary efforts to keep the aircraft in service in Rio Cuarto.

By then, four other aircraft (the C-409, 410, 411 and 412) had reached the port of Buenos Aires on 28 December 1978 aboard the MV Eshkol; on 29 January 1979 arrived C- 407, 408, 413, 414, 415 and 417 aboard the Turmaline Bay.

On numerous occasions and due to the lack of pilots, the transfer of aircraft from AeroparqueVIII Brigada Aérea was completed with the assistance of Mirage III pilots, as Mayor Eduardo Costa, who performed the short ferry flight after a brief cockpit familiarization.

Tandil: Dagger's permanent nest

On January 26, 1979 by BAR (Reserved Aeronautical Bulletin) 1999 was created the Air Defense Command, commanded by Major Brigadier Antonio Lopez. It consisted of the VIII Air Brigade and its two weapon systema (Dagger and Mirage III), 1 Air Surveillance Group and the Antiaircraft Artillery Group based at Tandil Military Air Base Base (BAM).

Meanwhilc, the four pilots, Robles, Ratti, Senn and Herlein, who conducted the flight course in Argentina with the Mirage III, made their solo flights in M-5 (Dagger) on 30 January 1979 (Robles) and 24 January (the others). The instructors Pergolini and Arnau would return in June and February of that year, to the ranks of the Mirage III Squadron.

While the Dagger Squadron continued to operate from the ARMACUAR as a host unit, the staff was evaluating alternatives for its definitive base, since VIII Brigade did not have space enough to accommodate all the air material, coupled with the increased activity was being generated on the outskirts of Buenos Aires.

By then, the BAM Tandil located south of the province of Buenos Aires, was chosen as the future site of the Dagger, as defined by Directive 135/79 "Reactivation of the VI Air Brigade".

To accomplish this task was created the Operations Group "Project Dagger" being its chief Commodore Theodore G. Waldner and Vicecommodore Horacio J. Viola, his assistant, who previously served in the General Staff of CATON.

In March 1979, Major Roman, Dagger Squadron C.O., was replaced by Major Luis D. Villar, who had extensive experience in the Mirage III had been reposted to the VIII Air Brigade after being assigned as assistant to the FAA Commander in Chief of the. On March 28, Villar would make his first solo flight in a Dagger.

Two days later, on March 30, on a training flight aboard MIIIDA I-001, the aircraft suffered an Enghien stopage while making touch and goes at Moreno airflied, both crew Captain Jorge Huck and his student, Vicecommodore Viola. Despite ejecting at low altitude, both were unharmed. In those moments, Viola was making his habilitation in Mirage III and then start flying the Dagger, performing his first solo in the Israeli jet on May 1.

BAM Tandil had held at the time the Gloster Meteor F.Mk.4 of Fighter Interceptor Groups 2 and 3 between 1948 and 1960 (with a brief period between 1952 and 1955) and later hosted the Search, Rescue & Special Tasking Squadron. The latter began operating in 1961, equipped with Grumman HU-16B Albatross and from 1968 with Douglas C-47/HC-47, DHC-2 Beaver and DHC-3 Otter. The activity of this unit ceased in 1971 when the Beavers and Otters were phased out and the Douglas transferred to other units.

Originally it was planned to base BAC Canberra B/T.Mk.62/64 light bombers in Tandil, as indicated in the programme Aviation Activity (PAA) for 1970. However this did not come to materialize, as the Canberras went to the II Air Brigade in Paraná (Entre Rios). The Albatross, in turn had begun to operate from Morón in 1970, so it was only an Antiaircraft Artillery unit and a solitary Cessna A182J (PG-341) for liaison.

The infrastructure of the future Dagger base was far from be able to accommodate a group of modern fighters and their respective support services. This situation was being corrected with the passage of time as the base facilities were adapting gradually. Much of the Officers Mess had been closed for many years, so the effects of humidity were important. The Air Squadron facilities were installed in a small building located near the taxiway called affectionately "the red shack" because of the color of its roof. The Service Flight, as it was called the first line maintenance, which depended from the Air Squadron during the first two years in Tandil and then moved to the area of Technical Group, was located in a trailer on the side of the control tower. These locations were temporary pending the completion work on the future Air Group. The only runway had only a VOR and some time later an ILS was installed.

On April 3, 1979 four aircraft arrived (C-416, 418, 420 and 422) aboard the vessel Alt. Stewart, while the final batch (C-421, 423, 424, 425 and 426) did the same on 7 July 1979 on the same ship. One Dagger, C-419, would remain in Israel to perform various tests of what would be the future SINT Project (Integrated Navigation and Weapons System), whereby these machines would be equipped with an autonomous navigation system and attack without ground or satellite support.

While the core of the future Fighter Group (the increase in the supply of aircraft imposed that on arrival at Tandil the Squadron was carried to the upper structure) was operating from Rio Cuarto, as an advance to transfer the same to its final site three of the aircraft of the last batch received were deployed directly from Moreno to Tandil, initiating formal operations at the base. On 11 July, the Vicecommodore Viola made the first landing of a Dagger in Tandil at the controls of C-421. Completing the flight were Major Villar (C-423) and 1st. Lieutenant Mir González (C-424). The three jets were configured in Alpha configuration (clean, without external tanks) to lighten the weight of the plane and land safely on the runway, which had not yet received the emergency barricade.

As part of the process to increase the Dagger's, was evaluated during a routine exercise at the Antuna weapons range near the VAir Brigade, new weapons such as the 5-inch Zuni rockets used by the A-4B Skyhawks. In parallel, a photographic pod was evaluated for vertical and oblique high Speedy photos.

Meanwhile, on 5 June 1979, the Dagger Squadron reached the first 1,000 flight hours and took part in the Operational Ranquel planned by the newly created Air Defense Command. Carried out at the Area Material Rio Cuarto from 25 June to 4 July carrying out operations with the Daggers and Mirage IIIs from Grupo 8 de Caza.

On the occasion of the Air Force Day, it was organized an air parade over the city of Jujuy being deployed to airfields in the north types of the FAA. Six Daggers departed from Rio Cuarto

Flight reception moment of C-438 (even with Israeli serial 634) at Ben Gurion Airport on April 9, 1981. [IAI via Brig (R) Luis. Villar]

Major Luis Villar was responsible for conducting the reception flights of the second batch aircraft in 1981. [IAI via Brig. (R) Luis Villar]

to the Catamarca Airport on 4 August 1979, performing the show six days later.

Simultaneously, the same day came the second delivery of machines to Tandil, which departed from Rio Cuarto with a team of minimal support, since part of it was in Catamarca. The next day, the six Dagger who participated in the parade took off from the north to Tandil on a direct flight, checking their fuel status over Moreno airfield; completing subsequently the transfer of the remaining aircraft that were at ARMACUAR and the VIII Air Brigade.

By that time, they began to be used in a mocking nicknames "rich cousins" and "poor cousins" referring to the personnel operating the Mirage III and Dagger respectively. This was mainly due to the similarity of both machines but emphasizing different forms and circumstances in which they were purchased to serve both aircraft of the Mirage family.

The first acquired new from the factory and as part of a contract covering all aspects related to the incorporation of the aircraft. The second, used aircraft, with a war on their backs and some shortages as a result of the urgency of delivery.

On August 16, 1979, the Commander in Chief of the FAA, Brigadier General Omar Rubens Graffigna presided in Tandil ceremony in which the Group 6 Operations "Dagger" under Commodore Waldner was established as a unit housed in the BAM Tandil and subordinate to the Air Defense Command ceased to be part of Operations Group VIII of the VIII Air Brigade.

This first stage was marked by an intensive pilot training and the solving of technical issues encountered with the aircraft. To this end, with the support of a group of Israeli technicians led by Arie Lavion and composed of Jacob Nagar (airframe Specialist), Eli Mishal (electrician) and Nachum Ben-Arie (engineer).

The first operation carried out from its base in Tandil, would take place atPatagonia, by deploying eight Dagger sto BAM Rio Gallegos in October 1979.

As they reached 2,000 flight hours, the unit would suffer the first loss when C-406 fell to the ground in Estancia Santa Lidia, belonging to the Partido de Azul (Buenos Aires) on November 26, 1979, exactly one year after that jet touched Argentine soil. The accident was caused by the stoping of the GTR (Turbojet Group) during a training flight and after repeated attempts to restart theengine with negative results, the pilot 1st. Lieutenant Cimatti ejected safely.

The incorporation of air assets to the air base, prompted that BAM Tandil was again called VI Air Brigade on 10 December 1979 by BAR 2019/79, under Commodore Waldner. Its air component would be the Fighter-Bomber Group VI led by Vicecommodore Viola formed by two squadrons whose Commanding Officers were Major Villar (Operational Squadron) and Major Sapolsky (Training Squadron). In the latter, Captain Donadille was appointed as Operations Officer; and as instructors Captains Dorado and Mir Gonzalez. The structure was completed with the technical unit, the Group Technical 6 (GT6) under Commodore Rizzo Corallo and support unit, the Group Base 6 (GB6) under Commodore John C. Casado.

As part of the festivities related to the creation of the Brigade and coincident with the ac-

Major Villar besides C-431 after finishing his flight acceptance. Note the Star of David on the air intake and the covered serial number under the windshield. [IAI via Brig. (R) Luis Villar]

tivities planned by the Aeronautical Week and Open Day was organized for the first in Tandil. The primary purpose of it was to show all the capabilities of the Dagger, displaying it and its weapons to the citizens. The response from the public was important filling the Base and its surroundings. Air demonstrations consisted of a spectacular display of acrobatics performed by Major Villar in a Dagger in Alpha configurations, taking advantage of an old shooting range that Gloster Meteor used by the side of the runway, a Dagger flight made up of Major Sapolsky, Captain Puga and 1st. Lieutenants Musso and Ratti thundered the crowd with firing their 30mm cannons.

Material assigned to the new unit also included a Services Squadron consisting of a Cessna/FMA A182J (PG-341), a Douglas C-47 (TC-18, then briefly replaced by the FMA IA-50A GII T-125) and a Aerocommander 500U (T-134). The Air Activities Programe for the following year, provided for the incorporation of a Hughes 369/500 for search and rescue tasks, which only years later would materialize with the addition of 369HM H-26.

With the initial problems practically solved, the G6C began 1980 with a large air activity. The first class of pilots trained in Tandil, consisted of 1st. Lieutenants Carlos Moreno and Osvaldo Battioni who performed their solo flight on January 2 and January 3 respectively. On March 14 completed his first solo Commodore Waldner, Brigade C.O. and July 3, would do likewise four junior lieutenants, Juan D. Bernhardt, Gustavo Aguirre Faget, Pedro I. Bean and Ricardo H. Volponi. On September 5, another new student, Lieutenant Cesar Roman, also conduct his solo flight.

That year different exercises from Neuquen (Aries) between 18 and April 30 were executed, Comodoro Rivadavia (Centaur) and Rio Cuarto (Golondrina II) between 5 and 12 September, in what would be the operational training for Mobile Air Squadrons, which should be completely autonomous in regard to operations and maintenance.

During Operation Centauro, June 4, C-420 crashed during the landing at threshold of runway 25 of Comodoro Rivadavia. The aircraft was damaged 3% due to the rupture of the uprights of the landing gear and three days during the same exercise, there was another accident when Dagger C-413 skidded off runway during landing. Both aircraft were recovered, the fisrt having be repaired in Rio Cuarto.

The first Dagger to be subjected to a major inspection (ICM), which also coincided with being the first ICM carried out in Argentina to a Mirage was C-415. It began to be held at the premises of the Maintenance Group Area Material Rio Cuarto on May 22, 1980 and lasted until October 15, when he made the post maintenance flight with Captain Donadille at the controls.

On July 9, 1980 on the occasion of the celebrations for the Independence Day, eleven Daggers participated in a parade that took place on the city of Buenos Aires operating from Ezeiza Airport. They made it, returned to Tandil where they made a pass over the city forming a "escuadrillón". On August 10, 1980 participated in a new parade, this time in the city of Rosario, on occasion of the anniversary of the creation of the Air Force.

Also in 1980 the capability for nighttime operation of the unit would be reached, but in the context of such training would be seriously damaged one of precious two-seaters. On October 7 when conducting a training sortie aboard C-425, Captains Mir Gonzalez and Maffeis engaged the emergency barricade while performing an ILS approach then reset without landing. While both drivers were unharmed, the plane smashed into the runway causing 70% damage after it caught fire what led to being wfu.

While the border crisis with Chile had been formally overcome, some friction continued in the border area. On 7 and 8 September 1980 the Argentine government denounced an "act of provocation" by units of the Chilean Navy, who tried to interfere with the activities of an oil platform, Interocean II rented by Yacimientos Petrolíferos Fiscales (YPF) in Argentine territorial waters near the eastern mouth of the Strait of Magellan.

This time, a Chliean police helicopter landed on it to suggest to the authorities of the platform should be moved from that spot since it hindered navigating the narrow, difficult access. That request was not carried out for obvious reasons and days later, two Chilean torpedo boats were present in the area with the same demands.

Argentina's response was swift so it was decided to install Military Air Base Río Gallegos a Westinghouse TPS-43 radar, its CIC (Center for Information and Control) and an anti-aircraft battery. Also, the FAA ordered the execution of a series of exercises in the south on a regular basis. These operations, called "Checking South" held in Rio Gallegos, began during that year and saw the active participation of FAA combat aircraft including the Daggers that deployed south in early October and for 45 days, under the name Airmobile Squadron M-5.

The deployment of all the support staff and spare parts for these types of operations, required the support of a C-130 Hercules and one or two Fokker F-27s. Each deployment to a forward base involved transferring at least two/three starting cartridges for each aircraft, a compressor for filling them, one or two Harlan tow vehicles, 1.300 litres drop tanks, bomb racks, cannon chassis, boxes with hydraulic fluid, oil, bags and test benches of different systems, tools, spare parts and a complete engine, plus the technical team consisting of not less than 30-40 men.

During this "Checking South" exercise two new incidents took place of utmost importance that showed the constant tension that existed with Chile despite two years of the completion of the Beagle crisis. In the first, TPS-43 operators noted that it was being jammed, so it led a Dagger that was on a surveillance mission in the area of the Beagle Channel, under Captain Donadille, to the focus of the interference was thought to be a helicopter.

Once at low level, he detected a ship mailing with here flag foldedMade the descent a ship sailing under its flag collection was detected. With the landing gear deployed, Dona-

The IAI team carrying out the work of aircraft delivery resides the Argentine pilot. [IAI via Brig (R) Luis Villar]

dille made several passes, identifying the Wessel as the MV Coastal Transport. After this episode, the jamming ceased and it was determined that the ship was flying the Liberian flag.

In the second incident the Daggers were also envolved. This time two aircraft were on three minute alerto n the Tarlac, creced by Captain Donadille and 1st. Lieutenant Dellepiane, the CIC ordered them to take off to intercept an unidentified echo moved northwards in the Rio Turbio, west of Rio Gallegos on the border with Chile. Guided by the CIC, the section intercepted its target turned out to be a Douglas DC-6B, registration 986, Chilean Air Force flying over Lake Argentino, being forced to leave the Argentine airspace.

At that time, coinciding with the replacement programme in the IDF/AF of remaining Neshers remaining by Kfir C-2, the Israel Aircraft Industries offered a second batch of aircraft.

In this case it was eleven single seaters and a pair of two seaters that would be acquired under the contract DAG/ 2 dated September 22, 1980 for a total of U$D 62,891,800 and the price of machines was set at U$D 4,353.800 for the fighter and U$D 7,500,000 for the combat trainer.

To continue the planned upgrade project, it was established that the tests be carried out on a machine of this last contract, and that C-419 that remained in Israel had to be delivered to Argentina, which took place on 23 December 1980. the SINT project, thus, continued on the first jet of the new contract, which would later become C-427.

In late 1980, VI Air Brigade had a strengh of 24 pilots who flew 2,900 hours during the course of that year. In 1981 several solo flights were made, the first of which took place on April 13, by the Vicecommodor Tomáss A. Rodríguez who would take over as new Air Group C.O.. The second course consisted of the 1st. Lieutenant Hector Luna and Lieutenants Mario Callejo and José Ardiles as students, and its instructors Captains Mir Gonzalez and Dellepiane and 1st Lt. Dimeglio. Finally, on 30 November, three new sublieutenants performed their first solo, Daniel Valente, Luis Cismondi and Carlos Castillo. It can be said that throughout the history of the Mirage at the FAA, the VI Air Brigade was the first to receive personal with so little flying experience to train them on a plane which represented a large demand for pilots.

"A very special maiden flight," Major (R) Guillermo Posadas

As she was ready for delivery at IAI's the first two-seater (C-438), Major Villar asked if I could assist as a flight engineer for the test flight. With great pleasure I accepted and so on April 9, 1981, we completed the routine.

Before that, the IAI maintenance staff of asked if I ever had flown on Mirage, to which I replied that yes, I had in Argentina. Then they

First flight of C-431 in Israel. It already has the SEA (South East Asia) as requested by the FAA. [IAI via Brig (R) Luis Villar]

C-429 landing in Tandil. Note Technical Group 6 patch painted on the vertical fin. [VI Air Brigade]

Dagger Weapon System badge. [VI Air Brigade]

asked me if I had flown Dagger in Israel and at my negative reply I was told then that by the end of the flight I was going to be"baptized" according to tradition.

Upon landing without incident, after a beautiful flight which reached 62,500 feet, I was waiting on a tank barrel, from those used to empty the fuel tanks of aircraft, allegedly with water. I took off the anti-g, and life jacket and was introduced in the "water" ... but it was actually JP4 fuel!. They kept me head so I could not leave the tank and I swallowed fuel through the nose, ears and mouth ... I thought I was dying until I managed to sneak from one side and exit. I could not speak, I went straight to bath and soap did not make lather as grease was tremendous. Finally someone handed me detergent for washing aircraft and managed to get off me the fuel that had stuck to the skin, which I had completely red, as if burned.

From there I went to the infirmary of the factory and the doctor said I was fine and sent me home. That night I was "flying" of fever and had an impressive otitis and it took one month get over that incident.

Of course explanations were requested, including the Air Attaché in France asked to receive a written reply and as stated, someone got "wrong" and put a fuel tank instead of water. Of research conducted by our team we determined that it was in retaliation for our zeal to receive the material in conditions and that they made them waste time and awards.

Grupo 6 de Caza

In order to receive the new batch of aircraft acquired a new technical committee under the command of 1° Teniente Posadas and five experienced NCOs (SM O. Tolini, SA H. Gimenez, SA Maldonado, Saux. JC Villarreal and SAux Pozzi) was appointed..

For flight evaluation trials of the SINT project Mayor Villar was commissioned to who arrived at the time of delivery of the first four Dagger. This second commission was marked by many difficulties and problems generated by IAI staff. Corresponding to the revision contracted in most cases issues they were not met or were continually checked.

Modifications and agreed checks included a further inspection of the aiframe, placement of engines overhaul performed, placement of Collins radio and navigation system, modernization of instruments by placing ADI and HSI and unpainted and painted complete with the colors requested by the FAA.

Dagger C-428 arrived in Argentina on June 22, 1981. Almost a year later would be destroyed during the Falklands War. [Brigada Aérea VI]

C-404 operating in Tandil. This first batch Dagger would be lost during the Malvinas/ Falklands War. [Brigada Aérea VI]

Soon after arriving the Argentine commission, IAI tried that it received four aircraft ready, so and before the contract clause requiring inspection tasks by Argentine staff, but the Argentines proceeded to thoroughly review the aircraft.

Thus it was found that the earlier painting had not been removed, had canopy ejection cartridges corroded without replacing filters and expired due, among other issues.

This situation led to many brushes with IAI Project Manager, Mr. Gershoni and his technical staff, having started work again. Even, on numerous occasions, it was found that some elements had been changed after inspection by the Argentine commission, which brought about further delays and complications. The delay in delivery by Collins avionics elements produced more changes in the delivery.

The flight of the first two-seater Dagger completed, C-438, was held on 9 April 1981 by Mayor Villar and 1° Teniente Posadas. Once the inspection of the first six aircraft completed, they began to prepare the transfer to the port of Ashdod, complex task due to the need to pass through very narrow streets and plenty of power and phone lines that corssed them.

The last Daggers

Daggers (C-428, 429, 430, 431, 433 and 438) were on board the ship ELMA General San Martin and arrived in Argentina on 22 June 1981. Finally, the last six Daggers,

C-432, 434, 435, 436, 437 and 439 were embarked on the vessel ELMA Tucuman reaching Buenos Aires on 21 October 1981.

Teniente José Ardiles (center) posing in front of C-413 after making his solo flight on June 12, 1981. To his left is Capitán Ruben Dimeglio, his instructor, accompanied by Teniente Mario Callejo who also made his solo flight on that date. Ardiles, was KIA during the war, after being shot down by a Sea Harrier [Brigada Aérea VI]

Escuadrón Dagger pilots when operating in Rio Cuarto. Even they war the original blue scarf. [Comodoro (R) Carlos N. Martinez]

Like the previous year, over 1981 were carried out several exercises, the first of them Zonda II and Zonda IV conducted between 28 May and 6 June, operating from the IV Brigada Aérea at Mendoza.

Between 2 and 9 October Operating Blazon I, which mobilized the entire Air Force to the north of the country and consisted of an to opposing sides exercise. The G6C (Grupo 6 de Caza) sent an airmobile squadron with six Daggers to Jujuy Airport as a central base of operations, continuously redeploying overnight at other airfields in the area to keep the element of surprise on the enemy side.

Between 21 and 28 October the Dagger deployed back to Jujuy to carry out with the Argentine Army Coya III exercise, operating in the area of San Antonio de los Cobres. By year end, more precisely in December 1981 the Daggers deployed to BAM Rio Gallegos was performed in order to carry exercise Sur III.

It is also noteworthy participation in the Joint excercise Chapaleufú, made with the Argentine Army in the vicinity of the city of Azul where live ammunition was used, which also involved the Dagger, within which the C- 415 flown by Capitán Donadille was configured with 500 litre tanks MADNAP bomb racks, dropping in salvo fourteen 125 kg bombs, being one of the few opportunities that this configuration was used.

During this first phase of operations, the Daggers accumulated a total 8,557 flight hours (3,205 for 1981). In this period to the end of 1983, the presence of Israeli advisors was highly appreciated by the VI Brigada Aérea staff, especially Moshe Shani, an expert in first-line maintenance. In turn, the instructor Shlomo Erez rendered valuable services in the Air Group, managing to convey to the Argentine pilots his great experience in air-to-air combat. His identification with the Argentine cause cause during the Falklands war was such that he volunteered to fight with the rest of Dagger the pilots, which obviously was not authorized.

At the end of 1981 Brigadier Robert F. Camblor assumed command of VI Brigada Aérea, while Comodoro Thomas A. Rodríguez was the new C.O. of Grupo 6 de Caza. Meanwhile, Comodoro Pedro Martinez took over Grupo Técnico 6, on the other hand Mayor Carlos N. Martinez was appointed Escuadrón Operativo II, replacing Mayor Villar who had moved to Israel to fulfill three tasks of paramount importance: SINT design and integration in the Dagger, receiving the second batch of Daggers and operational design of flight simulators that the FAA had acquired.

In 1982, with the start of the activity in the military year, the G6C continued with the incorporation of new pilots, this time Captain Luis Demierre, 1° Tenientes Carlos Antonietti, José Luis Gabari Zoco and Jorge Reta. In turn, Vicecomodoro Oscar Aranda Durañona and Mayor Gustavo Piuma Justo joined the unit, initiating the planned training and the following year they planned to take over as head of Group and Squadron respectively.

Hard at work without the vast majority of the members of the unit having any knowledge, 2 April 1982 dawned with the news of the recovery of the Malvinas (Flaklands) Islands by the Argentine armed forces ...

Anecdotes. "Logistics in bus" Brigadier (R) Luis D. Villar

During the first months in which the Dagger Squadron was based on the Area Material Rio Cuarto, we had to implement a rather curious supply system. Through a telephone call that was

On October 15, 1981, Captain Donadille had the privilege of making the acceptance flight of the first Dagger (C-415) that recived a major cycle inspection (ICM) in Argentina, being accepted in the Area Material Rio Cuarto on 22 May 1980. [Via Brigadier (R) Ruben Dimeglio]

made every day between 11 and 12, we asked the Brigada Aérea VIII (distant 800 km from Rio Cuarto) spare parts needed to continue the operation of the aircraft. In the afternoon we received them through a bus line and turn the same way we sent our stuff. All went well, and we never had problems, never lacked anything.

"They do not know how to stop..." Brigadier (R) Carlos A. Moreno

In late 1979 I joined the Training Squadron with 1° Teniente Battioni. Also later, already in 1980, four lieutenants joinded us: Aguirre Faget, Volponi, Bean and Bernhardt and later also in that year, ten came, a while later Cesar Roman also was posted. Sapolsky was the Trainign Squadron C.O., and the instructors were Donadille, Mir Gonzalez, Dellepiane and Dorado.

One day I left to fly in C-407 in a section with Mir Gonzalez. On landing, the jet veered to the Leith 45 degrees , when I started to slow down, it Leith the runway, a continued for about 300 metres over the "green". The aircraft was not damaged, not even the airframe was stressed.

That day Sapolsky formed his squadron and we were "challenged" telling "students know not stop the Mirage". The next day they checked the plane and apparently had nothing and came flying Sapolsky, makes two abortions burns off and the brakes because he raised temperature. The next day was for flight again. I played out with Mir Gonzalez and me reallocated the C-407. yet still sensitive by what had happened, Mir told me to change the plane. We went out, we did air-to-air, and when we landed, Mir Gonzalez - who was the "master of the master" - he went off the runway when braking. After a more deeply investigation about the causes of this new incident, it was discovered

Grupo 6 de Caza pilotos, from left to right t César Román, Ruben Dimeglio, José Luis Gabari Zoco and Carlos Rohde from of the Air Group facilities with Israeli advisor Moshe Shani in early 1982. [Via Brigadier (R) Ruben Dimeglio]

that the aircraft had one intermittent bug that caused that one of the wheels blocked, ie the brake system called Ministop failed, similar to ABS found in cars. Luckily I had changed the Aircraft., and that if he throw me, surely I had been fired by "useless".

"Close Encounters" Brigadier (R) Luis D. Villar

During one of Dagger's second batch the acceptance flights, while performing the last part of it, which consisted of a leg in supersonic flight from sea to land (Tel Aviv) and subsequent low-speed maneuvers, I noticed that F-15s closed on me, believing they were pilots of the Israeli Air Force who knew me I started doing the classic combat maneuvers (scissors) to make them overtake me, then I got radio a call from ground control, where I was ordered to fly straight and level and follow their instructions strictly. The F-15 escorted me to landing, and already on the ground I heard that as IAI had not passed my flight plan, the defence system saw unidentified flying going supersonic at 50,000 feet, and not having other information scrambled the fighters. By then coming down and making other controls, and almost give me ... The pilots were unfamiliar with the aircraft in the new camouflage schme and a Star of David in light blue.

Grupo Técnico 6 badge applied to some Daggers.

Grupo 6 de Caza in the postwar

After the Falklands War in June 1982, Group 6 was forced to reschedule the activity for the rest of the year under the normal routine of peacetime, ending interrupted training courses and planning new deployments and exercises.

The incorporation of the ten AMD-BA Mirage 5P (known within the Argentine Air Force Force - FAA - as M-5P) to within the VI Air Brigade represented a major breakthrough that allowed recompose the fleet again aircraft to prewar levels. The M-5P acquired from Peru were not assigned to a new air squadron and began to be flown by pilots more experienced as there were some differences between this jet and the Dagger.

However, the general state of the "Peruvian" Mirages was pretty bad, so a process to put them at suitable service began. Pursuant to the differences presented with Dagger, on November 13, 1986, these machines as part of

Operation "Kaolin" were deployed and assigned to Squadron 10 Hunting with a seat in the X Air Brigade (Rio Gallegos) , replacing the IIICJ Mirage acquired in Israel after the South Atlantic Conflict. The Mirage IIICJ would be transferred to Squadron Cruz and Fierro Group 4 Game of the IV Air Brigade Mendoza, unit which unified the operation of this model, achieving alternative optimization in the logistics.

On the other hand, immediately after the cessation of the conflict, the SINT project was restarted and, over the years were entering service Finger - that the new name of the project - in a process that lasted until 1989 where the cars Dagger survivors were modernized through the standard Finger I, II, IIIA to finish in the final version Finger IIIB. Thus, the FAA began to identify their two seat Daggers as M-5D and the new Fingers as M-5F.

Operational activity

The impact resulted in international public opinion the performance of the pilots of the Argentina Air Force and his fellow Naval Aviation and Army Aviation Command, led the visit of different personalities of the aviation world to our country and more specifically to Air Force units.

Indeed, the October 23, 1982, Colonel (RE) Pierre Clostermann, French ace of World War II, visited the VI Air Brigade to congratulate in person to the Argentine pilots for the bravery and courage shown during the conflict against United Kingdom.

Between 1 July and 9 July 1983 took place in Tandil the first exercise of air-to-air between aircraft different performances (dissimilar combat) in which they operated A-4B Skyhawk, IA-58A Pucará, Mirage IIIEA and M-5.

As an indication of the activity carried out by the unit since its inception, December 7, 1983, were completed 16,000 hours of flight, maintenance 235,000 hours and 17,500 outlets by the M-5.

Moreover, a series of exercises were planned immediately after the war in order to apply the lessons that emerged from it and deepen the analysis of the capabilities and shortcomings of different weapons systems.

After the Falklands conflict, the Dagger returned to his peace time base at Tandil and resumed their normal training activity. In turn, it started the modernization process that led to the Finger standard. [Collection Vladimiro Cettolo]

Deployments Finger Squadron I were permanent during the 80. Here it can be can C-415 taking off from the Nuequén airport, operating under "Aike". [Angel Bertogna]

The Finger IIIA C-424 preparing for a bombing and gunnery practice operating from the IV Air Brigade in Mendoza, September 1988. Set in version Golf (two tanks of 1,300 liters] with two pumps BK-125 BR Nafgan support in the ventral and two pumps CES1 bomb racks exercise in seasons 1 and 7. [Angel Bertogna]

In an intermediate step towards the total elimination of external identifications, some machines retained tuition and enrollment in the bow, eliminating the badge, shield and reducing the size of the rear license plate, as in the C-427 seen in Tandil in April 1991. [Horacio J. Clariá]

New policies aircraft identification applied after the Falklands War made it virtually impossible to externally identify Finger, who lost all its markings except the national flag, as seen in the C-429 photographed in the VI Air Brigade in December 1989. [Jorge R. Figari]

The two-seater C-439 deployed in the X Air Brigade of Rio Gallegos in April 1994 Hotel configured version with two tanks of 1700 liters. [Carlos A. Garcia]

Until the mid-90 remained the last Finger painted in the original SEA scheme, this being replaced by low visibility. In the photo C-405 and C-412 behind with the later scheme. [Carlos A. Garcia]

The Finger IIIA C-424 in Tandil platform in December 1989. This jet would not be changed to standard Finger IIIB and left to serve after reaching the expiration of his cell in 1997. [Jorge R. Figari]

Despite not being involved in combat, the Dagger B C-426 received the silhouette of the Falkland Islands and for a vessel in his left intake. [Jorge R. Figari]

In this context, the June 30, 1984 was held in the IV Air Brigade Operational "Zonda 84". It consisted in a new theoretical and practical air-air exercise between aircraft of different performances to update and devise operating procedures use the material supplied combat. Participating aircraft A-4B/C Skyhawk, Mirage IIIEA/DA, F-86F Sabre and Pucará while Group II Air Surveillance and Control deployed a three-dimensional TPS-43 radar Westinghouse. The VI Air

The Dagger B C-439 at a time entered the Hangar 1 Squadron Workshops Technical Group 6 where it would be painted in the gray air superiority scheme in June 1997. It was the last operational jet to preserve the original scheme. [Horacio J. Clariá]

Brigade Mendoza sent his Dagger and the Finger II C-405 that had recently entered service.

The flight line was diminished on May 16, 1985 when the Dagger C-431 crashed into the sea in the range of Mar Chiquita in the province of Buenos Aires. Under the command of Captain Robert Prior had taken off from Tandil to make an issue of air-to-ground (dive bombing at 45 ° and shooting guns). After the release of exercise bombs of 25 pounds, the pilot felt pitch with sudden movements that became ungovernable off the plane. Unable to recover the pilot ejected at low altitude, being rescued by a helicopter search and rescue station. This oscillation mode suffered the plane is a variant of the short period known as Dynamic Instability Longitudinal (Porpoising) and was a characteristic phenomenon of Nesher, given the location of the center of gravity. Since 1980 they had reported seven cases of Porpoising, all aircraft of this type, but not as severe as those suffered by the C-431 and its consequences.

The IV Air Brigade hosted a new year exercise named "Zonda" between 9 and 16 June 1985 with the participation of the M-5D/F, where continued training the pilots in dissimilar air combat maneuvering.

That same year, more precisely on September 4, then President Argentina, Dr. Raul R. Alfonsin visited the unit and aboard the C-438 made a flight of 30 minutes under Major Mir Gonzalez. Under the indicative "Homeland" she took off Dagger B becoming the first flight of an Argentine president in an aircraft of the Mirage family.

In March 1988 were transferred to the VI Air Brigade Mirage IIIEA / DA from the Eighth Air Brigade. Since then, both jointly operated weapons systems deployed simultaneously on different operating that followed until today. [VI Air Brigade]

Finger IIIB C-415 landing at VI Air Brigade's runway, while deploying the cruciform braking parachute. [Horacio J. Clariá]

On 13 November 1986 the M-5 met its first 25,000 hours of flight, a fact that led to a series of celebrations in the Brigade.

Gradually, he began to apply a new policy aircraft identification, which began eliminated rosettes, plates and unit markings, remaining only the national flag at the helm, giving the aircraft an absolutely anonymous appearance.

On June 12, 1987 in a field near Tandil ground he rushed the Dagger C-418 while on routine maneuvers, eyectándose its pilot, Captain Fernando Robledo, uneventfully. At that time, the captain Robledo took off as Section Chief to complete a topic of air-to-air combat and while conducting tactical maneuvers vertical combat, his plane went into a flat spin and after several unsuccessful attempts to regain control of the plane, he decided to eject resulting in the completely destroyed on impact with the ground machine.

Another outstanding participation was recorded to mark the 75th anniversary of the creation of the Argentina Air Force on August 10, 1987 where a major flyover in the I Air Brigade of El Palomar was performed. Group 6 of Hunting displayed their endowment Finger and Dagger in service biplazas Dr. Mariano Moreno Aerodrome (home of the Air Brigade VIII) where he also attended the Mirage IIIC IV of Br. Ae. and Mirage 5P X Br. ae., joining the MIIEA / lo-

A squadron of M5F / D operating from Pajas Blancas (Córdoba Prov.] From where they took off for air shows during the Open Days in October 1996 at the Military Aviation School. [Horacio J. Clariá]

The Finger IIIB C-434 rolling after completing a training flight, set to Bravo version with two supersonic tanks of 500 liters. This configuration is often used as training for air to air combat. [Horacio J. Clariá]

cal DA, taking place the highest concentration of the Mirage family history of the FAA.

A strong involvement of devices Group 6 in routine exercises continued during the year. Indeed, for the September 8, 1987 Squadron I was deployed to the X Air Brigade, where it operated until 13, then leaving for the airport Neuquén to complete the operation "Aike" navigation and attack military targets simulated until the 19th of that month.

As part of a broad restructuring of the Air Force, March 7, 1988 took place the dissolution of the Eighth Air Brigade and the transfer of Fighter Group 8 Tandil. Thus Fighter Group 6 was formed by two Squadrons (I and II) equipped with Dagger / Finger, Squadron with Mirage III IIIEA and Training Squadron operate the two-seaters of both models.

That year, a new loss would affect the unit when the C-435 fell to the ground on 19 November 1988. The machine under Captain Daniel R. Justet had taken off from the X Air Brigade to make a navigation flight back to navigation Rio Cuarto when he noticed clear signs of an engine failure. Unable to recover the situation, the pilot successfully ejected, resulting in the totally destroyed aircraft.

From 1990 it began to be used a low visibility camouflage to Fighter Group 6 jets to replace the traditional Southeast Asian and after various assessments light gray air superiority, which completely covered the plane was chosen as had started be implemented shortly before the fleet of M-IIIEA / DA.

As the Finger began dating Inspection were completely painted with this scheme, although four aircraft (C-401, 411, 414 and 421) would never come to receive this coloration for being out of service and seriously cannibalized, wearing traditional in three colors until his deprogramming.

Between 26 and 29 November 1992 took place in the IV Air Brigade and the Tactical Shooting Range "Antuna" Competition and Shooting Tactical Evaluation "Dragon I". The VI Air Brigade earned him the 1st prize General "FAA Cup" and the 1st Bombardment Prize in Picado with M-III and M-5 aircraft.

The provision of Finger suffered a new low on 25 October 1993. This time, while the C-427 is it effected a test engine in mamelón point fixed Area Material Rio Cuarto, the plane began to catch fire product of engine failure. Despite the action of anti-fire services, the damage was so great that determined their release. The front of the plane did not suffer major damage so was repaired and transformed into a testbed for the fuel system on the hard drive.

A new operation called "Air Defense" was carried out between 13 and 18 September 1993 in the X Air Brigade in southern Argentina, where he again participated the M-5F and M-III along with local M-5A Mara in a direct air defense exercise Sector defense GAL.

On May 31, 1994 took place an accident to Finger IIIB C-405 on the runway of the VI Air Brigade with 98% destruction. Under the command of 1st Lt. Fabian Costanzi, Finger was in the thresold to start off for a bombing exercise in the weapons range of Mar Chiquita. The aircraft was configured in the Golf version with two underwing 1,300 liter tanks at the start of the takeoff, the pilot noticed an engine failure, so he decided to abort the takeoff and address the barrier was deployed. However, the barrier down and the Finger could not stop the remain-

Interesting view where you can see the wing configuration of Finger C-408 while walking the runway for take-off position at the head. [Horacio J. Clariá]

ing part of the runway ending about 400 meters from the area to stop. The pilot suffered minor injuries and the aircraft was destroyed by the subsequent fire caused by the off track.

Another accident affected Squadron M-5 the following year, when the Finger IIIB C-413 was destroyed on September 14, 1995 while conducting air-to-air combat maneuvers on the outskirts of Tandil. The plane went into a tail-spin and unable to regain control of the aircraft, the captain decided eyectarse Raul Gomez, reaching land without consequences.

Between 12 and 18 October 1995 took place in Neuquén Operational "Escort" in which participated the Finger and Mirage III G6C. From there they performed the various presidential escort aircraft that landed at the airport of the city of Bariloche on the occasion of the "V Iberoamerican Summit of Presidents".

During 1996, more precisely on 18 and 19 greater than 1996 M-5 and M-III were deployed to Naval Air Base Commander Espora to participate in the major Open Days organized by the Naval Aviation called "Spore 96 ". The C-415, commanded by Captain Juan José Janer, held an exhibition by the M-IIIEA I-008, 1st Lt. Marcelo Del Punta, which showed their performances against the Super Etendard local. This show was one of the largest made in recent times and was attended by all the military aircraft Argentine.

The rest of the year, continued performing routine exercises as part of the scheduled annual activity, including the Operational "Napaleufú" dispersion consisting of aircraft and darkening in Tandil Base completed October 9, 1996.

In October of the same year it was held in the premises of the Military Aviation School in Cordoba a new air show. It included the organization of a private company and was a success both by the audience and by the great flight activity was recorded. It was conducted on 4, 5, 6, 11, 12 and 13. In the first three days, airshows aircraft of "Delta" family were in charge of the Mirage III (I-003, 007 and 012) while on the last weekend three Finger (C-415, 416 and 434) and Dagger B (C-438) made spectacular passes. This time, in their respective weekends, both weapons systems deployed at Pajas Blancas International Airport under the length of the runway of the EAM not allow them to operate safely.

For the month of December 1996 closing the X Air Brigade, which fell into the category of Military Air Base and the dissolution of its air component, the Squad 10 Hunting "Cruz and Fierro" was available - also known as "Ice Warriors" - given the small overhead lines in service (three M-5A Mara) and the logistical difficulties involved in its operation. In a ceremony held on December 19, these aircraft were officially transferred to the VI Air Brigade which decided to create a new squadron of instruction, which would maintain the spirit of its name, identifying himself now as Squadron 10 Examination "Ice Warriors". In addition to aligning the M-5A Mara, also it operated fleet seaters (M-5D and M-IIIDA) on training missions becoming the "School of Supersonic Hunting" where the pilots who then would integrate the Esc formed. I M-5F or Esc. II M-IIIE. To differentiate itself from the other two squadrons of Mirage, the pilots used a handkerchief white color.

After the launch, the pilot checks the correct operation of the moving surfaces of Finger C-429 (August 1999). Subsequently, this device would be destroyed in an accident on 18 October 2000. [Horacio J. Clariá)

In order to participate in the aeronautical parade it was held on August 13, 1997 on the I Air Brigade to mark the Day of the Air Force, Group 6 Game deployed part of its means to Ezeiza International Airport, participating one Total sixteen machines Mirage (Five Finger family - C-408, 415, 416, 420 and 434 - two Dagger B - C-426 and 439 - two Mirage IIIDA - I-002 and 021 - five Mirage IIIEA - I-003, 005, 007, 008 and 013 - and two M-5A Mara - C-604 and 619 -), showing a notable effort of the Technical Group 6.

19Oct 17 to 97 took place Mantenar exhibition organized at the headquarters of the Military Aviation School. The event combined an exhibition of aircraft maintenance with an air show attended by various weapons systems FAA. The participation of aircraft VI Air Brigade was in charge of a Dagger B (C-439), an M-5A Mara (C-604) and a Mirage IIIEA (I-003) that operated directly from Tandil. They performed numerous solo and in formation past the delight of the public.

On 7 November the same year in the VI Air Brigade commemorated the 25th anniversary of Mirage IIIEA in the Argentina Air Force. This requires a great feast was held in the unit where the Mirage and staff who operated from their arrival until then were his protagonists. The other relatives of the Mirage family could not miss the celebrations began with a series of low-level flights by a squad led by a Mirage IIIEA (I-008) with a Finger IIIB (C-434) and Mara (C -619) as numerals, who performed last in training and individually, with stunning breaks off the platform where the public was invited.

Cancelled upgrade

During that year it had also conducted the study for the upgrade of several subsystems. Basically the replacement of the gyroscopic inertial platform by a girolasérica center and support GPS, change communication equipment was sought, the installation of a RWR associated with a pitcher of flares and chaff and the adoption of a probe for refueling flight. a budget of $ 39 million was estimated, but finally the project would be canceled.

Finger in Tandil

In early August 1998, twentyone aircraft of the Mirage family again moved to Ezeiza to parade on the Day of the Air Force at El Palomar.

They were then redeployed to the IV Air Brigade (Mendoza) from where they operated while maintenance was done on the runway of Tandil which would remain closed for three weeks.

The 16th of the same month, four Finger IIIB and four Mirage IIIE left for the V Air Brigade, Villa Reynolds, to participate in the Combined Exercise "Eagle I" where they operated alongside the A-4AR Fightinghawks of Grupo 5 de Caza and the

F-16C/D Fighting Falcons of the 160th Fighter Squadron, 187th Fighter Wing belonging to the Alabama Air National Guard based in Montgomery.

The operation consisted in the formation of an aerospace defense sector around the Bri-

Cruzex 2002 was the first international operation in which Escuadrón I deployed its M5Fs, allowing the Finger to operate with different models of the Mirage family belonging to Brazil, Chile and France. Among the planes sent by the G6C was C-423. [Javier A. Mosquera]

gade, participating means of combat and support of both countries. This exercise was an excellent opportunity to evaluate the performances of the weapons systems of the Mirage and A-4 family in front of the most advanced F-16. It was the first participation of US F-16 aircraft in the country and was a preparation for a possible future Argentine participation in Red Flag exercises that are held periodically in the US, which at the time was still not materialized.

In late 1998, more precisely in the month of December, the 20th anniversary of the weapon system Dagger/Finger was commemorated that by then had accumulated 43,267 flight hours. An emotional ceremony attended by many of the pilots and technical staff who worked with the Dagger from arrival in the country was conducted.

On 10 August 1999 the Air Force Day was celebrated in the facilities of the I Air Brigade with a major flyover followed by a weekend with Open Days. This time the machines pf Grupo 6 de Caza took part in the flypast operating directly from Tandil. That morning, on the taxiway of the VI Air Brigade they lined twenty Mirage to take off to Buenos Aires. The impressive flight line consisted of nine Mirage IIIEA/DA (I-002, 004, 005, 006, 007, 008, 011, 013 and 021), eight Dagger B/Finger IIIB (C-408, 415, 417, 420, 426, 429, 438 and 439) and four M-5A Mara (C-609, 610, 619 and 628). It is interesting to note that for this event and for a while until any of them entered an overhaul period, the entire fleet of of five two-seaters was available. This was not often the case for several years and the unit could take the time to fully exploit the available hours in the precious combat trainers.

Between August 30 and September 2 joint operations with the Naval Aviation were made.

Finger IIIB C-420 during Exercise Eagle II developed in the V Air Brigade. This machine was the only one to take Argentina Air Force titles in the low visibility scheme. [Javier A. Mosquera]

Finger operating in Kilo configuration (two tanks of 1.300 litres and one of 880 liters] for Air Force Day Parade on August 10, 1999 held in the I Air Brigade of El Palomar. [FAA via Christian Amado]

Dagger B C-426 taking-off from Tandil to participate in the parade on August 10, 1999 where 21 aircraft participated G6C. [Horacio J. Clariá]

Overflight of the Andes as part of a deployment south of the country during Operation "Chaltén" in September 1999. [Juan J. Janer Com.]

It was a bombing exercise using the shooting range of Isla Verde (in the estuary of Bahia Blanca, south of the Province of Buenos Aires). Grupo 6 de Caza took part with its Fingers, Mirage III and Mara, alongside the Super Etendards of 2ª Escuadrilla Aeronaval de Caza y Ataque.

On 23 September 1999, G6C, with their M-5F/M-5D (C-408, 417, 420, 426, 429 and 439), M-IIIEA/DA (I-004, 005, 007, 011 and 021) and M-5A (C-609, 610, 619 and 628), deployed to BAM Rio Gallegos to perform operation "Chaltén" for about one week (until 30 September), basically consisting of launching weapons on the range of of 11 Artillery Group Argentine Army and tactical navigations. During the event, 1st Ten Carlos Marenzi, at the controls of C-408 had to make an emergency landing at the airfield in the town of Puerto Santa Cruz after presenting engine problems which led to its replacement at the aerodrome.

After five years without major accidents, October 18, 2000 Squadron I lost Finger IIIB C-429 when Captain Alejandro Anzuinelli was on the take-off run from Tandil. When the jet veered from the runway, immediately the Leith main landing gear wheel detached. Unable to make an emergency landing as indicated by the Mirage family procedures manual, and after ejecting tanks and consume internal fuel, he made a successful controlled ejection.

Training Squadron 10 was deactivated on 11 November 2000, and the M-5D two seaters were returned to Escuadrón I, which also was assigned the M-5A. In this short time, Major Vicente Autiero, Luis A. Briatore and Roberto Andreasen had been the successive squadron commanders.

Later that year, between November 27 and December 1 was carried out a major exercise of air-to-air combat in Tandil. The same was the first deployment to the VI Air Brigade of the A-4AR Fightinghawk from Villa Reynolds, where

six of these jets, five M-IIIE Three Finger and two Maras performed several dogfight exercise. This training was an update for major combined operation a few months later that would be conducted with US aircraft.

Indeed, a new edition of Combined Exercise "Eagle II/Southern Falcon" was developed in the V Air Brigade from 18 to 28 April 2001. Again Squadron I M-5F participated in the same, deploying a M-5F flight consisting of C-420, 423 and 434and a two-seater F-5D (C-438) while the United States did the same with eight F-16C/Ds of the 121st Fighter Squadron, part of the 113rd Fighter Wing of the Air National Guard based in Maryland, Columbia. In addition to the local A-4ARs, also involving weresix M-IIIA/ DAs (I-002, 007, 008, 011, 013 and 017) and two Maras (C-610 and 628).

A section of Fingers overflies the lakes in southern Argentina, near the border with Chile, August 1999. [Juan J. Janer Com.]

Multinational exercises conducted in the Southern Cone countries would take on a new dimension since 2002, when the important exercise "Cruzex" was held. In succeeding years similar maneuvers combined in Chile and Argentina they would be held.

To raise the level to the optimum required to participate in an exercise of this category, the FAA organized the Operation "Pre-Cruzex" in Reynolds. Between 8 and 12 April 2002 different air combat maneuvering and flights package (- LFE - Large Force Employment) a new concept for the use of air assets began to be incorporated into the FAA and its South American col-

A pair of Fingers during a tactical navigation in Hotel configurations. It provides the maximum range (over 2,500 km] due to the lower resistance of these tanks against India configuration (three 1,300 litre tanks]. [Juan J. Janer Com.]

During the deployments to BAM Rio Gallegos, the Fingers often perform long-range navigation to attack simulated targets, flying hundreds of kilometres of Patagonian steppe. [Juan J. Janer Com.]

Grupo 6 de Caza Finger taking-off from the Cóndores Air Base (Chile] during the combined exercise "Salitre 2004". [FAA]

Participation in t operation "Salitre 2004" allowed the Esc M5 make an interesting exchange of combat procedures within the framework of tactical flight in Large Force Employment. [FAA]

leagues) was executed with Fightinghawks between the V Air Brigade and deployed Mirage unit (two Fingers two Maras and three M-IIIEs).

A few weeks later, Squadron I M-5F deployed five jets (C-408, 412, 423, 432 and 434) and a two-seater (C-438) to Brazil to participate in Operation Combined "Cruzeiro do Sul/Cruzex 2002" conducted between April 29 and May 11. The exercise was carried out in Canoas Air Base (Porto Alegre) where fighter aircraft the Air Forces of Brazil, Chile and France participated. This was a new challenge for the unit where its pilots operated alongside the Mirage 50 Panther Aviation Group No. 4 of the IV Chilean Air Brigade, the Mirage 2/2 2000-5F the Cote d'Or and 2000B of the EC 2/5 of the Armee de l'Air (by a KC-135FR ERV 93 of Istres and Boeing E-3F Sentry EDA 36) and Tiger II F-5E 1st Group Aviação de Caça and Mirage IIIEBR 1st Defesa Brazilian Air Group. It was an exercise where

Esc Finger pilots walk to the first line shack for de post flight debriefing. [Horacio J. Clariá]

Training in bombing missions was constant and numerous training sorties awere conducted throughout the year, using both real and practice bombs, as the Mk-76 that can be seen in the photograph. [Horacio J. Clariá]

Pilots of Squadron I prepare to take their place in the cockpit of a Dagger B for a flight training as parto f the conversión course to the Finger. [Horacio J. Clariá]

the two sides Finger attack missions conducted ground targets demonstrating the SINT effectiveness and accuracy having incorporated. In turn, this deployment was the first out of the Dagger/Finger abroad after 23 years of service.

That same year, between 13 and 18 October, was held in the V Air Brigade (Villa Reynolds) Exercise "Checking COA 2002". Participants all weapons systems FAA, making the aircraft of the Mirage family practice air-to-air, simulated attacks and real weapons delivery in the shooting ranges of the unit (Shooting Range of Exercise "Vcom Correa") combat and Tactical Shooting Range "Antuna" located 200km from Villa Reynolds. From Tandil they involved three Squadron I Finger IIIB and three Squadron II Mirage IIIEAs, Pucarás operating with the Third Air Brigade, Pampa and Morane Saulniers MS.760 of the IVAir Brigade and the A-4ARs of the V Brigade. The Fingers mainly placed in fighter-bomber role using 1.300 litre drop tanks and racks for practice bombs, while in other sorties droppend free-fall and parachute retarded 250 kg bombs..

Another highlight of 2002 was the visit of Air Chief Marshal of the Royal Air Force, Sir Peter Squire in what would be the first visit by a senior RAF officer after the cessation of hostilities in 1982.

Indeed, on December 9, 2002 and in the framework of a two-day stay in Argentina, the Chief of Staff of the RAF, visited the VI Air Brigade accompanied by the then Secretary General of the Air Force, Brigadier Horacio Mir González, a veteran Dagger pilot during the conflict over the Falkland Islands. In the unit, the then Chief Brigadier, Commodore Carlos Moreno (also veteran M5 pilot in Malvinas/ Flaklands) he made the delivery of Lt Nick Taylor personal documents, who died when their Sea Harrier FRS.Mk.1 (XZ450) was shot down May 4, 1982 during the South Atlantic Conflict. A special request Squire himself, made a flight in a two-seater Dagger (C-438) with Major at the controls Marcelo Cattani while Commodore Moreno did the same in another two-seater with Captain Carlos Moriones. This historic event marked the meeting who 20 years ago had fought on opposite sides.

On October 31, 2003 the ceremony was held in Tandil to commemorate the 30th anniversary of Mirage in Argentina. On that date the incorporation of Mirage IIIEA/ DA who began arriving in September 1972 was recalled, making the first flight in January 1973. The guests arrived aboard Boeing 707 TC-91 escorted on his leg to Tandil by Dagger B C-438 and Finger C-415.

On June 21, 2004 Finger C-434 crashed, after suffering an engine stop after initiating the Lansing circuit in the Area Material Rio Cuarto. Its pilot, 1st Lieutenant

Finger Squadron pilots posing in front one of its jets. The scarf with blue and red checkerboard is one of the hallmarks of the unit. [Fighter Group 6]

Sebastián González Iturbe successfully managed to eject, after repeated and unsuccessful attempts to restart the Atar 09C5A engine.

Overlooking the participation of a new international exercise, the FAA organized operation "Phoenix" carried out between August 26 and September 1. The headquarters of it was Villa Reynolds and participated the Fighter Group 5 Fightinghawks, Attack Group 3 Pucarás, four Pampas and four MS.760 Paris from Fighter Group 4 and Fighter Group 6 Mirages (four Mirage IIIs and four Fingers).

Between September 25 and October 10, 2004, Fighter Group 6 deployed three M-5F

Two M5F flying in close formation around the VI Air Brigade. [Hunting Group 6]

The Finger of the Argentina Air Force spent 37 years of service. However, it is not clear yet what will be its replacement, made of should be defined in the short term. [Hunting Group 6]

In April 2008, the C-426 had an accident while performing practice touch and go in Mar del Plata Airport. [Collection Mauricio Chiófalo]

Finger (C-412, 415 and 423), two M-IIIE (I-013 and 018) and an M-IIIDA (I-021) to Iquique, in northern Chile, to participate in the Combined Exercise "Salitre I". Operating from CóndoresAir Base, along with aircraft of the Chilean Air Force (six Mirage Panteras, eight Elkans, eight F-5E Tiger IIIs, eight A-37Bs), the US Air National Guard (Six F-16C Fighting Falcon of the 188th Fighter Squadron - 150th Fighter Wing, New Mexico Air National Guard - and two Boeing KC-135R Stratotanker from the 106th Air Refueling Squadron - 117th Air Refueling Wing, Alabama Air National Guard -) and Força Aérea Brasileira (six

Tiger F-5E II and Boeing KC-137), the operation of an air coalition was simulated in a low intensity conflict. It was a new opportunity to increase the interoperability of the participating Air Forces and practice planning and execution of joint air operations following NATO procedures.

Dagger & Finger in Argentine Air Force service

Traditional deployments to southern Argentina started again in 2005. Indeed, between 8 and 16 March took place Operation "Falcon" at BAM Rio Gallegos in which participated ten Fighter Group 6 aircrat (Finger, Mara and Mirage III).

At year's end, between 12 and 25 November was held a combined exercise with similar characteristics to "Salitre" organized for the first

Finger C-412, veteran of the Falklands, looks into its nose the kill-marks of the frigates HMS Brilliant and HMS Arrow. [Group 6]

Group 6 in full during the year "Pre Salitre 2009". In the photograph may be five models operated by the FAA Mirage: Finger IIIB, Dagger B, M5A Mara, and Mirage IIIEA / IIIDA. [Santiago Cortelezzi]

Finger C-408 parked on the tarmac of the Reconquista airflied, home of III Air Brigade where the unit participated in the "Pre Salitre 2009" along with the A-4AR, Pucará and Pampa. [Santiago Cortelezzi]

Two M5 from Esc I M5 performing escort to the Boeing 707 that brought the guests who attended the celebration of 30 years of the Mirage at the FAA on 31 October 2003. First may be the Dagger B C-438 with nose painted Black, Finger style. [Horacio J. Clariá]

TFinger C-423 set to Alpha configuration, no fuel tanks, prior to an air-to-air sortie with guns in Rio Gallegos, on June 3, 1993. [Carlos A. Garcia]

time by the FAA. With the name "Ceibo 2005", the main activity was held in the premises of the IV Air Brigade, participating the G6C with their machines (Finger C-412, 420 and 423 - Mirage III I-007, 011 and 013 and Mara C-603), together with the rest of the combat units of the FAA, which were joined by five Air Group 8, Chilean AF, Mirage 5MA/MD Elkan six AMX A-1A/B1/ from 10th GAV of the Brazilian Air Força and three Cessna A-37B Dragonfly from Air Squadron No. 2 (Fighter)) of the Uruguayan Air Force. In addition to the Mirage aircraft family, operated A-4AR Fightinghawk FMA IA-58A Pucará, Morane Saulnier MS.760 Paris and FMA IA-63 Pampa trainers, C-130 Hercules and Fokker F-27 transport and Bell 212 helicopters for SAR tasks, all of the FAA. The number of participants totaled 52 aircraft.

Dagger B C-426 taking off from the runway of the then X Air Brigade (current BAM Rio Gallegos) on 11 June 1993. This jet was one of three two seaters in Group 6, of a total of five acquired. [Carlos A. Garcia]

A Finger and Mirage 5A Mara (left) performing a navigation on the Argentine Sea during deployment south of the country made in June 2009. [Collection Santiago Cortelezzi]

The proximity of Tandil with the Argentine Sea encourage constant interaction between the Grupo 6 de Caza aircraft and Fleet units of the Argentine Navy when the latter go to sea on maneuvers. Between 21 and 23 April 2006 Mirage IIIs and Fingers conducted mock attacks on air defence and support ships that were sailing in waters south of the Province of Buenos Aires. They should remain alert during the three days to counter air attacks, readying their threat detection systems, while the FAA aircraft perfected raid tactics against naval targets.

As of April 28, 2006 and at BAM Rio Gallegos, it was conducted Exercise "Pegasus", where tparticipated Finger C-415 and C-423 a Dagger B, C-438, plus two M-IIIEAs (I-017 and 018), an

Finger C-423 landing at BAM Rio Gallegos. The delta fighters operated detachments since 1978 from this southern Argentina airfield, until they were phased out. [Collection Santiago Cortelezzi]

Before dawn began enlistment tasks by mechanics on the platform of Rio Gallegos in June 2009. In the photo, the two-seater C-439. [Collection Santiago Cortelezzi]

Rio Gallegos operations were interrupted by a surprise snowfall that blanketed the platform and even the C-423, in June 2009. [Collection Santiago Cortelezzi]

In November 2008 the Group 6 campaigned shooting with live ammunition. In the picture it can be seen a squadron of aircraft for staring up their engines. In the foreground the BK-BR 250 kg bombs placed without the tail, waiting their turn. [Group 6]

M-IIIDA (I-002) and six A-4AR the G5C supported by a Boeing 707 from Squadron V, I Air Brigade and one Bell 212 of the VII Air Brigade for SAR tasks.

The operation consisted of combat training in offensive and defensive techniques with the use of flight package taskings. The operation took place until May 4, interrupted only on May 1 for participation in a flyover ceremony commemorate the FAA's Baptism of Fire, held this time in the town of Puerto San Julian.

During the months of June and July 2006 Fighter Group 6 was deployed to the Resistance airport (Chaco provice) in northern Argentina. They did it to participate in Operation "Pulqui" that each year takes place in the area where alternately different systems of the Force are involved, such as Morane Säulner MS.760 Paris when they were still in service, Pampa, the A-4AR, the Pucará and the "deltas". The aim of the operation is to control the airspace in the northeast of the country to deal with illegal flights mainly carried out by drug traffickers and smugglers. For 15 days in June primarily they operated the Mirage IIIs of II Squadron so that later in July was the turn of the Dagger and Finger. During the same yime Squadron I managed to intercept four TAI (Irregular Air Traffic), these intercept operations were supported by a mobile Westinghouse TPS-43 radar deployed permanently at the airport.

In 2007, to commemorate the 25th anniversary of the recovery of the Malvinas/Falklands Islands. on April 2 took place in the city of Ush-

uaia (Tierra del Fuego province) the central ceremony that included a land parade by veterans and **members of the** three armed forces The flyby was in charge of the Mirage (two M-5D/F - C-412 and 426 - and three M-IIIDA/EA - I-003, 006 and 021 -) that deployed to BAM Rio Gallegos few days before .

In turn as part of the reminders, the Argentine Mail printed a series of stamps, one of which represented the baptism of fire of the Argentina Air Force, which occurred on May 1, 1982, illustrated for three Dagger flying low over the sea towards their goals. The art of the seals was made by the renowned Argentine artist, Carlos A. Garcia.

On April 28, 2008 there was an accident whose protagonist was the Dagger B

C-426. When performing practices goaround at the airport of the city of Mar del Plata (Pcia. Of Buenos Aires), during one of these aircraft hit too hard against the track causing a loss of hydraulic fluid. After trying to replicate Tandil and check that the ruling was important, the pilots decided to return to Mar del Plata to make an emergency landing. At the time of playing track, the front folded and Dagger ended his career perched on fuel tanks on one side of the runway, no injuries pilots. The two-seater was subsequently taken to the Area Material Rio Cuarto for repair.

On August 28, 2008 was commemorated the 30th anniversary of the creation of Dagger Squadron M-5 in the FAA. The emotional ceremony held in Tandil, attended by the highest authorities of the FAA. As part of the celebrations two Finger IIIB Vcom at the controls of Diego Garcia and Guillermo Llana Ten 1st performed a routine with simulated and skimming past attacks.

On the occasion of Combined Exercise "Cruzex IV" to be held in Brazil where participate the A-4AR Fightinghawk of the V Air Brigade and replenishing Lockheed KC-130H Hercules of the I Air Brigade, the FAA organized an operational training to optimize the degree enlistment of the media. Dubbed Op-

Staff Armament Section of the Technical Group 6 installing two 250 kg bombs in the Nafgan ventral support, placing in the ventral station 4. [Hunting Group 6]

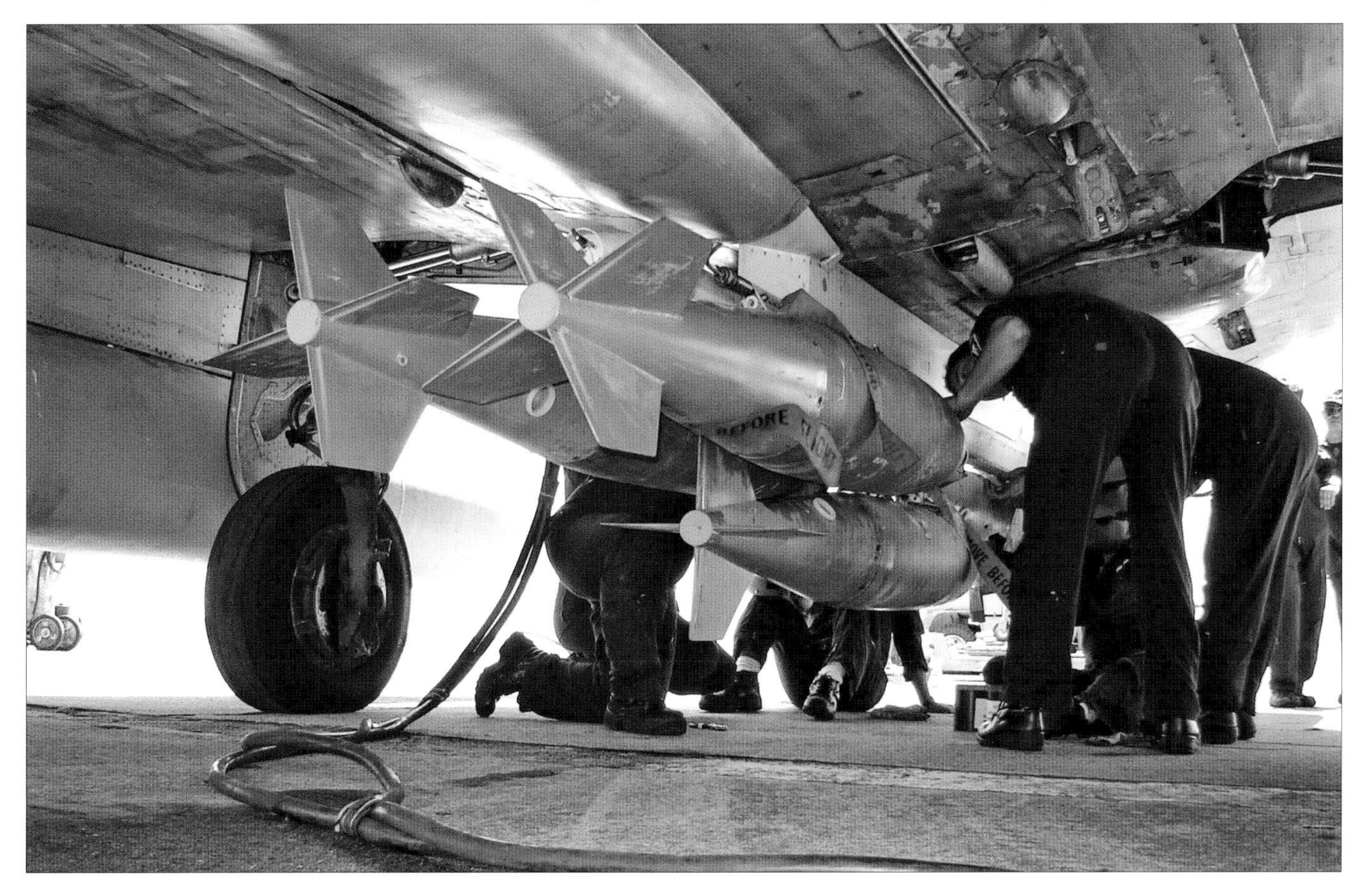

Armourers loading this Finger with five BK-BR bombs with smooth tails on the ventral PRR support. [Hunting Group 6]

After the placement of the load, the armourers perform final checks. [Hunting Group 6]

The bombs' safety pins will be removed on the runway thresold. [Group 6]

Operation with weapons of war requires caution. The first aircraft left in minutes will start its Atar engine engine. [Group 6]

eration "Pre-Cruzex IV" took place between 1 and 5 September 2008 at the Third Air Brigade (Reconquista). Media G6C deployed to the base in the north of the Province of Santa Fe to perform various practices dissimilar combat and flight package. After this training, the Finger remained in Reconquista fortnight to participate Operating "Pulqui" control the airspace. Finally, the participation of the Argentine air assets in the important exercise in Brazil would not take place due to the unexplained delay of the Ministry of Defense and the Argentine Parliament to obtain authorization for the departure of the aircraft.

The tight budget constraints incumbent on the Argentina Air Force for several years and in 2008 prevented deployment south of the country was made. In 2009 despite continuing with the same situation, the VI Air Brigade made a major effort to bring out their aircraft back to Patagonia. Thus on June 13 he started from Tandil Airmobile Squadron "Mirage" to Rio Gallegos. The return would take place on June 20. Participated in the exercise M-5D / F 423 and C-439, an M-5A Mara C-630 and M-IIIEA / DA I-002, 006 and 021. The machines Squadron I made tactical missions and navigations attack while the Mirage Squadron II officiated interceptors supported by Westinghouse TPS-43 radar stationed permanently in the BAM Rio Gallegos. During navigation, a squadron of F-5 had to land at the airport of El Calafate, previously designated as the alternate aerodrome briefings. This was because in time they started back to Gallegos, the wind on the track became excessive and out of standard, between 30/35 knots, preventing the realization of a landing safely. Thus, from Gallegos it had to leave the ground support needed for the next day returned to the base.

Between 12 and 19 August 2009 the G6C operate from the premises of the III Br. Ae. together with the other media to FAA participating Operating "Pre-Salitre", aiming to train in combined air operations, both in its planning and tactical development thereof and having as the purpose of preparing the means Combined Exercise subsequently participate "Salitre II", in the north of the Republic of Chile, where deployed this time the a-4AR Fightinghawk. In the "Pre-Salitre" participated the M-5D / F (C-

Start up!. Flight line staff interacts with the pilot for the checks before taxying. [Group 6]

Taxying to the active runway. The Finger has seven points for attaching bombs, missiles and additional tanks. In the picture may be five of them, because the stations 3 and 5, located at the rear ventral part are not installed. [Group 6]

A section of Finger flies to the Argentine Navy weapons range located in Isla Verde, south of Bahia Blanca (Province of Buenos Aires.]. [Group 6]

Finger making a turn to start the gunnery pass. [Group 6]

After the weapons practice, the section returns to Tandil. [Group 6]

408 and 438), an Mara (C-630) and two M-IIIEA / DA (I-002 and 018), along with four A-4AR four Pampa four Learjet 35A Pucara and the Second Air Brigade.

During the month of May 2010 many celebrations were held in Argentina to commemorate the 200th anniversary of the May Revolution. Under the "Bicentennial" the FAA participated in the same conducting two days of flyovers on Avenida 9 de Julio in Buenos Aires. Aircraft Group 6 Game could not be absent, and this is how the May 19 deployed from Tandil to Ezeiza Airport four machines (a Finger - C-420 - a Dagger B - C-439 - a Mirage IIIEA - I-018 - and a Mirage IIIDA - I-021 -), also present were four A-4AR Fightinghawks of the V Air Brigade.

By weather issues could only make the last day May 25 before thousands of spectators who were present at the Avenue of July 9 to enjoy the important homeland festivity.

SINT Project, the Finger is born

In 1978, unable to acquire the IAI Kfir C-2, the Argentina Air Force (FAA) sought alternative solutions to be provided with a machine with similar technology.

With the offer of Nesher, IAI offered a modernization that lead to these airplanes to become a "Kfir with Snecma engine" according to the expressions of the company itself.

Actually, that statement was not so far from reality in its initial form and in fact expected to include some more modern systems than those used in the Kfir.

The programme was named SINT Project (*Sistema Integrado de Navegación y Tiro* Integrated Navigation and Attack System) and although initially thought to use Dagger C-419 for testing, the delays in the initial definition of systems, prompted the machine to be sent to Argentina without modification on December 23 1980. C-419 was part of the first batch of 26 Daggers acquired, which were delivered in late 1978 and early 1979.

However, the decision to equip the Dagger with modern avionics, had another less known origin. In the mid-70s, the FAA considered the possibility of equipping with modern avionics and an up front control panel and - Head Up Display to its fleet of

A-4C Skyhawks recently incorporated. Even the possibility of providing them with radar to replace the obsolete AN/APG-53 was evaluated. At that time, a committee of the FAA visited different countries, including France and the United Kingdom, to take cognizance of the various navigation systems and shooting available at the time, to take knowledge about these posibilities, the commission submitted a report on the feasibility of the project.

Test bench for inertial unit. Technology transfer produced during the development of SINT/Finger Project was very rewarding for the Argentina Air Force. [IAI via Vcom Erasmo Zabala]

Stand where technicians carried out their activities at the IAIA facilities of. [IAI via Vcom Erasmo Zabala]

Overview of the test bench partially installed in one of the huts. [IAI via Vcom Erasmo Zabala]

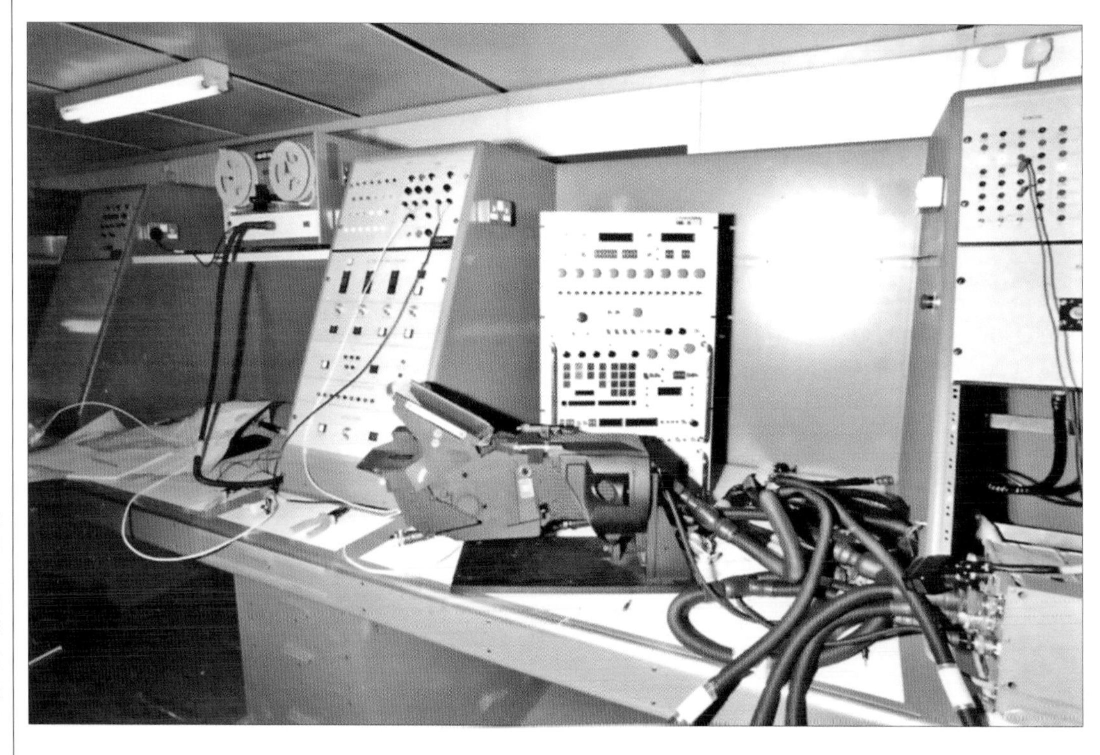

Head-Up (or PDU, Pilot Display Unit] in the Marconi company calibration process. It would then be replaced by a French Thompson CSF due to the embargo produced by Falklands. [IAI via Vcom Erasmo Zabala]

With the acquisition contract of Dagger up and added to the fact that the Skyhawks were technologically surpassed machines by the IAI product, it was decided to allocate funds for the modernization of the Dagger and face a less ambitious programme for the A-4C .

The British company Marconi Avionics Ltd. (MAV) was chosen to supply the main hardware, which was the same platform as the the USAF Lockheed F-16A Fighting Falcon. At first tried tried to incorporate a laser inertial platform, however it was extremely expensive, so it was decided to use a gyroscopic platform manufactured by the French company Thompson CSF associated with a doppler radar thus creating a hybrid platform.

Simultaneously with SINT Project, in October 1979, the FAA signed a contract for the purchase of two flight simulators, one of the Mirage IIIE and the other of the Dagger (with the SINT incorporated). The contract was called SIMAR project and initially involved companies MAV, IAI and a subsidiary thereof, Mabat (MBT).

Vicecmmodore Juan Carlos Candeago was appointed as the responsible of the SINT Project, while his deputies were Major Erasmo Zabala and Captain Julio Gómez while the FAA test pilot would be Major Villar, with extensive experience in the Mirage III system. The first requirements of the final SINT configuration were issued in late 1980 and in February 1981 the

The Argentine team in Israel (Major Zabala, Major Villar and Captain Gmez] With two assistants posing in front of the prototype IAI SINT, in the process of conversión, the Kfir nose already installed. [IAI via Vcom Erasmo Zabala]

first meeting of coordination with the companies involved (MAV, and MBT IAI) took place in England.

The planned SINT specification transformed the system into one of the most modern and innovative of its time. This was due to incorporating the first real "Head Up" in the world. Until then, several airplanes and used the HUD concept using a front PDU (Pilot Display Unit) which presented information to the pilot superimposed on the external image information. However the same controls were in a separate console in the cockpit so the pilot had to look down to operate. The characteristic of SINT was that incorporated the console (NCU - Navigation Control Unit) just in front of the pilot, below the PDU, so he did not need to lower his head.

Major Erasmo Zabala working on Nesher "599" (then C-427] during its conversion to SINT in IAI facilities. [IAI via Vcom Erasmo Zabala]

Argentine and Israeli personal posing in the prototype SINT project cockpit. [IAI via Vcom Erasmo Zabala]

In turn, the HUD had the distinction of being the first with "smart" features. That is, if when you turn on the computer, the pilot made a mistake in loading data to perform the mission, the same system will automatically detect it, preventing him continue programming until the error was corrected.

Another important feature of the design was that the system was made very pilot friendly and it was very important the close involvement that had Major Villar with engineers both Argentine, British and Israelis who raised them to the various problems of flight and suggestions on how the system should work to facilitate the work of the pilot, and engineers translated them technically to raise the solutions together.

The results of this methodology were highly satisfactory, achieving an extremely versatile and functional the pilot system. An example of this was programming of calculating fuel consumption. different algorithms for different stages of the flight, such as takeoff, descent and cruise, which was extremely accurate, with an error not exceeding ten litres was made. That is, an insignificant mistake considering a version Dagger in India configuration (three1.300 litre tanks plus complete internal fuel) totals over 7.210 litres The system also incorporated a system of ten *Bingos* that in case of lack of fuel or problems en route, indicated the pilot told him ten alternatives to go.

All these elements transformed the SINT in one of the most advanced in the world at the time and many of its features were later incorporated into the Kfir C-7 and other aircraft.

In March 1981 construction of the Electronics Workshop began in the Area Material Rio Cuarto (Córdoba Province) and some of these facilities would incorportate test benches for Project SINT. At that time, this workshop was to the latest world standards and was one of the most advanced in South America, along with the one belonging to the Venezuelan Air Force.

The SINT initial configuration included a telemetric radar, associated to the hybrid doppler platform with telemetry functions integrated up front control panel, the new mission control system and avionics updated with an inertial navigator. The Air Defence Command also requested to be included in the package, the Emergency Heading System (BCCS).

This whole package would be mounted on a new Kfir C-2 type nose section. It was also evaluated the possibility of equipping the aircraft with canards allowing the Finger to incluye two additional weapons stations, ahead of the numbers 3 and 5 below the air intakes. However this was already ruled out as the performances did not significantly improve since using the Atar 09C powerplant of lower thrust that the J79 fitted to the Kfir C-2, and in turn, the installation of such surfaces would consume about six additional months of work by jet.

With the advancement of the project the first contract airframe DAG/II, the Nesher No.

599 (c/n S-48) that would be subsequently registered as C-427 was selected.

Upon completion of the SINT design work, began the integration process, at first on the ground on a mock-up and then on the aircraft.

The first flight of the prototype took place on 28 May 1981 with Major Villar at the controls, initiating the Phase I trial programme, consisting of eleven assessment flights. In this first stage an aerodynamic study was conducted to see if the addition of the heaviest nose Kfir aircraft altered behavior, especially in spins, since the center of gravity position had changed.

The project included a trials stage to be completed in Israel and a final one in Argentina, more precisely in the Area Material Rio Cuarto.

Incorporating SINT to the FAA was a new challenge with the incorporation of advanced electronics and technologies unused to date. To support this programme was planned construction of testbeds and different elements to operate and maintain the new aircraft, radically different from the basic configuration of Dagger.

Thus, the construction of a test bench (RIG) was completed in England and was taken to Israel during the month of June 1981, while construction of the NOVA-4 computer that would allow analysis and programming hired test flights to be held in Argentina.

During the month of August 1981, the final meeting was made where the final configuration was established. At that meeting took part IAI (in charge of the construction of the nose section and the integration of the entire system), Marconi (HUD, EU - Electronics Unit - ADC - Air Data Computer- and ADR - Air Data Recorder) ELTA Systems Ltd. (EL/M2001B radar), Société Française de Instrument de Mesure - SFIM - (ISU - Inertial System Unit), TRT (radio altimeter) and Canadian Marconi Co. (doppler radar).

For thatinstallment, he was sent to Argentina the weaponry (rockets, bombs and ammunition) to be used in the tests.

In early November, a group of technicians and mechanics ARMACUAR and the VI Air Brigade traveled to England, France, Canada and Israel to perform the courses in maintenance of the different systems that made the SINT while England made course about ADC, EU and PDU Marconi facilities.

Moreover, in France they conducted courses ISU and SFIM system and in Canada the doppler radar courses, culminating in Israel with training courses on servocontrols in IAI and Elta for the radar.

Phase II of flight tests began in Israel in December 1981 and the last test flight took place on 28 January 1982. Once this phase of testing was over, C-427 was dismantled and prepared for transfer to Argentina which would continue the approval phase. It arrived at Rio Cuarto on February 26, 1982 aboard Lockheed C-130E Hercules (TC-61) after taking off on 24 Febru-

Major Luis Villar in the cockpit of Nesher "599" calibrating the NCU (Navigation Control Unit] system, also known as UFCP (Up-Front Control Panel]. [IAI via Vcom Erasmo Zabala]

ary from Tel Aviv and stops at Las Palmas (Spain) and Recife (Brazil).

Once arrived in the country, the assembly of the aircraft was conducted and Phase II of the project was continued. Thus was formed in ARMACUAR, as host unit, the Flight Test Center SINT (CEV-SINT) led by Vicecommodore Villar and Captain Rohde and 1st. Ten. Ardiles as assitants. This unit would then give rise to CEASO (Test Center for Armaments and Operating Systems) that still operates currently.

Next to the first prototype, arrived the first kit to make the upgrade in country, as well as the IAI technical team came from Israel, led by Abraham Einey andformed by Ishai Almaz (electronic technician radar), Abraham Turshi Ehud greidi, Tzvi Tal-Haim (technical airframe fitters), Shmuel Pupko, Badichi Moshe Haim Zaltzman, Barash and Carmel Abramovich (electronic engineers).

The team was completed by British engineers from EASAM company, responsible for the installation of RIG at the Electronics Workshop.

To carry out the first national modification aircraft C-408 was elected as previously had been admitted to ICM (Major Cycle Inspection) to ARMACUAR on 5 March 1982. To this end, facilities in the Maintenance Group were adapted in order to prepare the SINT assembly line.

However the works were abruptly interrupted by the start of the conflict in the South Atlantic when his conversion was performed at 60% and the second aircraft, C-411 at 20%.

As expected, all assistance from Canadian Marconi and Marconi was cancelled. Specialists of these companies withdrew from the country and Argentine personnel who at the time worked for such companies, was quickly hired by the Air Force to go ahead with the project. The material of French origin (SFIM) was suspended although the contract was not terminated.

Some maintenance personnel from Rio Cuarto was sent to Tandil and deployment bases to serve during the conflict and the same happened with pilots Villar, Rohde and Ardiles. The first was initially moved to Tandil torehabilitate to Stage III readiness, to pilots who were in other postings and continue the instruction of new students. Rohde and Ardiles joined the I Squadron deployed in Rio Grande.

Given the need for as many planes to the conflict, the work of conversion in

C-411 were suspended and was reassembled in its original configuration, departing April 24 for Tandil. Due to the urgency of the case, it was sent without having gone through the paint shop, so his fuselage was covered only with the green primer. Nicknamed "the parrot" upon arrival at the VI Brigade, it was hastily applied brown and green stains over the primer and titles and registrations in black.

The prototype C-427, meanwhile, remained in Rio Cuarto inside an hangar throughout the conflict since it made no sense to use a single machine that was not yet fully tested and would not represent a significant contribution in operations.

Arrival of Finger I C-427 to the Area Material Rio Cuarto aboard C-130E Hercules TC-61 on 26 February 1982. [My Brig (R] Ruben Palazzi

C-408 was the national prototype of the Finger I conversion part of the avionics were of British and Canadian origin. After the embargo caused by the conflict in the South Atlantic, the project was reformulated with components of French and Israeli origin, but suffered significant delays. [via Juan J. Martinez]

After the conflict with the United Kingdom, the SINT project froze and had to be severely reformulated. Vicecomnodore Sapolsky was posted to CEV-SINT later arriving Major Cimatti and Captain Callejo who were responsible for conducting verification aircraft out of production lines flights as, in addition to running the flights for approval of the various intermediate versions emerged as a temporary and necessary solution to reach the final system configuration.

Thanks to the efforts of staff and the reestablishment of delivery of French material in the month of August 1982, the first national SINT emerged from the workshops of Rio Cuarto in October. Because of the actions taken to obtain certain components missing from English origin and that this task could be achieved even circumventing the blockade boundary conditions at the initiative of Commodore Candeago, it was decided to be name SINT as Project Finger, for obvious reasons.

Administrative closure of contracts with Marconi (MAV I, MAV II and MAV V) was held for the month of December 1982 as indicated by the Materiel Command and the impossibility of getting a replacement adapting these systems (basically the HUD) it was decided to continue with a small number of "hybrid" machines without that component.

Indeed, at the time of suspension of the delivery of equipment by Marconi, a supplier of equipment that were the heart of the system, it had in Rio Cuarto three PDUs, eleven EUs and eight ADCs. The main problem focused on three PDUs already in use. One of them in C-427, the other in C-408 and the remainder had been placed in the Finger simulator that was in the process to be manufactured.

For this transition variant named Finger II were selected the aircraft intended originally to be converted to Finger I so the C-405, C-422 and C-424 were for inspection major cycle were selected, they were taken to that standard as a temporary solution.

Finger I C-408 production ended in October 1982 and in the same month made its first flight and then return to Fighter Group 6 strengh where would continue his evaluation.

As part of the trials carried out with the two Finger Is, the position of the belly VHF antenna was modified, moving it to the tail of the aircraft due to the interference caused by the doppler also located at the bottom of the nose. This change was made first in C-408, and finally on C-427 and Finger II C-405, leaving the rest of the aircraft production line with this amendment incorporated.

During November 1982, C-427 began to perform weapons trials. This machine, like C-408, was equipped with an ADR (Air Data Recorder) for data collection and subsequent analysis using the NOVA-4.

As part of the search for solutions to replace the Finger English avionics, Material Command drafted the REI Project (English Replacement Equipment) and sent requests to various companies.

In early 1983 tenders were accepted for the provision of materials and services and after studying them in September was signed

REI-1/83 contracts with Thompson CSF for the provision of the EU and the PDU and REI 2/83 with the Israeli company Astronautics, for the provision of the ADC.

Finger Technical characteristics

Dimensions:

Length (including pitot tube): 15.61 m.
Wingspan: 8.22 m.
Height: 4.55 m.

Weights:

Empty: 6,800 kg.
With internal fuel (clean): 9,550 kg.
Maximum takeoff: 13,500 kg

Engine:

Snecma Atar/Bet Shemesh 09C5A with maximum thrust (test bench) dry 4,300 kg with maximum afterburner (PC) 6,000 kg. Its weight is 1,400 kg approx. equivalent to 20% of the weight of the aircraft. Using the PC equivalent to an increase of 28% thrust engine at full dry powere.

Performances:

Indicated maximum speed: 750 knots or Mach 2.03 (above 33,000 feet). Operational Ceiling: 50,000 feet.

Armament:

Internal: two 30 mm cannon gun with 250
External loads: seven hardpoints for external fuel tanks, various weapons and missiles.

From Dagger to Finger

Similarly, in March 1983 a new campaign was launched approval and adjustment with the C-427. At this point, the total technological independence was what makes software control and operational logic programming system, a fact that enabled successive months in new campaigns as new editions of the software are generated are made. All software and inertial HUD in its final form would be an entirely Argentine development.

The Finger II modifications to the C-405 was completed in July and the 14Nov was delivered to the VI Air Brigade after completing flight tests, remaining even in producing the C-422, 424 and 420 in February of that year had entered a special modification line.

The C-405 also would be used for various tests carried out by the Flight Test Center, acting as commission for such aircraft housed in the then Military Aircraft Factory in Cordoba unit.

In December ICM entered the C-402 and its modification at this level it is also envisaged. In turn, we proceeded to plan the successive changes in the rest of the planes as they entered the ICM and not on special effects not reduce the number of aircraft in service in Tandil lines.

A Finger Fighter Group and Falklands veteran, during a deployment to Rio Gallegos.

The Directorate General of Aeronautical Material in its Annual Report of 1983 established different conclusions about the SINT Project. Among the advantages cited above that it could overcome the problem that threatened to disrupt the project, caused by the definitive suspension of the provision of the EU, the PDU and the ADC, vital elements of the system. Furthermore, the replacement material, hired that year, the SINT placed within the most advanced systems of time. Another advantage was that was completed successfully the target set in 1982 to achieve self-sufficiency in SINT software control, having obtained the total capacity of handling thereof and consequently the technological independence. Finally it was found during the approval of SINT prototypes, equipped with HUD Marconi, high quality material and software, its high reliability and very good accuracy of the system, which exceed the specified values, both in shooting and navigation .

In 1984 he began to introduce the amendment Finger IIIA in the production line with the addition of the ADC and PDU provided by Astronautics and Thompson respectively. Finger II for May that were in production had been delivered to the VI Air Brigade, except the C-402 that would be directly taken to the Finger IIIA standard.

In August the prototype C-427 Finger I began to be recovered to transform the prototype of the Finger IIIA, performing its first flight 18Oct such a configuration, while the Finger II C-422 began to be taken to the same standard.

Completed test flights, the 08Dic both machines were delivered to the VI Air Brigade, where four days later was made a presentation to the Air Group and the Technical Group on the performances of the system and maintenance procedures.

Finger IIIA variant began to be introduced in 1984. The C-405 passed this configuration the following year after being the prototype version of Finger II. [Javier A. Mosquera Collection]

1985 Finger IIIA endowment increased to seven units with the delivery of the C-402, 405, 420, 424 and 429, adding two C-416 and 411, by the middle of next year.

The Finger IIIB, final version of the project, began to be delivered in 1986. The main difference with previous versions, it was that was equipped with the US company Thompson, computer replace the Marconi selected in the original design.

The C-414 was the first to come out with the final configuration of the line of Rio Cuarto the 21Ago86, being delivered immediately to the VI Air Brigade. That year also were given the C-412, 415 and 423.

Finger IIIB endowment increased during 1987 with the delivery of eight additional aircraft (C-401, 408, 417, 432, 434, and 435) which are added two Finger IIIA reconverted (C-405 and 402).

At the end of that year it took place the final approval of the system. It was conducted by the Cap. Mario Callejo, CEASO test pilot, with the collaboration of Cap. Gabari in the VI Air Brigade, for which the release of ninety bombs was performed on the weapons range at Antuna

Still bypassing the ARMACUAR painting workshop, the C-415 completed various tests for CEASO weapons in 1994. [Via Manuel Vilchez]

The Finger I C-427 during the approval of throwable weapons in Rio Cuarto in Nov82. Note the initial position of the VHF antenna at the bottom of the nose. [Via Manuel Vilchez]

(San Luis), and various checks for air-to-air shot using cannons and Shafrir II missiles were performed.

Three other jets were converted to Finger IIIB during 1988 (the C-413, 421 and 420 - the latter was a Finger IIIA) and in 1989 the last two appliances delivered were the C-429 (Finger IIIA previously) and the C-416 the 22Dic.

Four machines (C-411, 422, 424 and 427) remaining in the Finger IIIA version, not becoming converted to the final variant, because only seventeen Thompson acquired electronic units.

A final version, called Finger IV was also projected. It looked equip the Finger IIIB with a radar warning system (RWS), thanks to the experience gained during the Falklands War.

Such assessments had begun in FEB85 with SINT-TERO Project, carried out on the C-412 which was for a P inspection in Rio Cuarto. this machine was selected as previously had been modified to bring the RWR antennas on a project carried out in 1982 (and then canceled) and still retained the modification of the electrical installation.

Despite the need to equip these jets with this defense system, it was decided to cancel the project and applying these systems to the Mirage 5P under FAS 430 amendments, which led to these aircraft to Mara standard between 1988 and 1991.

Finally, the C-412 was delivered as Finger IIIB in December 1986 retaining lobes receptors in the vertical fin, which were later removed, leaving only the wiring to them.

However, delays in obtaining the funds to purchase a replacement for Finger produced the project to equip these aircraft with a RWR system will resume on several occasions, most recently in the year 2004 but without positive results.

The SINT

The system is centered around a mission computer called EU (Electronic Unit) associated with a Head Up Display (HUD) and fed by a series of subsystems via digital serial links (Digital Bus). Thus, using the commands that are available to the pilot, it can access all the necessary information that allows you to fly "head up" at all stages of the mission.

The EU controls the main means of communication between the subsystems that allow to obtain, in real-time navigation information and shooting. This computer is the main component of the system, since in it all the information is centralized and most calculations are then presented to the pilot performed.

The HUD is constituted by two elements that interact with the EU permanently, they are the NCU and the PDU. The NCU (Navigation Control Unit), which can also be called UFCP (Up-Front Control Pannel) is the interface between the SINT and the pilot.

Using a keypad located to the center-top of the dashboard, it allows control and programming of the different functions of the system through displays in the PDU and the opticadores. The PDU (Pilot Display Unit or Unit Presentation Pilot) presents the pilot superimposed on the external image, the information necessary for navigation and shooting developed by the EU, being composed of a cathode ray tube that projects the symbols required on the display.

The EU performs calculations receiving data and interacting with the other subsystems that make up the SINT. One of them is the ISU (Inertial System Unit or Unit of Inertial System) composed of the BEN (Boite Electronique of Navegation -Box Electronics Navigation-), BGA (Bloc Gyro Accelerometrique -Box Giro-acelerométrica-) and BCCS equipment (Boite Computation of Cap Secur -. Box of Emergency- Rumbo Computing). The ISU made posture information, position and speed of the three axes of the plane, necessary for piloting, navigation and attack modes and is based on a giroacelerométrica platform (BGA) containing a set of accelerometers mounted on a gyro-stabilized platform. The information in attitude, heading, and horizontal and vertical speeds are developed by BEN where speeds are compared with those

Finger IIIB C-412 taxying at Tandil in May87. Note the RWR antenas on the fin and registration in small size near the nozzle. [Jorge R. Figari]

Cockpit front position of a Dagger T. Note the difference regarding Finger equipment. [Horacio J. Clariá]

obtained by the Doppler and elevation changes sensed by the ADC. Thus, very accurate velocity components in short term and very good average value is obtained. The BCCS is used to switch the heading information automatically in case of failure or BGA BEN.

Doppler velocity sensor measures the speed of the plane relative to the flight horizontal and vertical axes. For measurement of speeds, the receiving antenna transmitter (located at the bottom of the nose in front of the front axle) radiates energy toward the ground through four beams. The return of each of these beams is received by a corresponding antenna and it's component plane relative speed of the earth is extracted along the beam direction. Since the incorporation of an inertial platform was extremely expensive at the

Finger IIIB cabin stand out clearly where the PDU and NCU front and the GPS on the top right. [William P. Gebel]

time, it was decided to incorporate a Doppler radar to ensure inertiality ISU. The latter has the task of comparing and correcting errors in electronic form in the long term inertial gyroscopic core speeds.

The ADC (Air Data Computer Data) processes anemometer data (static and dynamic pressure, ambient temperature) transforming them into aerial data (barometric altitude, Mach number, -IAS- indicated airspeed, true airspeed -TAS-, air temperature, angle of attack, rate of ascent, etc.) required by different systems. Atmospheric data are collected through various outlets static and dynamic pressure, and air temperature sensors and angle of attack (AOA).

The telemetric radar Elta EL / M-2001B provides basic information to the EU for calculations shooting missions. In air-to-air mode, it provides the distance and speed of zooming relative to a moving target with an operating range of 150 meters within 5 km. In the air-ground mode, its range is 10 km.

The SINT provides the pilot three modes of basic air-ground attack. One of them is the CCPI (Continuous calculation Impact Point) mode that provides information permanently impact the point where selected weapons if released at this time, allowing greater freedom and flexibility to the pilot to select the target. The pilot maneuvered the plane, once selected target, match the symbol with white aiming to beat and release the weapons when you achieve such a coincidence.

The second mode is the CCPL (Continuous calculation Launch Point) that provides guidelines aim and maneuver to beat previously designated targets at a distance. The system displays the guidance information to navigate to the computed release point, where the release of the pump will occur automatically.

The last mode is the CNPL, also known as "shot over the shoulder" which provides the information necessary for the release of weapons in designated targets inertially, and normally maneuvering in ascending order without viewing them. It is noteworthy that this way was entirely developed in Argentina since it was not included in the initial contract.

For air-to-air shot, the SINT includes two modes: CCLT (Continuous Calculation of the Line of Fire) known as "hot line" and LCOS (computed line of sight) that resembles the look gyroscopic predictor.

Other Modifications and Projects

After the ceasefire in Jun82, it was concluded that the Dagger should adopt a system of autonomous startup, such as that equipped the Mirage IIIEA / DA. Consequently it carried out Microturbo modification that was to incorporate the engine Bet Shemesh / Atar 09C5A a small reactor by which the required power is generated to start the engine ignition sequence. In addition to the changes in the front warhead Atar engine also they had made another in the internal structure of the aircraft to accommodate the reactor whose length was greater than the Microturbo contain. The first device with such modification, C-401, left the workshops ARMACUAR 24Oct83.

The autonomous system boot was joining all aircraft as these entered to inspection. Another advantage that reported this modification was that the provision could be standardized engine with 09C3 Mirage IIIE Atar of.

By the end of 1982 in the Area Material Rio Cuarto work began to be held in the C-412 in order to equip it with a warning system radar (RWS) under the project called Modification Countermeasure Electronics for which the FAA acquired ten MGN-80 kits of Israeli origin but by then was in the market the most advanced MGN-200.

In a small hangar, which would then be used by the paint shop, he was executed the same with total secrecy by staff Avionics Workshop attended by Israeli technicians.

The works included the installation of omnidirectional receiving antennas (RWR - Radar Warning Receiver) on the nose and tail, and primary and secondary containers chaff and flares were located one behind the tank rear fuel ventral pointing down, and two oblique to the same height in the fuselage, pointing backwards. In Sep83 they concluded such modifications and ground testing and flight began. The Israeli personnel only participated in the installation of equipment starting before they began tests to verify proper operation.

However, when the trials began, it was found that the radar warning did not work. In the absence of Israeli technicians, he began to analyze the reasons and found that the RWS was loaded with radar frequencies of Soviet origin as this was the origin of the weapons from neighboring countries to Israel. However, in South America there was only Western equipment and to solve this problem, took Tandil a complete battery of anti-aircraft missiles Roland and radar guided Skyguard a coming weather radar Center Flight Test and 3D radar TPS-43 with the idea of recording data from different computers. After this operation, the frequencies captured and began analizarle how to load them into the system were recorded.

In October they completed those tests and the plane was then moved to Tandil for compatibility with SINT, performing simulated at different speeds and heights attacks. Chap. Gabari souk was responsible for executing the first demonstration of this system against the authorities, in which the aircraft successfully detached a string of flares on the unit. Chap. Demierre after also conducted a similar test.

The 17oct83, the C-412 together with the prototype Finger I (C-427) to Rio Gallegos deployed for further flight tests. In one, the aircraft went into the ocean bound for Falklands intending to "click" the English lobe radar surveillance and record their frequencies. At that time, the radar detected ordering the immediate takeoff section Phantom FGR.2 who were on permanent alert. The Argentine aircraft started back to the mainland. Later it was announced that both Phantom resulted injured after colliding with each other during takeoff, the plane derecognised registered XV484.

The project to provide the other RWS Dagger with significant delays suffered mainly due to the lack of software and interface problems that prevented feed the system with the frequency data. By then, the project was well

advanced Finger and Finger planning IV held in 1985 foresaw the incorporation of this same system to Finger IIIB. However, the inability to solve the above technical problems gave ground the idea of giving the Finger with RWS. The C-412 will be dismantled computers when it left the assembly line as Finger IIIB Rio Cuarto, preserving a while receiving antennas in the drift. The kits were stored, and years later, interface problems solved, were used in the modernization made the Mirage 5P that led to the standard M-5A Mara.

At the request of the IDF / AF, the Nesher had a sequence of specially configured fuel to make it more unstable. This condition was the most suitable aircraft for air-to-air combat, but did not favor its use in air-ground missions.

The sequence causes the Upper consumption of 465 liters tank located behind the cockpit, empty it first then followed by the leading edge wing tanks. Thus, by reducing the weight on the front of the plane, the center of gravity back reducing the margin of longitudinal dynamic stability (determined by the location of the center of gravity and the aerodynamic center), and therefore the plane is less stable. In Argentina, this feature allowed in the training of air-to-air type "dogfight", the Dagger beat in most times more stable Mirage IIIEA, whose nose was heavier due to the installation of the radar.

On the other hand, in air-ground missions this feature could cause oscillations almost impossible to control by the pilot. The purposing or Longitudinal Dynamic Instability is therefore caused by the combination of a center of gravity backward and certain conditions of speed, altitude and attitude changes of the aircraft. Such instability subjected to high accelerations plane that can exceed 10 positive and 4 negative Gs Gs.

Precisely this was the cause of the loss of C-431 on May85 and several minor incidents earlier. After analysis of the accident, preventive measures until a solution to this problem is found, as on flights with tanks 1,700 liters (delaying the center of gravity) and limit the speed to 450 knots for flights below set out 500 feet.

The Flight Test Center was asked to assess possible intervention solutions, one of which is to alter the sequence of fuel consumption. However, the incorporation of the avionics SINT to Dagger introduced a weight of 80 kg in front of the center of gravity. Thus, the new configuration on the weight of Finger determined a more stable centering which made it unnecessary to change the sequence of consumption and release the restrictions mentioned.

In parallel to SINT Project, the FAA implemented the SIMAR project which consisted of the acquisition of two combat flight simulators, one of Mirage IIIE and the other Finger. The contract was signed in Oct79. In Feb81 they finished programming tasks simulators and August 1983, after overcoming the problems caused by the conflict in the South Atlantic, concluded partial acceptance tests Finger simulator.

In October 83 the simulator were delivered to VI Air Brigade, and Captain Gabari and 1st Lt Callejo were responsible for making the ATP (Acceptance Test Procedures).

Another development carried out in the country would be building of external 1700 litres tanks.

One of the developments carried out by the FAA was the feasibility of building additional underwing tanks of 1,700 liters. The Directorate of Aeronautical Development Area Material Cordoba produced a single sheet identified as TLX-01 which was approved by the Flight Test Center [AMC via Juan J. Martinez]

At the request of the FAA in 1987 they began in the Area Material Cordoba tasks aimed at obtaining documentation, execution of prototypes and approval of such tanks being tested successfully on one of the Fingers of G6C.

In late 1991 the FAS was crystallized project through which 510 were delivered to the VI Air Brigade manufactured in the country. The joint venture agreement between the Directorate General of Systems, dependent of Materiel Command, and Tecno Dinamica SA resulted in the production Air Blanc White Towable Tecno 500 to be used interchangeably in the Finger or Mirage IIIE. It has similar characteristics as the white SECAPEM 90 acquired by the FAA in Mar75.

In 1992, studies began to be made to equip Finger and Mirage III aircraft with refuelling system and CPT system (Load Pressure on Earth). The latter allowed load of fuel from one mouth both internal and external tanks.

The project began as a concern of Brig. Eduardo Martinez, then Commander of Material, who formed a working group composed by Cap. Guillermo Piuzzi, the SM Luis Segura and Ing. Bortis, later joined by 1st. Lt. Julio Ayup, Petty Officer Geuna and PC Horacio Jorge Torres and Hugo Gaveglio. After gathering information began designing the probe and all the fuel transfer system by the Area Material Rio Cuarto.

Finally it was decided that for operational reasons, recipients would Finger aircraft of this modification.

As part of this development, visits were made to the 2nd. Fighter/Attack Naval Air Squadron and Central Workshop (both based in Naval Air Base Commander Espora) to study the system that had the Super Etendard. By 1996, a visit to the Maintenance Service (SEMAT) of the Peruvian Air Force based in Lima was carried out to study the characteristics of French resupply kit that equipped the Mirage 5P4/DP4 of the force.

According to preliminary studies, the unit cost would amount to national kit U $ S 150,000, significantly less than U $ S 650,000 it cost to complete the purchase from a manufacturer abroad.

Another important advantage was that the envisioned system would fill the axuliary tanks, made the system did not consider what Dassault.

The importance of the project led to the creation of a development FAS (Air Force Systems), identified as FAS 840. In 1997 it became lodged in the Air Force in the ARMACUAR, with the presence of the Chief of General Staff , Brig. Gral. Ruben Montenegro and Systems Director, Com. Raul Diaz. For this event, a mock-up of the refueling system, which was placed in the nose of a Finger mounted on a IIIEA Mirage was built. the fuselage of the aircraft and not a Finger was used as the latter, at that time were at an advanced stage of inspection, precluding their use for this purpose. Externally, the system was composed of a fixed probe and located

Evaluation flight for the towed white Tecno 500 gunnery target developed by the company TECNODINAMICA Argentina SA. [TECNODINAMICA]

right in front of the windshield, attached to the fuselage between frame 1 and 2, and two outer pipes carrying the fuel to the tank upper. These pipes were similar to those that can be seen in the M-5D or M-IIIDA seaters that these devices are part of the ventilation system of avionics housed in the nose.

Despite the technical feasibility of the project evidenced in the initial design stage, it was canceled for budgetary reasons and political nature, without actually materialize the construction of a prototype.

Airframe and description of its main components

The fuselage of the aircraft is of conventional semi-monocoque structure and pursuant to rule the area is close to the center of it. The engine air intakes are provided with boundary layer traps. They force of the airflow to the fuselage to cool the engine and cooling supply air to the air conditioning system. Cones shots (semi-conical shaped body also called "suories") moving within the air intakes forward and backward as the Mach number, regulating the mass air flow. They are automatically controlled by the ADC (which can also be operated manually) and begin to move forward to Mach 1.25. When the cones out, decreases the air inlet so that the air flow is continually adapted to the demand of the reactor.

The fuselage has three compartments containing: 1) the front of the belly which is mounted chassis cannon and ammunition, 2) In the ventral rear, is a fuel tank and the compartment camera bombing; and 3) Behind the cockpit, which is mounted a fuel tank (Upper), the bottles of oxygen and fuel tank inverted flight.

The delta wing configuration is constituted about three stringers. Has a total theoretical surface 34.8 m2, positive arrow on the edge of 60 ° 36 ', thickness ratio of 3.5 to 4.5% and 235 kg load wings / m2 with half the internal fuel . Command surfaces are composed by two elevons that function as a set of pitch and roll command and a damper (inner surface) which assists the pitch control. The plane has no flaps.

The internal fuel capacity is 3,460 liters distributed in tanks located in the fuselage and wings. The tanks are two of fuselage (left and right) of 515 liters each are located on either side of the fuselage above the chassis canyon, the Upper 465 lts, two full tanks of wings (right and left) of 680 liters each (including tanks edge 130 liters each), the tank lts inverted flight 60 and the rear fuselage ventral tank (soute-arriere) of 545 lts.

In the outstations may hang external tanks 500 and 1.700 liters (stations 2 and 6), 880 liters (est. 4) and 1,300 liters (est. 2, 4 and 6). With India version of three additional tanks of 1,300 liters the total amount of fuel amounts to 7,360 lts.

The ejection seat Martin Baker is a JM-6 features 0-0, that is operable at a minimum height of ejection of 0 (zero) meters (with the stabilized plane) and with a minimum speed of 0 knots. The theoretical maximum speed of ejection is 600 knots while the optimum is 250 knots in smooth ascent. The overall weight is 95 kg. During ejection, the maximum acceleration is 12 Gs and the maximum speed is 24 m / sec. The seat has a survival kit consisting of a self-inflating life raft and other survival items such as medicines, foods, etc.

The aircraft has seven stations suspension arms numbered from 1 to 7 from left to right. Station 1, located at the extreme left wing has a load capacity of 150 kg being commonly used to carry a missile Shafrir. Station 7 at the end of wing has the same characteristic. Stations 2 and 6 are located in the central part of the wing and having a capacity of 1500 kg each. 3, and 5 stations located left and right in the rear belly up to 250 kg each. Finally, the station 4 is in the centreline of the stomach and has a 1,250 kg load capacity.

Military loads are fixed to the suspension points by pylons, bomb racks and adapters that allow for mechanical and electrical coupling to the aircraft.

Anecdotes of the operation of the new Finger. "Thrifty By" Brig. (R) Luis D. Villar

The 02Abr the British Marconi who were working on the project in Rio Cuarto SINT left, so then had to redefine it, to replace the English components that were nothing less than the mission computer and display. As the original contract provided logistical support for 10 years and the British had considered that it would be cheaper (for them) have two Argentine engineers to support the maintenance of aircraft, to ship by that time two English, the company took England and provided them with technical information about the project development, necessary for subsequent maintenance, which otherwise we would not have had access. To this end they participated and worked on the development of SINT system itself. That capacity acquired 180 planes joined the system that came with the prototype, was what allowed to continue the successful development of the Finger in Argentina.

"The acid test" Brig. (R) Luis D. Villar

Many people distrusted capabilities and accuracies, especially older SINT system. Always distrustful of the new. Thus, one day being in Tandil with the C-427, the first prototype of Finger, showed them what this aircraft was capable of. Two senior officers gave me the points of navigation which we had to spend, I marked a bridge, a point at sea, then another point in the sea, then appear over the port of Mar del Plata and return to Tandil. I proceeded to take the coordinates of these points and pointed them to tell me what time wanted to be in them according to the speed of aircraft navigation and after scoring all that in a form to that effect, I boarded the plane without any mapping. I loaded the data into the navigation system, and took off. They accompanied me in two Dagger, with all navigational charts and navigation and computed marked by doubts.

Dagger in Malvinas/ Falklands, first blows to the British fleet

On May 1, the first sortie of the unit come with the O.F. 1,101 for ana ir cover mission with the call sign Fierro, configured with Shafrir AAMs, full ammunition for the cannons and three tanks of 1,300 liters (Configuration "India").

The pilots deployed to achieve the first mission of the unit were the Cap. Diaz (C-421) and Ten. Aguirre Faget (C-403) who could not take off because of errors in the implementation leaving the leader alone at 12:00 pm. Once airside, twice the radar Stanley Diaz directed toward the enemy PAC, which shied away from combat, returning to San Julian at 14:30 pm.

At 15:30 came the O.F. 1,105 ordering the attack on four ships plying 17 km north of Port Stanley. With the indicative Torno, the squadron consisted of Cap. Dimeglio (C-432), 1st. Ten. Roman (C-407) and Ten. Aguirre Faget (C-412) and armed with two pumps Expal machines BRP 250 kg with braking glue stations 3 and 5, complete ammunition for the guns of 30 mm and three supplementary tanks of 1,300 liters.

The OF 1107, indicative Fortin, watching the air cover of the lathe with a pair of Dagger armed with Shafrir and the command of Cap. Donadille (C-403) and 1st. Ten. Senn (C-421) who took off with the lathe at 15:55 pm.

16:30 pm near the Torno took by surprise a naval training cannonading positions in Puerto Argentino, consisting of two frigates HMS Alacrity Type 21 (F174) and HMS Arrow (F173) and the destroyer HMS Glamorgan County class (D19). The latter received damage by two bombs that hit on both sides of the waterline while the frigates received minor damage. The return was made in height due to insufficient fuel, adopting three different levels to hinder the possible interception by the PAC. Actually, a PAC approached the lathe, but Fortin escort section managed to put to flight the Sea Harriers that were short of fuel.

Some sources indicate that the ship attacked by this squadron, was actually the de-

Dagger C-407 seen with a Rafael Shafir II IR-guided AAM mounted on the right outer pylon.

Moments of joy in San Julian. In a makeshift dais, the My. Juan Carlos Sapolsky celebrates the arrival of My. Gustavo Piuma Just after being recovered after ejection aboard the C-404 on May 21. [Gustavo Brig Collection Piuma Justo]

stroyer HMS Sheffield and damage caused by Dagger led to the sinking of the ship days later. According to these versions, the AM39 Exocet missiles launched from the Super Etendard of Naval Aviation on May 4 would not have had an impact on the ship but in the light aircraft carrier HMS Hermes (R12).

As part of a climate of euphoria, the five aircraft returned without inconvenience to San Julian, having to then change the VHF antenna C-432 that had received bullet impacts. As a result of the attack, it was decided to paint on the left side of the participants aircraft silhouette of two vessels, filled in half to represent the damaged ship.

However, the euphoria would quickly disappear when knowing the loss of the 1st. Ten. Ardiles (the First Squadron) and Cap. García Cuerva (M-III Squadron deployed in Rio Gallegos).

At the end of the day they arrived at San Julian, the C-401 with Vcom. Luis Villar (Nandu) and the C-420 with Ten. Carlos Castillo. The same occurred and at night, with the penalty that the track had less than 2,000 meters cash beaconing, highlighting the certainty with which the operation was performed taking into account the limited experience of Ten. Castle on the plane.

The activity scheduled for May 2 (O.F. 1,129 and 1,130) was annulled by bad weather. On May 3, two planes arrived from Tandil, the C-415 and C-434 with My. Piuma Justo (cricket) and the Cap. Dellepiane (Piano), arriving Squadron to a fleet of ten aircraft and all service. Just Piuma far south 24:50 hs with little experience in M-5, which did not prevent that it would join combat operations.

By then he began to glimpse the ejection of 1,300 lts tanks soon would leave them to the entire Group 6 Game. Thus, contacts with Israel for the purchase of these tanks were initiated by triangulation via Peru in order to avoid blocking actions against the operation. Similar efforts were made with Venezuela which also operated Mirage 5 aircraft.

Moreover and to increase operational flexibility, it began to evaluate the possibility of us-

Armourers placing the cannons chassis on C-420, then the cenerline 1,300 litre drop tank. San Julian Daggers used during the conflict this configuration, while those at Rio Grande used two 1,700 litre drop tanks. [Collectio Brig Gustavo Piuma]

A pair of Daggers from Airmobile Squadron II prepare por a misión (Fragmentary Order 1.277); at the control s of C-421 is 1st Lt Musso and in C-416 1st Lt Román, photo taken at BAM San Julián on JUne 4, 1982, for attacking British troops located 20 km from Port Stanley/Puerto Argentino, both were loaded with four BRP 250 bombs and in "Golf" configuration with two 1,300 litre tanks. [Collection Brig Gustavo Piuma]

ing tanks of 1,700 liters of IIIEA Mirage. On May 5, around noon, Cap. Dellepiane left with the C-403 to Rio Grande, to test 1,700 liter tanks with the modification of the electrical connection tab already made. Finally it was decided to prioritize the use of tanks in Rio Gallegos 1,700 and 1,300 in San Julian.

This setting fuel ("India" version) would be the standard for operations by Airmobile Squadron II. For missions cover such a configuration was completed with a pair of Shafrir II missiles and full ammo for guns (although for this time of conflict, the Dagger would be used only in attack missions) while setting the usual surface attack the warload included two Expal BRP-250 250 kg bombs - with different types of fuze - and full ammunition for the guns of 30 mm. Unless otherwise these combinations of weapons were used in missions described below.

On May 6, the Southern Command Air Force planned four attack missions. However, the British fleet did not enter the radius of the Dagger, so the O.F. 1,166 (call sign Fierro), close fire support with four aircraft, O.F. 1,167 (call sign Tucano) and O.F. 1,186 and 1,187 (indicative Poker and Coral) to attack naval targets with six aircraft were canceled.

Until 9 May, only some flight training and testing of weapons were made, when at 13:30 pm came two fragmentary orders for AON (Naval Attack Target). Puma, (O.F. 1,175) squadron was composed of the My. Sapolsky (C-401), 1st. Ten. Senn (C-407), Cap. Diaz (C-432) and 1st. Ten. Callejo (C-412) while the O.F. 1,176 (indicative Jaguar) would be completed by the Vcom. Villar (C-404), 1st. Ten. Roman (C-420), Cap. Dimeglio (C-434) and Ten. Aguirre Faget (C-415).

Both squadrons took off from San Julian from 13:40 pm with an interval of five minutes, but after sailing to the west of the island Great Malvina, who was covered with 8/8 low clouds and heavy rain, no to establish contact with the

Remains of the rear fuselage of Dagger C-404 which was shot down on May 21 by a Sidewinder missile fired from the Sea Harrier flown by Lt. Steve Thomas. The Argentine pilot, My. Piuma Justo, managed to save his life miraculously given the extreme conditions in which the ejection was performed. [Gustavo Brig Collection Piuma Justo]

Pilots I Airmobile Squadron Dagger, including 1st. Ten. Ratti (1st on the left), The My. -Head Of squadron Martinez (3rd to the left), Cap. Cimatti (4th on the left), Cap. Mir Gonzalez (3rd to der), 1st. Ten. Gabari Zocco (2nd to der) And Cap. Moreno (far r]. Photograph taken in mid-June in Rio Grande. [Collection Horacio J. Clariá / Avialatina]

radar of Puerto Argentino, solve abort the mission, landing in San Julian at 15:10 pm.

A mention deserves the birth name Airmobile Dagger Squadron II. In meetings they held every time the activity permitted, pilots and mechanics, used to sing some songs with his guitar accompanying the 1st. Ten. Callejo, including one that was entitled "Marinete Squadron Dagger" and whose letter was the adventures of a pilot Dagger he wanted to "stick a shocker to some beautiful fragatita." Later, the Marinete materialized in the drawing of a lady scantily dressed provocatively sitting in on a Dagger. Since then, it was decided to name the unit as Airmobile Squadron II "the Marinete".

On May 20, there was the arrival of My. José Rodeyro, manager GT6 Control Squadron, who

Pilots Airmobile Squadron Dagger I end the conflict. From left to right: Squadron Leader, Vcom. Villar, followed by Cap. Maffeis, Dimeglio, the 1st. Ten. Musso, Roman, Callejo and Ten. Aguirre Faget and Valente. [Collection Horacio J. Clariá / Avialatina]

This photograph shows the conditions under which operated the Daggers at San Julian, in the foregournd an over aluminium matting, Spanish made EXPAL 250 kg bombs both with low drag fins (BR) and parachute retarded fins (BRP). [Collection Horacio J. Clariá / Avialatina]

came to take over the Chief Technical Squadron, 1st remaining. Ten. Posadas as his second.

May 21: New attacks on the fleet and first casualties of "The Marinete"

With respect to combat operations, increased activity was recorded until May 21, maintaining the squadron in a tense wait, held on the ground by the weather and the position of the English fleet, out of reach of the Dagger. Improved weather conditions allowed that day the execution of four missions planned for the unit.

The O.F. 1,183 (indicative León) ordered an attack naval targets and was conducted by the Cap. Dimeglio (C-404) and Ten. Castillo (C-407) while the third member, 1st. Ten. Senn, could not take off due to problems in the implementation of the plane. Liftoff took place at 09:50, arriving at the Strait of San Carlos at 10:40, which successfully attacked the destroyer HMS Antrim which was out of action.

The O.F. 1,184, indicative Zorro, ordered an attack naval targets and was conducted by the Cap. Diaz (C-412), the Ten. Aguirre Faget (C-415) and Cap. Dellepiane (C-434). The squadron took off at 10:00 am attacking the frigate HMS Brilliant and returning along with Leon at 12:30 pm. After landing, it was found that the

C-434 had received an impact on the cone making air and left C-412 suffered breakage VHF antenna also by impact of a projectile.

The following missions represent the first blow received by the squadron. At 14:00 take-off Squadron Mouse (O.F. 1,198) with Cap he planned. Donadille (C-403), the My. Piuma (C-404) and 1st. Ten. Senn (C-407) for an attack on ships in the Strait of San Carlos. Five minutes later, the squadron was off Laucha (O.F 1,199), commanding the 1st. Ten. Roman (C-421) and the My. Puga (C-412) and 1st. Ten. Callejo (C-415) as numerals.

The use of integrated by an official of greater degree as numeral of a modern leader formations, was used regularly to exploit the combat experience of those who had flown missions in return to training squadrons in peacetime where are led by the oldest official.

During the commissioning of aircraft, paragraph 2 of the Mice (1st. Ten. Senn) he had trouble starting up and to the delay, Cap. Donadille ordered the takeoff of Laucha first. This alteration would be fatal to his squad.

Indeed, over the Strait Laucha they entered without much opposition which attacked the frigate HMS Brilliant and successfully escaped.

However, two Sea Harriers of 801 Sqn. They were vectored against the three Dagger of the mouse approaching the Strait minutes after the Laucha. Lt. Cdr The. Nigel Ward (ZA175 / "004") and Lt. Steve Thomas (ZA190 / "009") approached formation while Dagger eyectaban bombs and fuel tanks to lock in an unequal battle, armed only with guns 30 mm.

Thomas snagged one of its AIM-9L Sidewinder Piuma on the plane making a direct impact, reaching the pilot ejected in boundary

Stunning images of a Dagger gun camera when attacking the Type 22 frigate HMS Boradsword (F88), on May 21 in San Carlos. Note position of the Sea Wolf launcher pointed towards the attacking jets, fomred by "Ñnadú" flight (OF 1.181) flown by Capts Rodhe and Janett, and Lt Bean who lost his life after being hit aby a Sea Wold. [VI Air Brigad]

conditions. While the Cap. Donadille effected a junction with the plane Ward, I firing their guns, turned impacted near the wing root by the second Sidewinder Thomas, losing control of the plane and eyectándose immediately. Senn Finally, after a brief bout was hit by the second missile launched by Ward successfully eyectándose.

The remains of the Dagger C-403 and 404 fell in the area of Green Hill Bridge, while the apparatus did Senn near Mount Carolina, both locations near Port Howard, east of the Strait.

The Second Squadron received the direct impact of the disappearance of three pilots who were given up for dead. A loss of three Dagger, the C-412 and C-415 amounted down for windshield cracked by impacts received during the attack on the Brilliant and the C-432 with engine problems. To further complicate the picture, there were only at the base, three auxiliary tanks of 1,300 liters.

The activity of the day ended around 19:00 pm when the commanders of the 1st Tandil came from the C-419 in transit to Rio Grande. Ten. Musso.

At dawn on May 22 they lived moments of tension when the base defense movements detected on the coast and began firing their weapons to the presumption of an attack command. However, most movements were detected and calm returned.

The possibility of attack from continental bases elite British units supported by the Chilean forces was dormant throughout the conflict. In fact and during a search mission for a possible enemy infiltration, he lost the Argentine Army Bell UH-1H AE-419 and all its crew in the area of Caleta Olivia on April 30.

Moreover, the appearance of the remains of a helicopter Westland HC.4 Commando (ZA290) of the Royal Navy in the Chilean town of Agua Fresca, 18 km south of Punta Arenas, on May 18 then confirmed these suspicions. Years later it was learned that the operation was an attempt to infiltrate elements of the SAS (Special Air Service) from Dawson Island (where the command center of British operations in Chilean territory was) for sabotage of the Super Etendard operating from Rio Grande.

Returning to the activities of the squadron, the two Dagger with problems on the windshield were sent for repair to Tandil on May 22 and sent as a replacement thereof the C-410 and 416 would arrive the next day. In turn, he commanded the 1st. Ten. Musso to remain in San Julian, along with the C-419 to restore the line squadron. Finally that day announced the news that the downed pilots were rescued and were in the BAM Condor, in Darwin, which significantly raised the morale of the unit.

At dawn on May 23, he landed in San Julian, a Boeing 707 carrying Aerolineas Argentinas a shipment of 1,300 liters tanks acquired in Israel and had been triangulated via Peru, partly by improving the critical situation of these elements. Along with the cargo, new new fuzes acquired by the Materiel Command to solve the problems caused by the bombs that did not explode. These fuzes, the Kappa E, were fed by a battery of 9 v. I had a time of 2.6 seconds armed, after which exploded on impact and if not, automatically operated at 3 sec. Since the use of these fuzes, all BRP bombs dropped by Dagger exploded upon impact with the target or near it.

Moreover and because of the danger caused by the missile radar guidance (Sea Dart, Sea Wolf, Sea Slug, Sea Cat and Rapier) used by British forces, alternative solutions were sought to equip Dagger some protection against these . The partial solution was obtained using traditional tailoring strips of foil to be used as chaff, which in the absence of containers on the plane were located in the housing of the speed brakes to be released by actuation thereof. The charge of testing them was the Vcom. Villar who by then had replaced in command of the unit to My. Sapolsky. The addition of these elementary chaff was performed successfully in both squads and provided a certain additional protection during missions.

Meanwhile, from Tandil and Rio Cuarto efforts they were made to commission as many planes as possible. On May 23, they came to join the C-430 and 411 with the Cap unit. Demierre and 1st. Ten. Zoco Gabari who also joined the unit. During landing, the C-411 veered off track due to a brake problem finishing buried at the side of it and after multiple efforts to remove the plane from that position, he was in repairs.

At 12:54 the order for a new mission was received by O.F. Dagger 1216 indicating three armed in the usual configuration, although in this case the traditional pumps 250kg lead MU tail fuzes. The Coral squadron would consist of the Cap. Dimeglio (C-421), 1st. Ten. Roman (C-434) and Ten. Aguirre Faget (C-420). On reaching the Strait of San Carlos, the presence of British PAC reported by the radar Stanley decided the return of the squadron without completing the attack.

In the early hours of May 24, he was ordered to cover the yellow stripes on aircraft at the low effectiveness demonstrated by them. To accomplish this, he looked for the city green paint to perform this task, being only synthetic enamel in a bluish green hue. With frozen empennage and wings, it had a difficult task to be performed until the yellow was partially covered by the new color, giving a closer look at the turquoise green expected.

In the morning received O.F. 1,227 ordering an attack against ground positions (AOT) in the area of San Carlos Arm. La Plata squad was composed of the Cap. Dellepiane (C-434), 1st. Ten. Callejo (C-421) and the 1st. Ten. Musso (C-420).

In turn, the O.F.1.228 indicated an attack against naval targets in the Strait of San Carlos with the same configuration as above Squadron and Gold indication, training was composed of the Cap. Diaz (C-430), My. Puga (C-410) and Ten. Castillo (C-419) with takeoff scheduled for 10:20.

Once again and as had happened days before the Mouse and Laucha, a member of the first squadron had trouble starting up, so the starting order was altered, leaving the silver first.

As in the previous mission, Dellepiane, Callejo and they reached the target Musso throwing their bombs without problems, although receiving heavy fire from light weapons.

The Cap. Maffeis leaning out the cockpit of the C-420 Dagger in San Julian. In the picture can be seen clearly setting "India" with three tanks of 1,300 liters and supports 3 to 5 obliquely placed inside the fuselage in the rear. [VI Air Brigade]

While Gold approached the Bourbon Island, a PAC 800 Sqn. was vectoreada towards Dagger. Lt. Cdr The. Auld (XZ457 / "14") two separate AIM-9L shot, making overthrow the My. Puga and Cap. Diaz, while Lt. Dave Smith (ZA193 / "93") did the same with the plane of Ten. Castle.

Diaz and Puga reached eyectarse of its planes on time, dropping both planes sea north of the Borbon Island. The Ten. Castillo was not so fortunate and his plane disintegrated with the direct impact of Sidewinder, dropping some remains at the height of Mount First, near Sea Elephant Bay.

Puga spent about eight hours in the water and saved his life thanks to anti-exposure suit that he had tried during the early conflict in Tandil. Diaz fell quite battered on Bourbon Island, with two cracked vertebrae and a dislocated elbow product ejection off limits to more than 540 knots. Both pilots were rescued by personnel from the Naval Air Station Calderon and returned to the mainland in a Twin Otter

(T-82) it carried out a difficult rescue mission on 29 May. Meanwhile, in San Julian Plata they landed at 13:00 and after a reasonable wait gave a full squad lost again.

The situation of air assets was delicate, with a plane (C-434) with a broken windshield and other (C-420) with impacts projectile received in the left drop tank while the C-421 landed with a hung bomb because a failure in the launcher. This innovation was repeated on numerous occasions and in one of them, the fuse was armed with the danger of explosion. It was a wishbone type MU tail and after a tense work was disabled by the SA Quiroga with the assistance of Diaz and the 1st CP. Ten. Posadas.

The rest of the machines, the C-432 was returned to service after an engine change while the C-411 continued with brake problems and the C-434 was prepared for transfer to Tandil for windshield replacement. Moreover, again he began noticeable shortage tank lts 1300, having only twelve of them.

On May 26 came the O.F. 1,241 for the first time the Dagger would be used with a different configuration. In this case, the two members of the Poker machines squadron, commanded by Cap. Dimeglio (C-420) and Ten. Aguirre Faget (C-416) were configured in version Golf (two tanks 1,300 liters) and two pumps BRP 250 at stations 3 and 5 as commonly used, while a ventral support Nafgan (station 4) was placed to two other BRP 250, all with fuzes SSQ (Super Super Quick) and MU tail that would cause the explosion of the same one meter above the ground.

The mission required off at 13:30 for a 60° dive bombing against ground positions on San Carlos Bay. The final section was performed under the guidance radar Puerto Argentino, performing the attack successfully and returning both to San Julian at 15:30 pm.

Picture of the attack on the Type 22 frigate HMS Brilliant (F-90) held on May 21 in the Strait of San Carlos. This ship was attacked at first by Fox Squadron composed of the Cap. Diaz, Ten. Aguirre Faget and Cap. Dellepiane in the morning, and then to the late 1st Squadron Laucha. Ten. Roman, My. Puga and 1st. Ten. Callejo. [VI Air Brigade]

The next mission was completed on May 29 when the O.F. 1,264 ordered an attack on ground targets in the area of Goose Green. Homeland squad was composed of the Cap. Dimeglio (C-420), 1st. Ten. Roman (C-421) and Ten. Aguirre Faget (C-416) returning to the use of the usual India configuration and two BRP 250 bombs with fuses Kappa E. Addressing the takeoff, the plane Aguirre Faget had problems with the oxygen system, so he had to abort the exit , leaving the remaining two at 11: 00hs. However, when they were close to white, the air traffic controller ordered them back because they could not coordinate the attack with the own troops on site.

The next mission was ordered by the O.F. 1.269 and 1.270 consistent again against ground targets at a concentration of troops and helicopters, located 40 km west of Puerto Argentino.

The Puma squadron, composed of the Cap. Demierre (C-416), 1st. Ten. Callejo (C-420) and Cap. Dellepiane (C-421) took off with the Lion squadron, composed of the 1st. Ten. Roman (C-432) and Ten. Aguirre Faget (C-412) at 13:40 pm. This was the first mission of the Cap. Demierre who had only limited experience accumulated 45 hours of flight Dagger.

Upon reaching the mouth of the Strait of San Carlos, the Puma were intercepted by a PAC and after ejecting external loads returned to the continent. Having heard the warning, the Lion Squadron also returned to San Julian.

By a failure in the ejection system, a tank C-421 Cap is not detached. Dellepiane, being semi-hanging from its holder and landing without consequences despite initially fire to come off the tank by touching the track during brak-

Moments in the Cap. Maffeis aboard the C-431, attacks the logistical landing ship RFA Sir Bedivere (L3004) on May 24 in San Carlos Bay. Part of the Blue Squadron also integrated by Cap. Mir Gonzalez Robles and Ten. Bernhardt.

ing. In the post flight inspection of C-421, it was found that it had received the impact of a small calibre projectile in the left drop tank.

The activity in the following days was interrupted by bad weather conditions in the theater of operations, which were made only check local flights weapons and systems, leaving the six aircraft in service unit.

On June 4 came the O.F. 1,277 to complete an attack on a concentration of troops 20 km from Puerto Argentino. dive bombing (BOP) would be held at 60 to FL200 (20,000 feet), launching every aircraft configuration "Golf" four BRP 250 bombs with fuses SSQ. Pineapple squad was composed of the Vcom. Villar (C-432), Cap. Demierre (C-420), 1st. Ten. Roman (C-416) and 1st. Ten. Musso (C-421) and CARRY OUT the attack followed by two squadrons of Canberra T / B.Mk.62 / 64 (indicative Lince - B-108.111 and 112 - and Puma - B-105 and 101).

The formation reached the target guided by radar, without seeing the islands that were covered by a thick blanket of clouds which reached to 11,000 m. The planes came flying in line with a spacing of 1,000 m each other, and at the time indicated by the radar controller, made the descent and release 6,500 m inside the clouds.

The next day he received a new O.F., in this case 1,283 for an attack mission against naval targets and aircraft configured in India version with two bombs BRP 250. Cap Nene joined the squadron. Maffeis in the C-421, Cap. Demierre in the C-416 and the 1st. Ten. Musso with the C-432 who took off at 14:40 pm and after touring the north of the Strait of San Carlos, returned without finding the enemy fleet.

In an attempt to rebuild the ranks of Fighter Group 6, the Air Force received ten Peruvian Air Force Mirage 5Ps u to incorporate immediately to operations and thus replace lost machines. The task should be done as quickly and therefore responsible for receiving the planes that come to Tandil, prior stopover in the Province of Jujuy. While the Peruvian government offered to transfer the same to the south and even the participation of its pilots in combat actions -what it had happened in 1978 on the occasion of the pre-conflict with Chile-, the offer was rejected under problem generate in order not to generate International problemas by direct participation of other countries in the conflict.

For reception of these machines it was appointed 1st. Ten. Posadas who left San Julian on June 6 to Tandil on board the Learjet 35A LV-ALF along with Cap. Dimeglio and 1st. Ten. Roman who should receive instruction in shooting simulator air-ground missile radioguiado AS-30 arrived in the country along with the Mirage 5P and was already installed on the Brigade. Both drivers return south on June 9 to rejoin the squad. The state of M5P prevented his immediate transfer to the south, becoming in a position once the conflict is over.

Shares of June 8 represented as mentioned above, a critical time for British forces when paradoxically Argentine forces were carrying out the last attempts to stop the enemy advance, operating at the limit of its possibilities.

The Dagger of San Julian made paths missions that although were not intended to reach the target goal allowed the arrival of other squadrons who applied a harsh blow to the fleet. The O.F. 1,293 and 1,294 planned by the Cdo. FAS foresaw the use of two sqadron Daggers for a decoy mission over the area of Jason Islands (at northeast end of the archipielgo) to

HMS "Plymouth" (F126), a Type 12 Rothesay frigate on June 8 in pleasant Bay. The frigate suffered several 30mm hits from the Daggers. The frist attack was "Perro" flight formed by Capt Rodhe and 1st Lts Gabari and Ratti, followed later by "Yunque" flight formed by Captain Cimatti and Major Martínez.

Armoures fitting parachute tails fo EXPAL 250 kg bombs at BAM San Julian, near its main runway. [VI Air Brigade]

simulate a naval attack and attract the attention of the British CAP.

Charter Squadron, with Vcom. Villar (C-411), the Ten. Valente - on his first mission in the conflict - (C-412) and 1st. Ten. Callejo (C-432) lifted off at 13:20 in Golf configuration (two tanks of 1,300 liters) with full ammunition for the guns DEFA 552 as unique weapons.

The envelope with the Cap. Maffeis (C-416), 1st. Ten. Musso (C-420) and Ten. Aguirre Faget (C-421) with the same configuration departed five minutes later. The mission was a resounding success, as the PAC took to intercept the six Dagger, enabling the attack of the Bulldog and Mastiff A-4B Squadrons that successfully attacked logistic landing ships RFA Sir Tristram (L3505) and RFA Sir Galahad (L3005) and two squadrons of the First Squadron (Dog and Cat) did the same with the frigate HMS Plymouth.

The Dagger of La Marinete started back to Rio Gallegos, not San Julian, under the remaining fuel.

The last days

In parallel, the Command of the FAS decided to redeploy II Squadron to Rio Gallegos, in order to change the path to Malvinas, which was already known by the British while on the other hand, the A-4B operating in Gallegos were sent to San Julian, since they possess capacity to refueling could alter their approach routes to the objectives. The order came on the morning of June 9 and six flights of C-130H the order is complied with, supported by the Bell 212 LV-CHP.

From its new headquarters in Rio Gallegos BAM, flight training and testing new weapons they were made in an attempt to increase the capabilities of the aircraft. As part of the June 11 Cap. Dimeglio out in the C-432 for test flight equipped with four 125 kg bombs instead of the usual two 250 kg. The launch took place against the walls of the estuary near the base Rio Gallegos, successfully exploiting the same 12 seconds of impact.

The next day, in a transport IA-50A G II arrived three advisory Peruvian Air Force to assist in the operation of the ten newly acquired Mirage 5P and whose arrival in theater seemed imminent.

Finally, the next combat action came 13 jnuio when O.F. 1,317 and 1,318 ordered an attack on ground targets located southwest of Puerto Argentino in a desperate attempt to stop the English advance. The first consists of the Cap squad. Maffeis (C-411) and Ten. Valente (C-416) lifted off at 11:00 am toward the target while the 1st. Ten. Callejo (C-420) had to return due to problems with the landing gear. Ten minutes later they lifted off the Gauchos with Cap. Dimeglio (C-432) and 1st. Ten. Roman (C-421), while the Ten. Aguirre Faget had to abort the output engine failure in his plane. All aircraft were redrawn version "India" with two BRP-250 bombs.

Upon reaching the area of operations, the first squadron had to return due to the presence of enemy PAC. Meanwhile the Gauchos during the last leg of your navigation to the target, they came across a Westland Sea Lynx HAS.Mk.2 bound for the islands from a vessel southeast of Soledad Island. The pilots decided to attack the aircraft so they conducted a reemployment to use their guns with negative results. After it, they returned to the mainland under his presence had been betrayed by that enemy unit.

Thus it is closing the participation of Airmobile Squadron II Dagger "The Marinete" in the war. Command of the Southern Air Force planned 83 outlets throughout the 45 days of operations, reaching contact with the enemy in 39 of them, throwing 52 braking pumps Expal BRP 250 kg and 32 Expal pumps 250 kg normal tail and fuze SSQ. six aircraft were lost, recovering five of its pilots. The Ten. Carlos Castillo initialed with their blood the oath at the Military Aviation School: "Defend Homeland, even killed."

Professionalism and high degree of training of both units possible for non-operational accidents occur at their aerodromes deployment, especially San Julian and Rio Grande, whose tracks and infrastructure were far from ideal, to which one must also add the bad weather that prevailed much of the conflict.

Combat!

At dawn on 01May the first crew consists of Cap. Moreno and Ten. Volponi, received information indicating that at 4:30 am had to be ready for an out of air cover to an SP-2H Neptune of Naval Aviation to take off at 03:00 AM exploration mission. However the mission was canceled by Neptune which both were on alert for the next exit.

The arrival of the first Fragmentary Order (O.F.), the number 1,091, was received at 05:50 that 01May, ordering a mission of aerial cover over the islands.

Chap. Moreno (C-437) and Ten. Volponi (C-430) lifted off at 7:30 with the target configuration Toro in India (three tanks of 1,300 liters), cannons and two Shafrir II missiles. This configuration fuel would be initially used to combat operations and unless otherwise indicated, is used in all missions described below.

Coverage missions were conducted two missile gunships Rafael Shafrir II and full ammunition for the guns DEFA 552 30 mm, consisting of 250 rounds.

At 28,000 feet were vectored by radar Malvinas against two echoes that were in the area, down to 20,000 feet while the Harriers orbited 2,000 feet below. After a series of crosses that none of the CAP (Combat Air Patrol) came to see and having seen Volponi pass a missile between the two, the Dagger began to return to meet the minimum fuel to return to the mainland. The Sea Harrier FRS.Mk.1 belonging to 801 Sqn. of the Royal Navy, piloted by Lt Cdr. Robin Kent (ZA175 / 004) and Lt. Brian Haigh (XZ498 / 005) did the same and returned the aircraft carrier HMS Invincible (R05) while Toro landed in Rio Grande at 09:45 pm. Thus, it was for the I Squadron honored to have fulfilled the first mission of the Dagger and Air Force in the conflict.

At 10:00 pm came the launch of the Limon section for another mission coverage as required by the O.F. 1,099, with Squadron Leader, My. Martinez (C-435) and the 1st. Ten. Luna (C-429).

With your electrical system failures, Martinez Moon formed as a numeral, to go ahead with the mission and reach the area of operations were vectored against some echoes that turned out to be A-4B Skyhawk returning from an outlet. Later, they were led to what turned out this time an enemy formation, effected a crossing at different heights. As neither side changed its altitude to avoid losing the tactical advantage, the Dagger returned to the mainland landing at 12:15 pm.

The following output corresponded to the O.F. 1,100 on another mission air cover indicative Cyclone and off scheduled for 12:30 pm. Chap. Mir Gonzalez (C-430) and Ten. Bernhardt (C-437), guided by radar, made eye contact with

C-410 was named "Vikingo" upon arrival to San Julian, due to the nickname of its crew chief, caporal Miguel Paletta. On 24 May it was shot down, its pilot, Major Luis Puga ejected successfully. [Maj (R) Guillermo Posadas]

a section of Sea Harrier with which they were locked in combat. The Ten. Bernhardt entered a forced feature maneuver by the British apparatus (ringlet type) thanks to their greater maneuverability and control of its steerable nozzles, forced the opponent overchutaje, being in the tail of this. This maneuver was described by the Spaniards, who had made a written commenting reach the main features of the maneuverability of the Harrier, as well as its secrets in an attempt to lend some support to the Argentine actions.

Bernhardt, realizing that entered his game, broke contact and gained altitude to find more favorable conditions, but withdrew Sea Harrier.

The last departure of that 01May was the O.F. 1,113 with the indicative Rubio, also on a mission of air cover was provided with Cap. Rohde and 1st. Ten. Ardiles in the C-433. Section Chief failed to take off due to mechanical failures, so that according to orders of the command given above, paragraph solo off at 15:54 pm.

However, Squadron Leader tried to block the exit, as had been established that the minimum combat unit should be the section to provide some ability to fight against the enemy. However, Ardiles continued takeoff while Rohde tried to change his plane fruitlessly.

Once arrived at the islands the Malvinas radar guided him to an echo, which was transformed into two Sea Harriers. 1st. Ten. Ardiles locked in combat and fired a Shafrir against Lt. Martin Hale unsuccessfully, and was subsequently shot down by a Sidewinder launched by the Flt. Bertie Lt. Penfold aboard XZ455 / 12. Ardiles not managed to eject and only some parts of the C-433 in the Boungaiville Island, west of the Soledad Island found.

The news of the downing of Ardiles dealt a blow to the morale of the squad, although he was recomposed by news indicating that finally had been ejected and would have been rescued in the islands after the match. However, the Mirage pilot rescued according to information received from the theater, was actually the 1st. Ten. Carlos Perona, knocked down with his Mirage IIIEA (I-015) in a battle against an enemy CAP.

The next day, the squadron remained on alert, but no movements were recorded in the fleet that made possible an attack by Dagger or PAC enemy activity.

The 03May, the only mission would be conducted in compliance with O.F. 1,154, indicative Dardo, in order to provide air cover for the many A-4B and 4C A-missions planned for the day. They took off at 15:30 Chap. Mir Gonzalez (C-437) and 1st. Ten. Luna (C-435). They arrived without problems at 17:30 pm without being in contact with the enemy.

For 04May, with the indication chicken, it met the O.F. 1,161, providing air cover to the tanker KC-130 Hercules TC-70 resupply the Super Etendard 0752/3-A-202 and 0753/3-A-203 on a mission against surface targets located about 110 km southeast of Puerto Argentino.

Daggers of the Marinete Squadron holding off at the last chance area of Runya 07 at BAM San Julian [Com. (R) Carlos Maiztegui]

C-419 was named Boomerang by the II Squadron ground crew wishing to come bakc from combat, but sadly it was shot down on the first mission, killing Lt Castillo. [Maj. (R) Guillermo Posadas]

This output would result in the sinking of the destroyer HMS Sheffield Type 42 (D80), according to the official story released by the British. The squadron consists of the Cap. Cimatti (C-437) and Robles (C-414), took off at 10:20 pm returning to Rio Grande at 13:00 pm.

At 16:00 pm, by O.F. 1163 indicative Talo, air cover for the return of Neptune 0708/2-P-112, which had led the mission of the Super Etendard attack mentioned above is required. Chap. Moreno (C-431) and Ten. Volponi (C-429), returned uneventfully at 17:00 pm.

The problem of shortage of 1,300 lts tanks produced by the same ejections during combat, prompted the possibility of using 1,700 liters tanks employing the Mirage IIIEA / DA will be

Dagger C-421 undergoing maintenance during the war, inside one of the HAS at BAM San Julian. [Com. (R) Carlos Maiztegui]

evaluated. The problem was that the latter used the French electrical connection tab instead of the American model that equipped the Dagger. The solution was carried out by the 1st Cape. M. Rinaudo and Cabos H. Alvarez and C. Sanchez, ending the first game on 05May. After carrying out tests positive result, it was ordered modify all aircraft to use these tanks, being for the exclusive use of the First Squadron, while in San Julian continued to use 1,300 liters simplifying logistics.

While these tanks airplanes operated with less fuel, less weight also accounted for takeoff from the precarious track, and in turn, improved performance by offering lower drag (drag).

The 06 May the following missions contemplated the use of the apparatus Squadron I were planned: O.F. 1,173 Eagle indicative air cover, two aircraft in India configuration, Shafrir missiles and guns; the O.F. 1,175 indicative Puma: attack naval targets, four aircraft configured in India with two pumps Expal braking (Alaveses Explosives) BRP250 and canyons; and O.F. 1,181 / 2 indicative Cobra and python to attack naval targets, five aircraft configured Hotel (two tanks of 1,700 liters) and armed with a single Mk.17 pump 1,000 pounds and guns. However, since the fleet remained beyond the reach of the means of combat FAA, none of the named missions were executed.

Before an air raid alarm late in the afternoon 07 May for a possible attack Vulcan bomber on Rio Grande withdrawal Squadron it decided to Com. Rivadavia. Due to the urgency of the situation, only they came to refold three aircraft at the controls of the Cap. Rohde and Janett and 1st. Ten. Bean, returning to Rio Grande the next day.

The 8 May Squadron was again required, taking off at 11:40 hs Eagle section, setting air cover in order to wear down the Sea Harrier CAP, equipped with three tanks of 1,300 liters. Cap participated. Cimatti (C-430) and Robles (C-437) who arrived at Malvinas to FL270 level, where they were led to the interception of a PAC, which withdrew missing about 40 km to the meeting. As early return to the mainland, over the sea, at a distance of 370 km from Rio Grande and 330 km from Puerto Argentino, was a routine operation of the guns. During that period, the numeral he remained connected impoverishing shooting (system to reduce engine power while cannons are fired to prevent the shutdown of it by gases produced by actuation of weapons), implying that engine thrust decrease by 25%, preventing him from keeping the flight line so it ejected the ventral fuel tank. However this action failed to prevent the loss of height, falling from 9,000 m to 6,500 m. When he was ordered to return to the islands to eject, the impoverishing system ceased to act, restituting power. Subsequently, less than 180 km from the mainland, the Head of Section will be lit indicator light minimum fuel (600 lit-

Engine change to C-401 by the technical staff from Airmobile Squadron II. [My (R) Guillermo Posadas / Avialatina]

ers) and was forced to eject the remaining two external tanks to lighten the weight of the aircraft and offer less resistance. Next on arrival, Robles suffered failures in their radio system, which he had kept in close formation to pass through a layer of clouds with a ceiling of 70 m. For failures ILS final approach was guided by radar, making eye contact with the track and very overwhelmed and must make a visual flow of 360 °, at very low altitude and low speed, relocating and landing at 13: 20 hours.

Dagger and Canberra crews towards the end of the conflict. From left. to r .: 1st. Ten. Ratti, 1st. Ten. Bianco (Canberra), My. Martinez, Cap. Juri (Canberra), Cap. Mir Gonzalez and Cap. Cimatti. [Com (R) Carlos Martinez]

Attacks against the English landing in San Carlos

Just the 21May Squadron would take action. In the early hours of the day, he had begun the English landing, protected by the bad weather in the area of San Carlos. Toward dawn

(8:30 am) it started to improve, allowing the FAA implement the planned attack plan.

For this moment and given the limited effectiveness demonstrated by Shafrir missiles and the limitation on autonomy Dagger, the use of the same was decided almost exclusively on attack missions against naval and ground targets.

For these missions began devices used in configuration with pendulous Hotel 1700 lts tanks and gunships with a single bomb Mk.17 British origin. This configuration, including full ammunition guns was used in the following missions, unless otherwise indicated.

In the first wave, by O.F. 1,181, indicative Ñandú, and the mission of attack naval targets, set out at 09:45 pm the Cap. Rohde (C-409) and Janett (C-436) and Ten. Bean (C-428).

The arrival of the Straits of San Carlos occurred at 10:32 pm where they attacked the Type 22 HMS Broadsword (F88) Leander Class frigates and Type 12 HMS Argonaut (F56).

During the attack, the Ten. Bean was shot down by a missile launched from SeaWolf HMS Broadsword, achieving ejected in marginal conditions. However, there was located by either side so it is assumed that died drowned in the waters of the strait.

Immediately after the ejection of the pilot, the C-428 recovered attitude and grazed the British ships to finally hit the water in the Bay area San Carlos. The remaining members of the squad arrived in Rio Grande at 11: 45hs.

At the same time that Ñandú, they took off the dog according to O.F. 1,182 for an attack against naval targets, consisting of the Cap. Moreno (C-437), the Ten. Volponi (C-418) and My. Martinez (C-435). Having reached the com-

Mechanical performing the configuration change in the C-401 platform in San Julian. [My (R) Guillermo Posadas / Avialatina]

bat zone at 10:31 pm successfully they attacked the light cruiser HMS Antrim County Class (D18), which was put out of action. Immediately run shot made a Sea Harrier CAP 800 Sqn., Composed by Lt. Cdr Hale and Lt.. Rod Frederiksen, was directed against the Dagger. Hale fired an AIM-9L, which failed to be released to limit its scope, making the M-5 landing with no consequences at 11:45 pm.

In the third wave of attacks, they again used the Dagger by O.F. 1,193, indicative Cueca for the attack naval targets, with Cap. Mir Gonzalez (C-418), the Ten. Bernhardt (C-436) and 1st. Ten. Luna (C-409), taking off at 13:55 pm.

Five minutes later he made the corresponding output the O.F. 1,194 Pound squadron, also for a mission to attack naval targets, with Cap. Cimatti and Robles (C-429). Due to bugs in its plane, Cap. Cimatti had to return to Rio Grande at 14:55 while listening to the situation, the Cueca in January ordered the 1st. Ten. Cap moon to join him. Robles as numeral. Arriving at the Great Malvina, they were detected by the frigate HMS Brilliant Type 22 (F90), who vectoring to a PAC by Lt. Cdr integrated. Frederiksen, the Sea Harrier XZ455 / 12 and S / Lt. Andy George with ZA176 / 76, toppling the leader to the 1st. Ten. Moon AIM-9L with, who managed to successfully ejected at 17:35 near the creek Teal (north of Soledad Island).

Luna had come to see the Sea Harrier, but a failure prevented his radio notify his three companions, who were persecuted to near the target, for safety where the CAP should withdraw.

Detail of Expal (Explosives Alaveses) BRP 250 Kg bomb with Electronic 2.6 seconds delay fuse. [My (R) Guillermo Posadas / Avialatina]

Among the throwable weapons used during the war bomb was the Spanish manufactured Expal BR-250 kg. In this case with braking parachute tail (BRP). [My (R) Guillermo Posadas / Avialatina]

A BR-250 bomb with 904 MU tail fuze modified delay 0 seconds mounted station 5 (ventral position right rear). [My (R) Guillermo Posadas / Avialatina]

Without knowing what had really happened with moon and thinking that he had struck a hill during approach to the target, the remaining Dagger successfully attacked the frigate Type 21 HMS Ardent (F184), demolishing the hangar with a bomb and destroying the helicopter Sea Lynx HAS.Mk.2 XZ244 endowment of 815 Sqn. while a second Mk.17 untapped stayed at the stern.

Successive attacks carried out by A-4B Skyhawk of Group 5 of Hunting and A-4Q Skyhawk of the 3rd Squadron Naval Air Attack Game and the Naval Aviation caused the sinking of the ship the next day.

The 22 May, bad weather on the continent prevented the takeoff of the air units, thus allowing the consolidation of the beachhead by enemy forces.

The next day, a first wave of attacks on naval targets could be met thanks to a slight improvement in time was ordered. With O.F. 1,205, indicative Puma, lifted off at 08:45 pm Chap. Cimatti (C-417), 1st. Ten. Ratti (C-418) and Cap. Rohde (C-436), and O.F. 1,206 Potro did likewise indicative Cap. Moreno (C-414), the Ten. Volponi (C-437) and Cap. Robles (C-435). However, poor weather conditions prevented

to contact the Learjet 35A T-23, which should make the guided toward the target, returning to Rio Grande at 10:15 pm.

For the second wave of attacks, he was given the O.F. 1,214, indicative Daga, again with the Cap. Cimatti (C-417), 1st. Ten. Ratti (C-418) and Cap. Rohde (C-414). After takeoff at 14:20 pm, the guide returned for loss of fuel continuing the other two to the frontcourt, and after not see any white, returned to base at 16:20 pm.

The O.F. 1,215 indicative Puñal, was conducted by Maj. Martinez (C-429), the Ten. Volponi (C-437) and Cap. Moreno, who got ready to leave behind the Daga. However, number 3 could not take off due to problems in the implementation, continuing the mission the remaining two, who finding no whites started back.

During the event, they were intercepted by a PAC of 800 Sqn., Composed by Lt. Hale (ZA194) and Lt. Cdr. Andrew Auld (ZA177 / 77), toppling Hale AIM-9L with the Ten. Volponi, who failed to eject, falling the plane to land in the area of the Elephant Bay Marino.

Some time later the remains of the unfortunate Ten. Volponi were found by Maj. Puga, who also would be overthrown, and were recovered with the help of members of the Naval Air Station Calderon repatriated to the mainland on a daring rescue mission Argentine personnel held on 29May by the Twin Otter T-82 (O.F. 2532).

The 24May continued attacks on naval targets on San Carlos in an attempt to cut off support to the beachhead.

Fulfilling the O.F. 1,225, indicative Blue, lifted off at 10:00 am Chap. Mir Gonzalez (C-436) with the Ten. Bernhardt (C-417), Cap. Maffeis (C-431) and Cap. Robles (C-418).

Arriving at San Carlos Bay at 11:02, and while conducting the attack on the logistical landing ship RFA Sir Bedivere (L3004), they were intercepted by a PAC, which attacked with cannon to paragraph 3 without reaching impacts. The squadron performed successfully escape receiving heavy fire from anti-aircraft artillery, arriving at Rio Grande at 12:00 pm.

First combat with the British Sea Harrier; Brig. (R) Carlos A. Moreno

April 30, 1982 was the birthday of Mir Gonzalez, so we went celebrate Rio Grande, the English Pub, a bar mounted three young couples from Buenos Aires, and after we arrived we changed the name for Bar Argentino. We also went to celebrate the birthday of Bernhardt was the next day.

We went every night to drink and that 30Abr had gone almost all drivers, returning at two in the morning. When I got to my bed, I had a sign that read: Talo (my call) morning at half past four has a mission with Volponi. Initially it was scheduled a mission to Neptune coverage of the Navy was going to leave at three o'clock, to give back to the Falklands to try to locate the British fleet. Our departure time was half past four to hook them in the farthest to make coverage until you return part, so I just slept one hour later... Neptune mission was suspended because

Another view of an Expal BR-250 bomb with low drag tail on a bomb rack. [Maj (R) Guillermo Poasadas]

our ships had already detected the fleet and we were waiting. At half past four we learned the first attack on Puerto Vulcan. Argentino and five-thirty came our Fragmentary Order. We had to take off at half past seven, mission air cover over the islands. We were set to release India (three tanks of 1,300 liters), two Shafrir missiles and cannons, exceptional takeoff weight, maximum almost 30,200 pounds, short track, wind 10 to 15 knots to 90 ° (cross), and low ceiling minima. We took off on time, still night and in the air we met radar Rio Grande. At quarter past eight, then forty-five minutes we were coming to the islands, with that weight we were at 28,000 feet, we contacted the radar Malvinas, told them who we were asked if we had fuel to hope, we told them whether. They were already languishing external wing tanks, and were directed here are some pigeons to you, I asked them to colocasen good front by the issue of AIM-9L Sidewinder, that if they could well pull in front, we had the maneuver intended to avoid him, which was different than the side that was putting all small motor. We were not going to do what they did the Israelis who planted, they had three seconds and reencendían to take all the heat. As we approached, we were changing course to be well in front, they were at 18,000 feet and we descend to 20,000 feet, the radar was singing us the distance and twenty miles before crossing eyectamos tanks wing and left the plant that still had fuel. We were going with supersonic afterburning because we planned to do if we saw a missile reduction front. About four or five miles before crossing eyectamos the last tank, there came what told the British pilots who thought he splurged a front Shafrir missile. We were in a side formation but without difference in level, which was in order to obscure the view of others, I asked the radar that I was asking about the fuel - 2,400 lts was our fly fuel on Puerto Argentino - but we had already past the islands, we were about 30 or 40 miles north. When we sang radar 4 miles without seeing us, we started a maneuver vertically. The important thing for us was that at their level, 15,000 feet, we must have low speed never, never less than 0.9 Mach (450 knots), so we went up and began to evolve in the vertical. As we saw them, we asked the radar if they could indicate where they were and this told us are the four together, I can not identify !. We continue to evolve, and in one of those evolutions Volponi I sang missile left !.

He had left behind, and that was that he got eight Gs and a half plane, and Volponi saw pass the missile between the two, since with this maneuver, however good the missile did not you could go because I had to put Gs I put but squared, what exceeded in his maneuver. At that time we asked for fuel and 2,400 liters saw, told us we Volponi maximum afterburning up. We were up and doing maneuvers so that they are not acomodasen, and radar told us that they too were at that time to the N-NO.

All have lasted three minutes, spend about 1,000 liters of fuel in combat, about three hundred liters per minute with afterburner.

We started the return, I at 41,000 feet and Volponi to 40,000, the radar gave us a first vector to head to Rio Grande, then came a dead zone in which did not take us any radar until about 200 miles we caught the radar Rio Grande. We were warned that it was under minimal and left for Rio Gallegos and we said no, we go to Rio Grande and we put at the end of the ILS. Sixty miles before we began the descent and they said the right turn start to fit in the end, to which I replied no, mine is turning left. 'I was confused 180 ° !!!, what quiet kid told me, here I am quiet, do what I say.

When we arrived it was all the waiting world, we had participated in the first combat mission of the FAA.

Dagger at war: stories of its protagonists

"A civilian in the war ..." Cap. (R) Carlos Musso

Having integrated Fighter Group 6 Daggers since 1978, two years later I requested the leaving the AF and entered Aerolineas Argentinas.

When the conflict started over the Falkland Islands, I called my house My. Puga who was in charge of a squad in DIL (Tandil) to see if I wanted to collaborate ... I said yes, because I knew there were very few people airworthy aircraft, and as the beginning of operations was coming, it would need many people. So it went my call for presidential and went to DIL. A Puga had been given the mission to create a reserve squadron if there was any contingency with Chile. I came to Tandil the 01May from Aeroparque in a Learjet company Ledesma. I was alone with my flight suit which was the only thing left me ...

Upon arrival, Puga told me to put me to study to see when I could start flying. The next day I talked to Ratti and told him I was not going to put to study at this time. So I went to the hangar, I talked to mechanics, I asked some things, and I said we left to fly so my rehabilitation would be faster. I did a tandem output Ratti, then a second and the next day left alone in the C-410.

One of the tasks we did was try some anti-exposure suits that were manufactured in Puerto Madryn (Chubut Province). At that time, this kind of suits were not part of the Air Force

Dagger C-420, -421 and -404 in Header 07 May82 early in configuration attack naval targets. The configuration "India" allowed the maximum fuel load but did not provide the maximum range, due to the increased drag that generated the three tanks of 1,300 liters. [My (R) Guillermo Posadas / Avialatina]

inventory. They were actually for underwater hunting. After selecting some models, successfully tested on a lake in the city of Tandil.

Some time later, the suit would save his life as he went down Puga, can remain in the water for more than six hours to reach the coast.

We also tried 500 kg bombs throwing them at the site of Mar Chiquita, flying low, with such sensitive fuzes... almost flies blast throw me for very low!

Service in Tandil would have six or seven aircraft. Initially, I had to take two planes to the south. The 14 May took the C-428 to Rio Grande and brought the C-414 with problems. The 21 May took the C-419 to San Julian, where I was because that day had shot down three pilots and needed people.

When I arrived it was night, all the people came to meet me... They were hoping it was one of the downed. They had spent more than five hours after they had left ... it was impossible. When they saw me they asked me down "Vos you doing here?" Because no one knew who had returned...

That said Maj. Sapolsky they'd just knock three drivers so I needed to stay. That night I went to the hotel, I had to sleep in the bed of Piuma, and next was Donadille bed. There I began to think "what am I doing here?, in bed two pilots are presumed dead". On the 24th I went on my first mission, in an attack on San Carlos. We were two squadrons, in a Dellepiane, Callejo and I and another of Puga, Diaz and Castillo. We managed to go in and make the attack and when they passed them, shoot down all three. They threw us all as had already consolidated their defenses. I happened to attack the port and saw the guide "spooked" I saw him... I kept tummy, I threw the bombs and output, so low that we were coming, I could see infants with AA missiles shoulder. Then I began to make evasive maneuvers between the elevations and suddenly I went into the water, then said "well... I saved myself," I kept ground, and headed to the mainland because until then I was going to escape Africa. Again I started thinking... "I'm stuck, I'm stuck." We spent two frigates that were there and threw him Callejo and failed. I landed and then came Dellepiane Callejo and... there we learned of the demolition Squadron Puga.

I made another mission, dive bombing on Mount Kent, guided by radar Malvinas. We got a course, and from the moment they said, began the descent, throwing bombs altimeter. We saw nothing... was all covered. Villar Squadron, Demierre, Roman and we integrated. We descended from 43,000 feet and 20,000 throw bombs and recover. I was all covered and I thought... "at any time and get a missile down to one". We were in fairly close formation to give a single white and if it appeared a missile, pass between us, confused.

The 08 June out with Aguirre Faget and Maffeis, in a simulated San Carlos, to allow a real attack another squadron attack on Pleasant Bay. We left San Julian and landed in Gallegos. The mission was very successful because squads that attacked B. Pleasant had no opposition. Gallegos returned to and left no more. Days later, the war was over.

So I went to see the Chief of Squadron and told him that drove me to Airlines... there was nothing to do... I was once again a civilian."

"Homemade Countermeasures"
Com. (R) Carlos N. Martinez

During the war, the only passive countermeasure we had was chaff, handmade and put them in bags in the hollow brake flight, and say "boys, when we are close to the boats, we open the brake to lay out bags that that speed break and distribute all the chaff and generate an echo. " We were forbidden to use the brake during the flight, but instinctively, to maintain training flight back to Malvinas, sometimes without realizing it we opened and we lost the only defense we had.

A Dagger section in air-to-air configuration at Río Grande, April 2982. C-436 would be destroyed by a Rapier missile on 29 May killing its pilot Lt Juan Bernhardt. [Brig (R) Roberto Janett]

"Automatic opening Mae West" Com. (R) Carlos N. Martinez

On 21May six aircraft took off on a mission to attack the fleet. When the Ten. Bean was shot down, I saw the ejection but his parachute; but the ejection speed and low altitude that it must have vanished, unable to activate the inflation of the lifejacket. Leaving the attack on Antrim, I saw Bean enter the Dagger of water, ie I saw him about 5 km before, but the plane flew on alone, ran over the ship and nosedived when we went out the attack. I saw it in top plan, he was whole. Obviously it affected commands, forcing him to eject. 21 made the maximum effort, but they exploited fine weather and night.

Following the Bean, a change came. When we climbed the plane the plane were binding those two cuerditas we had to activate it manually, so if we eyectábamos lifejacket is "automatically" activated. It happened once, that lowering the cabin we forgot to untie it, so we ended up coming down with the inflated vest, something very uncomfortable.

"Bad and good" Com. (R) Carlos N. Martinez

23May I arrived with Volponi to the Strait and we do not see any boat as close to the northern islands were, did a very broad and very fast turn on the left to see if we could find a ship. We had already seen Harrier aircraft patrolling up and we'd go back to the Falkland Islands, when Volponi told me that the Harriers were attacking us. I looked back and saw a fireball, about five meters in diameter, 200 meters behind and close to the water. I thought you had given Volponi, I accelerated, I came to the islands doing a very tight turn, where the plane had problems with over-G. When I reached the continent warned that Volponi had been shot down over the sea, about 5 km from the islands.

Three days later I was informed that appeared the remains of Volponi ground, which I began to think that he had seen was not his plane but a missile that had thrown me, which self-destructed 200 m before reaching my plane. Given that the missile flying at Mach 2, and I was going to 1,000 km per hour, missed less than a quarter of a second for impactase me.

"Poor Bean" Brig. (R) Roberto Janett

With Bean, usually we cover the first round of the alerts and when the shift changed, sounded the alarm and went who replaced us, and we, we accumulated stress not leave. In one of those nights, in the box, Bean said, "Lord, do not give more, but not again want to leave!". He had a little box in the window, with soil and seedlings of the islands that had brought one of the crosses made in April in transport aircraft.

Thus we come to 21May, we comply with the routine walk to bowling, and upon arrival, he began feverishly lived as the English were landing, and we came fragmentary orders, the first one, Rohde, Bean and me. At last it was time!

And on the islands, passing a small hill and veering right, we appeared on the channel. The sun was shining, it seemed an unreal show, Rohde and Bean were on the right to a Type 42 destroyer, while I, just to the left I jumped on a frigate Type 21. A great distance I began to pull my guns when I saw a "little fire" I snuggled in a straight line. I hit a palancazo on the left, and the fire disappeared on my right. While the ship tried to maneuver, I threw my English pump while still squeezing the trigger gun ... Since the escape, by radio frequency, I only managed to understand "the two ejected" unrepaired that "two" is he spoke. The voice was the "Napo" Martinez, who had been following us in another squadron, and watched as Bean was

reached on a plane and eyectaba, but more than 500 knots. He must have fallen badly wounded and in the channel, we never heard from him ...

Individual silent back up divisarnos and meet with Rohde, and realizing that two was Bean ... and from there I echoed his words: "I want to go out but not again!".

"Ejection at 540 knots ..." Com. (R) Raul A. Diaz

On 24May day I ejected on the island Bourbon. I fell on the ground and I was lying there about 30 or 40 minutes, I tried to move my legs. Her pretty battered borseguíes with evidence of having been damaged during ejection. He had a thirst and terrible pain. I fell looking up with his right arm under the body. At that moment such pain I thought I had something in the column but to move my feet, I realized that I had some other problem, but was not invalid. The problem was the arm, not sorry. I ejected over 540 knots and the seat manufacturer, Martin Baker, said that about 450 knots not guarantee that reach not amputate any upper or lower limb, so I thought "here does not have the arm". I started taking the jacket until he left the entire arm. He had feeling in his hand, but could not move because he had dislocated his elbow. When I eject the ring located between the legs, having his arm in the air, surely a blow air it pulled me out of place. With these two very serious injuries I tried to sit up, but could not. I could hardly breathe and had a terrible thirst, so I took water from the pouch I carried in my survival vest. I did not know I was going to do because the situation was very committed. This occurred at 11:15 am, and if getting dark, and if he did not retreat, perhaps not going to tell the tale. He was evaluating it could do. My idea was to go on the beach which was a few hundred meters in search of a village kelper, and I began to see what could take survival equipment to load the lowest possible weight.

At that moment I felt a noise of a vehicle, I looked and saw a Land Rover that came to me. An individual green with rifle got out to open a gate about 400 meters away. They approached the vehicle. I took my revolver 38 high with my left arm. If they were kelpers or English soldiers had to be prepared for any eventuality. Approximately 80 meters a person moving vehicle crouching behind it got. I met the anti-G, the diver, vest and scarf group, which was red and blue, coincidentally the colors of the Royal Navy. They kept coming at me, pointing and talking among themselves. At one point one of them shouted in perfect Spanish "Name?". Then I realized it was our people, I dropped the revolver and pedi approaching. There were two pilots of Naval Aviation who were in a village. Their machines had been destroyed by the British command in the 15May Elephant Bay. They helped me take off my equipment and parachutes, put him in the jeep and I got into the passenger seat. A cross-country, we headed to a place of stay about 8 km. We arrived, went through the track where the Pucara, Turbo Mentor and Skyvan were destroyed and then we got to put kelper. There at the command post, I was put on a makeshift bed. A midshipman "clinical" made me the first aid prior to the anti-exposure suit me removed by cutting with scissors. There

Part I Airmobile Squadron "The Wild Avutardas" in Rio Grande, before the start of hostilities. Above left. to right., the Squadron Leader My. Martinez, Cap. Mir Gonzalez, Cap. Robles, Ten. Bean and Cap. Rohde. Below, Chap. Janett, 1st. Ten. Ardiles, 1st. Ten. Moon, Cap. Moreno, Ten. Bernhart, Cap. Cimatti and Ten. Comas Martínez (doctor). [Brig (R) Roberto Janett]

The ejected pilots recovery represented a significant morale boost fro Grupo 6 de Caza. 1St Lt Luna, Major Piuma and 1st Lt Senn explain the details of their shooting down on arrival to San Julian on 26 May. [Via Brig (R) Gustavo Piuma Justo]

I learned that the plane Carlos Castillo of my squadron had not returned. I always assumed until then, it had intercepted a plane and we had thrown Puga and me. I thought Castillo had managed to escape to the mainland. They communicated with Puerto Argentino radio saying he was the Cap. Diaz, who had recovered and sent them to say he had seen the plane fell Puga without knowing the fate of this and then I asked what had happened to the third plane. I did not know what had happened until the next day when they went out on patrol and found Puga on the beach. They brought it and we are giving a big hug. I told him that I had seen when they hit his plane and he told me that when he told me to hit the Oro 3, he meant he had seen Castle blow up the plane. The explosion covered the plane and could not see any ejection.

Impressive image of cinema-machine gun of a Dagger at a time when attacking a Type 22 frigate HMS "Broadsword" (F-88) on May 21 in San Carlos. Note the position of pitcher Sea Wolf bow pointed toward the attacking planes, composed of three Dagger Squadron Ñandú (O.F. 1,181), manned by Cap. Rohde and Janett and Ten. Bean, who lost his life mission to be brought down just by a missile fired from the Sea Wolf ship. [VI Air Brigade]

We stayed there several days, I had a fissure in the fourth and fifth lumbar vertebra and dislocated arm to the elbow. I was pretty sore in pain. Over the day the arm was put bigger, more bloated, more black ... in this situation the transfer to Puerto Argentino was asked, but as the road was taken, the only way was by air.

The rescue was planned one night with a Twin Otter, with the support of an F-27, but found the island, so the mission was suspended and returned to the mainland machines. The next day, 29May82, were present Harriers and bombed the area as they had noticed some movement in it, because some lights marked the track for the Argentine aircraft could land. The Harrier threw bombs with delay in the morning on the track. When not exploring think that the English had problems with the pumps and peat. But in the evening, at 15 pm again and again Harriers bombed and this time it exploded ... When it was coming the Twin, who advanced a little, the bombs had been thrown in the morning if started detonate and were about a thousand meters from the runway. Seeing this, Puga that was dealing with communications, tried to tell the Twin who turned and they were exploding bombs, but the plane continued without any radio contact and was landing almost when arriving warned. On top of the problem of the bombs he had Harriers in the area. The plane was at the head of the makeshift runway and the pilots made immediately abandon the machine. At night they take me away in a jeep with the rest of the evacuees and took off immediately. The operation was very complicated as it was night, the track had no markings, the situation was very grim. To get away from Malvinas, they made a low flight over the sea and then take up and finally landing in Puerto Deseado. There we changed to F-27 support coming and went to Comodoro Rivadavia where the Relocatable Hospital FAA was. I spent the night in the hospital, after full chest and placed in a cast me succeed in reducing me a little dislocation. Seeing that the elbow was not good, they decided to move to Palomar in an F-28 for surgery. Finally it elbow recovered by placing successive casts without requiring operation. I spent two months plastering and after two months of recovery ... .volví to fly .cosa Mirage ... I never thought that I would give.

"Escaping from the Coventry" Brig. Mario M. Callejo

On 24May I participated along with Dellepiane and Musso of attack ships in the Strait San Carlos. During the output phase target low-flying, up to the northern mouth of the Strait San Carlos and in low visibility at times, I stumbled on the Type 42 destroyer HMS "Coventry" accompanied by a frigate Type 21 in evident

Different images of the attack on the HMS Plymouth -F126- (Type 12 - Class Rothesay) on June 8 in Pleasant Bay. The frigate suffered impacts 30mm cannons from the two Squadrons Dagger. The first attack was the "Dog" composed of the Cap. Rohde and 1st. Ten. Gabari souk and Ratti followed later by the "Jack" Cap. Cimatti and My. Martinez.

task of radar warning (Coventry would be sunk the next day by a squadron of a-4B under the command of Capt. Mariano Velasco). No weapons available on board, I looked for an exit to escape to the coast of the Falklands, just when the destroyer launched a radar-guided missile. I immediately ejected three tanks of 1,300 liters and empty and began a violent maneuver to the right looking divert the missile. Fortunately the maneuver was effective and the missile being passed over endless moments to reach the coast of the Falklands. Subsequently the flight back I realized smoothly.

"The ejected" - Brig (R) Roberto Janett

23May was a black day for the Dagger, as they shot down six planes, but fortunately five pilots survived:

Piuma, after seeing the enemy and after ejection, facing the sky awoke on malvinense earth, with black eyes and some injuries. It was the best organized to survive, finding a place to stay with lots of wool, where he spent the night ... The comic was the rescue helicopter, he had previously rescued an Englishman, and with the same suit model anti-exposure, so to see him asked "what is your problem?" to which Piuma tell them ... "what what is your problem or what the fuck! I'm Argentinean!"

Puga, who fell into the sea, he said ejection seat with doing "duck" and semi open parachute, swimming for more than six hours to reach the coast of Elephant Bay.

Donadille, pardon I should say DONADILLE (hewell deserves capitals) attempted a cross with a Sea Harrier, which he shot with guns and according to different versions this could have then fallen by the impact of projectiles of 30 mm in the engine while returning the carrier In combat, another Sea Harrier "blowed his exhaust pipe" ejecting and falling with several bruises, also ejected were **"Little Boy" Diaz**, who had arm problems ... and **Senn**, who was the most normal ejected, returning all of them to the mainland after.

Baptism of fire

34 years later, Commodore Gustavo Aguirre Faget narrates the mission in which for the first time, the Argentine Air Force would effect an airstrike during a war against another country.

On May 1, 1982, the Argentina Air Force had its baptism of fire, participating for the first time in a conflict with another nation. Among the missions launched that day, the lathe squadron, formed by three IAI M5 Dagger from Fighter Group 6 would be the first to make an attack mission. Commodore Gustavo Aguirre Faget was then Lieutenant and was part of that squadron, number 2, flying alongside their leader, Captain Norberto Dimeglio and 1st Lieutenant Cesar Roman. Today, 34 years later, he tells how was his first combat mission, in which he attacked the HMS Glamorgan.

Aguirre Faget was part of Airmobile Squadron II The "Marinete", deployed to the Military Air Base (BAM) San Julian and Torno flight was the second mission of

unit that day. Due to a problem with his aircraft Aguirre Faget could not take off with the squadron commander, Captain Raul Diaz, at the first mission. However, Diaz did not go into combat and returned.

In the afternoon, the County class destroyer HMS Glamorgan and type 21 frigates HMS Alacrity and Arrow approached the east coast

Dimeglio, Roman and Aguirre Faget besides C-412.

Roman Aguirre Faget and two mechanics.

of Isla Soledad (East Falkland) to bombard Argentine positions around Puerto Argentino (Port Stanley). Southern Air Force immediately issued Fragmentary Order 1105, which came to San Julian and sending Torno flights was ordered. Dimeglio flew in C-432, Aguirre Faget did in

C-412 and Roman in the C-407. Each aircraft was carrying three 1.300 litre drop tanks and two Explosivos Alaveses 500-pound bombs of the BRP type (parachute retarded) at positions 3 and 5. At 15.45 hours, Argentine time Torno took off from its base.

From the Strait of San Carlos flew low level at 420 knots, then we accelerate to 480 and I think in the last part were about 520. We tried not to exceed 540 by a limitation of fuzes. The three had to keep training, which was one 50 side meters online, it is difficult at very low altitude. At that time we had no radio altimeter and height visually estimated, was about 50 feet, although when we accelerated in the last stage and we had ships ahead, we may have gone up a little and training disarm.

We had two VHF, the pilot can select the green VHF, red or both, we had a common frequency to talk between the squadron, on the other had three different frequency, one had the Malvinas radar, another Malvinas tower and the other to relay aircraft, which was the HS-125 (LV-ALW Phoenix Squadron) was at 40,000 feet. When we passed San Carlos we were on the coast I heard 'boludos not shoot, stop' after I found out that was Captain Gonzalez, who officiated spotter near the Malvinas airfield and saw the Mirage IIIEA with Garcia Cuerva came to the landing and artillery antiaircraft was pulling him. When I heard that I looked south and saw the wires far enough fire tracers, into the clouds. They have been five seconds I heard that. I later learned that this was the moment they overthrew Garcia Cuerva. Surely made a general ejection and let the missiles, which make it inert, it is a situation that sees the people below, who had seen dead and wounded. We already knew we had to be careful with Darwin and Puerto Argentino, that except with special coordination these areas were forbidden to fly.

In combat

We walked from north to south, we passed the Berkeley Sound, theoretically they were there and we had little fuel. Dimeglio told us 'we are still two minutes', because we went through the target area and there was nothing.

In the shift in Berkeley Sound, on the side of the coast there was a helicopter, as a Sea King, was not a Lynx helicopter was a big adjustment was doing allegedly shooting. Number 3, which was Román almost collides in turn, passed very close. There had and saw the ships, we would be about 5 or 6 kilometers from the coast, so there are many witnesses to the attack from the shore, they saw the very young aircraft, but saw everything that happened.

Just surrounded the southern boundary of the Berkeley Sound, the pilots saw three ships ahead bombarding Argentine positions, southeast of the airport, it was 16:40 (19:40 GMT).

In addition the vessel to which I went, there were closer to the coast a ship diagonally in front of us had other good side. Roman told me that as He could not have thrown a few seconds of preparation and hesitated to throw because we were sure that the ships were not Argentine. Aguirre Faget chose the target was farther east, I was sure they

Aguirre Faget standing with other pilots.

An Expal 250 kg bomb in a Dagger in San Julian.

were British, when they had ahead to 4000 or 5000 meters did not have it in sight, it gave me in the water, so I got up to about 3000 feet I went down with negative G, I hoped to have it within reach of guns and pulled the stern and reaching level off, throw bombs and went to the east shooting the bow first and then nose down, reaching the stern. Immediately from the ship opened fire with 20mm Oerlikon cannons of both bands and GPMG machine guns wheelhouse. The vision of the artillery was like arrows with smoke and looked like they would stick all and when they were near the plane seemed that opened and passed around, I threw the focus of that. You have probably begun to pull out of reach because when you are pulling makes you start throwing before. After nivelé, I threw the bombs and went eastward, saw no one, nor Dimeglio or Roman, the ships were in a triangle and in my career I attacked him fore and aft. Since I poked my nose I was started throwing with a very concentrated fire, so I can not say as was the ship, I was focused on my plane, looks, speed not to overdo, as if in a shooting exercise, he wanted to keep the pumps performance for my stick, is not courage or cowardice, you're there and you get to do that, the best he could do was keep throwing with 30mm ammunition and bombs. I pulled and I dove into the water because my height was higher than we'd had in navigation and between the dropping of the bombs and my dive I made a porpoising eastbound and not if it saved me because I looked and kept shooting, there I saw smoke. Not how long but I think two or three minutes sailed towards the sea to escape the shots. According to witnesses saw from the coast, a missile was launched against Aguirre Faget at the time when he took up to attack, so it passed beneath his plane and did not see it.

Dimeglio captain, first lieutenant César Román, Deputy Mario Callejo and Aguirre Faget.

HMS "Arrow".

HMS "Alacrity".

Roman, Dimeglio and Aguirre Faget with C-432 the aircraft in which Dimeglio flew his mission.

Lieutenants Pedro Bean, Juan Bernhardt, Héctor Volponi and Aguirre Faget, the first three were killed in combat.

Interception

After the attack, about 5 or 6 minutes later Dimeglio said 'one' and I had to have answered 'dos' and Roman 'tres', but said nothing and then shouted 'answer boludos' then I said two Roman said three. Put forward towards San Julián it meant passing over Puerto Argentino and had a limitation in the area prohibited by artillery and missiles themselves. To gain altitude had to fly at 300 knots and expected level, initially at 20,000 or 23,000 feet and then continue the climb. The Dagger when you speed is a wonderful plane, but it takes time to accelerate. At that point I notified the Malvinas radar No. 2 had a Harrier he was being followed. I realized I had low speed, could have ejected the three tanks, but eject one, trying to bring back to the other two because I knew we had a few. I had to make a very polished navigation directions fuel. I could not level or change course, had to reach cruising level and that the plane would begin to accelerate.

When we finished the attack could put the transponder in active *or standby and when the English had so I turned back to me who confirmed the three were chasing and confirmed it was me. With the sun in front saw nothing, it was 5 pm, had no ammunition and had little fuel.*

In the ascent he continued persecution, first to 12 miles, then 9 miles and when I sang that were 6 miles and I began to breathe a little quieter because it was already accelerating the aircraft to continue in a better position, 0.9 Mach.

This flight was covered by Fortin (Fragmentary Order 1107), which was formed by Captain William Donadille (C-403) and 1st Lt.. Jorge Senn (C-421), which began orbiting about Gran Malvina at 30,000 feet. Before the persecution of the two Sea Harriers on Torno 2 they were sent to protect. They were placed behind the British planes, reaching about 2 miles, although they could not fire their Shafrir because flying with the sun in front and missiles were hooked on it. Donadille plane could not fire their guns were locked. On the Strait of San Carlos the Sea Harriers started a dive due south and disappeared from radar.

Excerpt from the "book".

FUERZA AEREA ARGENTINA

Nº 49092

INFORME DE VUELO — TRIPULACION

The return flight

Aguirre Faget almost returned to its base fuel and describes: in the Dagger you can not accommodate you if you get in bad landing and you have to take another turn where you consume about 150 liters of fuel. When we crossed landing came the

Dagger taking off from San Julian.

interminable clouds. When we were getting were starting to look radials other bases to see how far we were from San Julian. En route, near the coast I saw a plane, a trail, as parallel came to me did not know if it was a Harrier, but suspected it was a buddy of mine, but I kept silent radio, watching the behavior of the engine, seeing as it began the descent, because if miscalculated consuming more fuel and maybe I had to eject in the water. The concentration of the flight lasted until I cut the engine. I challenged ground mechanics because I could not believe it when I said the plane had no impact, but really had nothing.

After the mission

Due to a bug in the photometer of his plane, the film of the Omera 110 gun camera was veiled, *I could not believe it, because it would have seen that vessel was my angle shot, which ammunition was pulling me, what time pressed the button pump and output. The photometer has a screw showing how is accommodating to light and the head is moving, and the noncommissioned officer in charge told me after landing, 'if you saw that was fixed I should have touched, because maybe he was hard' but now, in the middle attack ... I wanted to kill him.*

Dagger in San Julian.

C-412 before its retirement t, with the marks of the attack on HMS Brilliant and HMS "Arrow". In fact, the Arrow was attacked by Dimeglio.

Commodore Gustavo Aguirre Faget in his office in 2010.

The Dagger flight which damaged the destroyer Glamorgan with 30mm hits from guns fired by Aguirre Faguet, while according to the British version, the two bombs exploded a short distance over the sea and caused some damage to the rudder and hull. The Arrow frigate had been hit eleven 30mm shot by Dimeglio and Alacrity was attacked by Roman. The ships stopped the bombing and firing and the destroyer changed course smoking. At night was a loud explosion in the direction in which the ship had retired. None of the planes were damaged despite the flak and all landed safely between 18:25 and 18: 40hs.

Another mission

Gustavo Aguirre Faget made seven missions during the war. *The only mission that went volunteers was an attack dive we did with Dimeglio over the Strait of San Carlos. We had told our boss that we had done the involvement of its ships and artillery that they would necessarily desaprramar that air defense. We said that maybe it was not so serious attack in height and could do a test pecking from 40,000 to 12,000 feet or 35,000 feet or 15,000 feet and then throw the bombs and escape. The squad leader said, 'good morning you go'. We left the next day, on May 26 and the beachhead was*

established and there were many ships. We had the concept that with good visibility, at that point one has time to see the missiles from afar. Great Malvina had a perfect view, but from the Straits of San Carlos was all covered. Like began the descent, we made a dive of 60 degrees, practically idle, brake out and we jump into a tailspin next to each other, when we got 18,000 or 16,000 feet Dimeglio said 'we', put brake and started to leave for San Julian and I kept. In this mission we had two tanks of 1300 liter four 500-pound bombs with fuse SSQ, which operates in surface before entering and has a better flight, better penetration. As we went back height and height we were comfortable fuel. I went ahead and threw the bombs without seeing. We communicate with the radar where we confirmed that we were at the point where we had to make the descent. White attack was near the hotel San Carlos, there had ships. Where they were to stop the bombs do not know, but I'm glad they have not fallen into the refrigerator Ajax Bay, because there were many Argentine prisoners.

Dimeglio threw his bombs back on the Savage Islands at 15:20 and landed safely at its base. Aguirre Faget that night called the Chief of Air Group, which was Rodriguez Thomas, who was in Comodoro Rivadavia, in South Air Force and thought I was going to challenge by throwing the bombs, but challenged him to Dimeglio for not having as we were lying on the white and in the end ended up pulling at sea before landing. "

The aircraft

Gustavo Aguirre Faget flew on that mission aboard IAI M5 Dagger C-412, this aircraft was built in 1973 as IAI M5 Nesher for the Israel Defense Force/Air Force with the number of S-49 series and on 28 December 1978 entered service with the Argentine Air Force, at a time when Argentina and Chile lived a great tension over a border dispute over the Beagle channel at the southern tip of the American continent. He flew seven missions in the Falklands and on May 21 by attacking the frigate HMS Brilliant suffered an impact of a light weapon in the VHF and another attack on the same ship, on the afternoon of the same day he suffered an impact on the windshield. After the war, the C-412 was modified to standard Finger IIIB and currently still in service in Group 6 of Hunting VI Air Brigade at its base in Tandil.

The last Grupo 6 de Caza exercise with the Mirages, the end of an era

After a career of 43 years, the history of the Mirage family in the Argentina Air Force has come to an end. As part of this last operational phase, the Mirage Squadron of Fighter Group 6 made a new deployment to southern Argentina, to continue training in air-air combat and tactical navigation.

The Mirages of the VI Air Brigade returned to operate in southern Argentina, but this was not an exercise more. It was the last operational deployment of the "Deltas" prior to being phased out, set for late November 2015. A deserved and necessary retirement deprogramming after 43 years of service, with more than

A Finger IIIB flying near the border with Chilean Andes. It was the last time these jets flew over this area, always "hot" between the two countries on many occasions, when fighters of a country approaching from the other side taking off another couple of planes to let them know they were not alone. [Photo VI Air Brigade]

A section of Dagger B/ Finger IIIB off on a dorgfight sortie under dGCI (Ground Control Interception). During this type of mission, the aircraft were guided and controlled to the "bandit" by radar operators who used the Westignhouse TPS-43D early warning radar located at BAM Rio Gallegos.

Dawns on the platform of BAM Rio Gallegos. The Mirages are ready awaiting the arrival of the pilotss, "Hotel" configuration with 1.700 litre drop tanks for the execution of navigation tactics over the southern tip of the province of Santa Cruz and Tierra del Fuego.

131,000 flight hours and much glory on their backs.

This was the framework that covered the Operation "Ariete" held between 3 and 11 September. A stage full of energy because of operating again in Patagonia, on the premises of the Military Air Base (BAM) Rio Gallegos in the south of the province of Santa Cruz, a place very dear for the history of the Air Force and country by the conflict in the South Atlantic. But in turn also because it was the last flight of these jets by those latitudes, wrapping everything with much emotion and feelings, which translated into an incredible teamwork to achieve all planned missions were met.

Whenever Atar engines ignited, mechanics and pilots were in the central Hardened Aircraft Shelters (HAS) area of the base from where they operated, they took to the platform to see the scene. Flight line staff carefuelly checked the aircraft, with its Enghien idling to finally give the last "ok", then the pilot began taxiing to the runway. All attentively followed with their gaze the whole process, which already knew and had seen hundreds of times before ... but this time they would not want to lose. The aircraft rolled down the taxiway towards the runway; while some climbed to the roof of the shelter sto see the takeoff from a privileged position. Once at the runway, after carrying out routine checks, pilots pushed the throtles and lit the afterburners. The noise was deafening. The heat of the gases coming out of the exhaust distorted the horizon, making everything seem a mirage ... And so let loose the Mirages brakes starting the takeoff roll to rotate and start climb right up to the shelters. A unique short film that will remain in the retina of all and that despite repeated dozens of times throughout the trading week, no one would stop to enjoy it.

Logistical support was provided by transports Lockheed C-130 Hercules and Fokker F-28 of Squadrons I and II of Group 1 of Air Transport I Air Brigade (El Palomar). The VII Air Brigade deployed a Bell 212 helicopter for SAR tasks. As part of air operations, the radar control was vital during exercise. To do this they had the early warning radar Westinghouse TPS-43E, installed permanently in the BAM Rio Gallegos and operated by Squadron personnel VYCA 2 Group 2 Air Surveillance and Control, the "Ice Bats." In addition, radar operators from Squadron VYCA Mobile Group 1 VYCA of the Directorate of Surveillance and Aerospace Control (based in the town of Merlo, Buenos Aires) were sent to support the tasks of guidance and support in navi-

"Garfio" Flight, making the final checks before takeoff at the head of runway 25. It will be a new tactical navigation that bring the to Calafate and Cerro Fitz Roy, on the border with Chile.

A pair of two-seater Mirages (Mirage IIIDA and Dagger B) roll to the plaform after a training sortie. The Mirage family ends his career with more than 131,000 flight hours.

A Finger IIIB taxying from one of the shelters to start a new air-air combat, carrying supersonic 500 litre tanks (Version "Bravo"). For these exercises, they operated jointly with the radar operators Group 1 and 2 Air Surveillance and Control, for training in tactics BVR (Beyond Visual Range).

A Finger from a different perspective, while leaving his refuge. The Finger (Dagger in its original version) entered service in late 1978, 39 machines (five of them two seaters) were purchased from Israel.

gation. The activity of this last unit was closely related to the history of the Mirage IIIEA M, when the interceptors formed part of the Eighth Air Brigade (very close to Merlo), and operating jointly, both units they provided air safety to the city of Buenos Aires.

Under the significance of this event, BAM Rio Gallegos organized the weekend 5 and 6 September. Open Days for the Mirage could say goodbye to the Patagonian people. The link of the Air Force and Mirage in these lands is very marked, not only by the actions of the Falklands War, but also because between 1984 and 1996, the base of Rio Gallegos was hoe to Squadron "Cruz and Fierro" (the legendary "Ice Warriors" equipped with Mirage IIIC on, Mirage and Mirage 5P and M5A Mara), and recurring host deployments for air exercises.

As expected, the response of the Patagonian citizenship was very important, filling facilities enabled the public at the local airport and at the entrances and surrounding routes, despite the bad weather the first day of exhibitions. It had a small static sample with a Mirage IIIDA as

Mirage Squadron pilots, which had the honor of being the last crew of the Mirage III and 5 in the Argentina Air Force, closing a chapter in its history, full of exploits, glory and sadness for those who did not return their missions.

Once completed the flight of the day, the staff of the Technical Echelon, as true worker ants, carefully review the machine to check for discrepancies, leaving it ready for the next day. If necessary, work can be extended into the night, but their goal is that the jet be operacional for the next mission.

the main attraction, adding air assets theArmy Aviation and Gendarmerie, the Aero Club of Rio Gallegos and the Provincial Directorate of Aviation Santa Cruz province, plus demonstrations flights of a Bell 212 and DHC-6 Twin Otter, both from the FAA. The ultra lowe level passes of the Mirage all the applause and words of the pilots made from their aircraft after landing from the last missionthe thrilled many to drop a few tears.

The first phase of the exercise involved the execution of air-air combat with coordination and radar guidance. The day after the arrival at the base of Rio Gallegos, the Mirage performed familiarization flights with the area and immediately began training flights, which were not interrupted during the weekend of the Open Days. The range of fulfilled activities was very broad. They trained in combat tactics employ-

ing BVR weapons to NATO level, in advanced air combat maneuvering (ACM - Air Combat Maneuvering) simulating an environment of high intensity with enemy electronic jamming. In these practices, 2 vs 1, the two-seater Mirage IIIDA and Dagger B "allied" interceptors while a Finger IIIB acted as "bandit". Complementing all this and in response to air threats rapid reaction alert (Quick Reaction Alert or "scramble" QRA) they were conducted. Mock "stand off" attacks were also tested, as well as radar and electronic warfare exercises (SIGINT, ELINT and COMINT).

A typical sortie consisted of a pre-flight briefing where participating pilots and radar crews finalized the details of the mission to fulfill, such as sectors of training, tactics and

Coming down from their machines a pair of pilots can not avoid commenting aspects of flight, while behind, the mechanics are working to recover the plane to the next sortie. This trio, pilot - mechanic - aircraft has been the fundamental and indivisible for these steel birds would soar and fulfill its objectives throughout all these years.

Mechanical "sparklers" of Technical Group 6, solve the flight line, with the Dagger B with its engine running, a last problema with the alternator.

Mirage Airmobile Squadron, led by the Air Group CO, Commodore Fabian Celotto inside a HAS for the final briefing of the exercise. A true joint team, which despite the adversities because it is a weapon system over 40 years old and ending his operational career, was able to meet all the planned objectives.

procedures used in aerial combat. Each sortie included five "rounds" of air combat (also called "Set Ups") where each different tactics were practiced. Victories in the air to air arena were determined by compliance with the rules of training, by studying the GPS recordings of aircraft, filming HUD (Head Up Display) and recordings of the air battle by the radar crew . In the latter, the role of interception air traffic controllers was critical for airspace surveillance and detection of marauders, and manage the air battle. The novelty of this operation was that since the new Aerospace Command of the Joint Staff evolution of real-time combat continued, thanks to the new Argentine satellites and communications links. This allowed the practice of command and control.

The new systems of data recording GPS navigation (similar to EHUD ACMI pod used by A-4AR Fightinghawks) allowed the representation of all air combat in a new computer software.

The real "Magos" Technical Group 6. A true team of specialists with very young NCOs and other veterans of the Falklands, creating a unique symbiosis. Despite 43 years of service with the FAA, the flying machines returned from thei missions withoutany problems, or at least no significant ones, another example of the dedication and efforts of technical staff added to the the toughness of this truly French champion.

Mirage IIIEA 25th anniversary in flight.

The second stage involved the execution of navigation tactics s throughout the south of the country. Different missions were planned in order to visit the different cardinal points and fly over major cities so their inhabitants could see them going through their skies and so say goodbye to this enigmatic plane. The news that the jets would perform these passages generated great expectation and that is how, for example, in the city of Calafate, many people gathered for an afternoon on the waterfront of Lake Argentino not to miss this show. They waited with Argentine flags, cameras and cell phones to capture the moment. Something very similar happened in the cities of Ushuaia, Río Grande and Piedrabuena ... nobody wanted to miss the last low level runs of the Mirages.

As part of this phase, interdiction missions were flown against bridges, roads and mechanized troops. Even the penultimate day of operations, an attack mission against a naval target was performed.

Operation "Ariete" was a true teamwork of radar crews and fighter pilots. Another part of ocourse was the technical staff of the Technical Group. On land, they awaited the return of the machines and prepared everything for the recovery of machines to let them ready for the next sortie. When the radio notified that the Mirages were in area and in minutes would land, like ants the personnel began to leave again to the platform and climb onto the roof of the shelters. As was always tradition throughout deployment, the return of each sorites, the

Mirage IIEA fighter from Grupo 6 de Caza with the lastest gray overall camouflage scheme.

ARGENTINE AIR FORCE MIRAGE IIIEA/DA, DAGGER A/ DAGGER B/FINGER AND MIRAGE 5P/A MARA

SERIAL	S/N	built	in service	status	original a/c	converted	
C-401	S-07	1971-12-14	1978-11-26	Struck of charge	M5D Dagger	M5F Finger IIIB	Gate guardian at Tandil AB, Buenos Aires province
C-402	S-18	1972-07-24	1978-11-26	Struck of charge	M5D Dagger	M5F Finger IIIB	
C-403	S-16	1972-05-03	1978-11-26	Lost 21/05/82	M5D Dagger		Took part in the South Atlantic Conflict with II Airmobile Squadron "La Marinete", shot down on 21 May 82 by Sea Harrier FRS1 (ZA190/"009") of 801 NAS flown by Lt S. Thomas. Pilot, Captain Guillermo Donadille ejected and was rescued by own forces
C-404	S-12	1972-03-23	1978-11-26	Lost 21/05/82	M5D Dagger		Took part in the South Atlantic Conflict with II Airmobile Squadron "La Marinete", shot down on 21 May 82 by Lt. S. Thomas in Sea Harrier FRS1 (ZA190/"009") of 801 NAS. Pilot, Major Justo Piuma ejected and was rescued by own forces. Parts of the Dagger fell in the Green Hill area, where they are still visible
C-405	S-03	1971-08-31	1978-11-26	Lost 31/05/82	M5D Dagger	M5F Finger IIIB	Destroyed in an accident on 31 May 94 after veering off the runway, while on the take off run. Pilot Lt, Fabián Constanzi suffered was lightly wounded
C-406	S-13	1972-03-27	1978-11-26	Lost 26/11/79	M5D Dagger		Destroyed in accident at 12:10 hrs on 26 November 79 at Estancia Santa Lidia, near the city of Azul, Buenos Aires provine, due to an engine failure. Pilot 1st. Lt. Amilcar Cimatti ejected
C-407	S-26	1972-11-06	1978-12-06	Lost 21/05/82	M5D Dagger		Took part in the South Atlantic Conflict with II Airmobile Squadron "La Marinete", shot down on 21 May 82, while on its fourth sortie, by Sea Harrier FRS1 ZA175/"004", flown by Lt. Cdr. Nigel Ward, CO of 801 NAS. Pilot, Lt. Jorge Senn ejected and was rescued by own forces.
C-408	S-09	1972-02-21	1979-01-29	Struck of charge	M5D Dagger	M5F Finger IIIB	
C-409	S-10	1972-02-22	1978-12-06	Lost 21/05/82	M5D Dagger		Took part in the South Atlantic Conflict with I Airmobile Squadron "Las Avutardas Salvajes". During its second sortie on 21 May 82 was shot down by Sea Harrier FRS1 XZ455/"12" flown by Lt. Cdr. Frederiksen. Pilot, 1st. Lt. Héctor Luna ejected and was rescued by own forces
C-410	S-06	1971-12-06	1978-11-23	Lost 24/05/82	M5D Dagger		Took part in the South Atlantic Conflict initially assigned to I Airmobile Squadron "Las Avutardas Salvajes", and later to II Airmobile Squadron "La Marinete", nicknamed "Vikingo". Only flew a combat mission, being shot down on 24 May 1982 by a Sea Harrier CAP from 800 NAS, flown by Lt. Cdr Ancy Auld (XZ457"14") and Lt. Dave Smith (ZA193/"93"), this later being credited with the kill. Pilot, Captain Luis Puga ejected, while the jet fell into the sea off the north of Pebble Island (Isla Borbón).
C-411	S-02	1971-07-07	1978-12-28	Struck of charge	M5D Dagger	M5F Finger IIIA	Took part in the South Atlantic Conflict with II Airmobile Squadron "La Marineta". When war started it was on the SINT upgrade line, being interrutped and readied for transfer to the operations theatre, with the green primer finish, being nicknamed "La Cotorra" (parrot), it was repainted at Tandil in a non standard scheme
C-412	S-49	1973-12-15	1978-12-28	Struck of charge	M5D Dagger	M5F Finger IIIB	
C-413	S-40	1973-08-28	1979-01-23	Lost 14/07/95	M5D Dagger	M5F Finger IIIB	Crashed on 14 September 95 as it entered an irrecoverable spin while performe ACM. Pilot, Captain Raúl Gómez ejected
C-414	S-41	1973-09-03	1979-01-23	Struck of charge	M5D Dagger	M5F Finger IIIB	
C-415	S-04	1971-01-03	1979-01-23	Struck of charge	M5D Dagger	M5F Finger IIIB	Preserved at the Malvinas National Museum, Olivia, Buenos Aires province
C-416	S-23	1972-09-28	1979-04-03	Struck of charge	M5D Dagger	M5F Finger IIIB	
C-417	S-47	1973-11-08	1979-01-29	Struck of charge	M5D Dagger	M5F Finger IIIB	
C-418	S-46	1973-10-24	1979-04-03	destroyed	M5D Dagger		Destroyed on 12 June 87 at Cabaña Los Tapiales (Tandil), while on an ACM training sortie; the Figer entered into a spin after a vertical scissors maneuvre, and as the out of control Finger reached the safety height (10.000 feet), the pilot, Captain Fernando Robledo ejected
C-419	S-35	1973-02-21	1980-12-23	destroyed	M5D Dagger		Took part in the South Atlantic Conflict with II Airmobile Squadron "La Marinete", baptized as "Boomerang", only flew one combat mission on 24 May 82, shot down by a Sea Harrier FRS1 CAP from 800 NAS formed by Lt.. Cdr. Andy Auld (XZ457/"14") and Lt. Andy Auld (ZA193/"93"), being credited to Smith. Pilot, Lt. Carlos Castillo did not ejected and was killed when the Dagger blew up after an AIM-9L direct hit
C-420	S-38	1973-07-10	1979-04-03	Struck of charge	M5D Dagger	M5F Finger IIIB	
C-421	S-45	1973-10-16	1979-07-04	Struck of charge 11/03/93	M5D Dagger	M5F Finger IIIB	Gate guard at Puerto San Julián city, Santa Cruz province

ARGENTINE AIR FORCE MIRAGE IIIEA/DA, DAGGER A/ DAGGER B/FINGER AND MIRAGE 5P/A MARA

SERIAL	S/N	built	in service	status	original a/c	converted	
C-422	S-39	1973-07-30	1979-04-03	Struck of charge	M5D Dagger	M5F Finger IIIA	
C-423	S-34	1973-03-01	1979-07-04	Struck of charge	M5D Dagger	M5F Finger IIIB	
C-424	S-17	26/05/1972 (o 25/5)	1979-07-04	Struck of charge	M5D Dagger	M5F Finger IIIA	
C-425	B-02?	1974-05-11	1979-07-04	Struck of charge 07/10/80	M5D Dagger B		Accident on 07 October 80 after engaging the emergency barricade during a night training sortie. The aircraft received 70% damage and was w/o. Pilots Captains Horacio Mir González and Carlos Maffeis, safe
C-426	B-05?	1974-06-11	1979-07-04	Struck of charge	M5D Dagger B		
C-427	S-48	1973-12-09	1982-02-15	Struck of charge 21/10/93	M5D Dagger	M5F Finger IIIB	Written off on 25 October 93 at ARMACUAR due to engine compressor exploding while starting up, during post maintenace tasks at the test pit, a FIRE was declared, affecting 70% of the aircraft.
C-428	S-31	1972-12-28	1981-05-29	Lost 21/05/82	M5D Dagger		Took part in the South Atlantic Conflict with I Airmobile Squadron "Las Avutardas Salvajes", only flew one combat mission on 21 May 82, shot down by a Sea Wolf SAM launched from the frigate HMS Broadsword. Pilot, Lt. Pedro Bean ejected but was never found.
C-429	S-27	1972-10-25	1981-05-29	Destroyed 18/10/00	M5D Dagger	M5F Finger IIIB	Destroyed on 18 October 00 after crashing into the ground near the VI Air Brigade facilities due to losing the left wheel during take off. After consuming the remaining fuel, and jetissoning the drop tanks, the pilot Captain Alejandro Anzuinelli ejected
C-430	S-25	1972-09-05	1981-04-12	Baja 24/05/1982	M5D Dagger		Took part in the South Atlantic Conflict with I Airmobile Squadron "Las Avutardas Salvajes". On 23 May 82 transfered to II Airmobile Squadron "La Marinete", with whom only flew one combat mission, being shot down on 24 May 82, by a Sea Harrier FRS1 CAP from 800 NAS, formed by Lt. Andy Auld (XZ457/"14") and Lt Dave Smith (ZA193/"93"), the victory was credited to Auld. Pilot, Captain Raúl Díaz ejected ouside parameters and Landed with some bruises, being rescued by own forces
C-431	S-32	1973-03-01	1981-05-29	Lost 16/03/85	M5D Dagger		Destroyed aftr crashing into the ground near the Mar Chiquita weapons range. The aircraft started porpoising after the gunnery run, and as he could not regain control, the pilot Lt. Roberto Prior ejected
C-432	S-20	1972-07-20	1981-09-27	Struck of charge	M5D Dagger	M5F Finger IIIB	On exhibition at the National Aviation Museum, Morón, Buenos Aires province
C-433	S-24	1972-09-20	1981-03-29	Lost 01/05/82	M5D Dagger		Took part in the South Atlantic Conflict with I Airmobile Squadron "Las Avutardas Salvajes", only flew one combat mission on 1 May 82, engaging a British CAP, being shot down by a SideWinder AAM fired by Sea Harrier FRS1 XZ455/"12" flown by Lt Bertie Penfold. Pilot, 1st. Lt. José Ardiles did not eject, parts of the Dagger were found in Bouganville Island, west of East Falkland.
C-434	S-51	1974-02-05	1981-09-27	Destroyed 21/06/04	M5D Dagger	M5F Finger IIIB	Destroyed in crash on 21 June 04, after engine failure, while staring the Lansing pattern at Área Material Río Cuarto. Pilot, 1st. Lt. Sebastián González Iturbe ejected
C-435	S-22	1972-08-01	1981-09-27	Destroyed 19/11/88	M5D Dagger	M5F Finger IIIB	Destroyed in accident on 19 November 88 near Estancia La Elisa, Santa Cruz provine, while on a tactical navigation sortie after a sudden loss of thrust in the engine, which finally failed. Pilot, Captain Daniel Justet ejected
C-436	S-29	1972-11-27	1981-07-29	Lost 29/05/82	M5D Dagger		Took part in the South Atlantic Conflict with I Airmobile Squadron "Las Avutardas Salvajes", shot down on 29 May 82 by a Rapier SAM fired from a battery located near the beachhead. Pilot, Lt Juan Bernhard did not eject and was killed
C-437	S-19	1972-06-01	1981-09-27	Lost 23/05/82	M5D Dagger		Took part in the South Atlantic Conflict with 1 Airmobile Squadron "Las Avutardas Salvajes", shot down on 23 May 82 by an AIM-9L AAM fired by Sea Harrier FRS1 (ZA194) from 800 NAS flown by Lt. Martin Hale. Pilot Ll Héctor Volponi did not ejected and crashed with his aircraft, in the Elephant Bay area. Later his body was recovered and moved to the mainland
C-438	T-04	1974-06-28	1981-05-29	Struck of charge	M5D Dagger B		
C-439	T-07	1974-07-18	1981-05-29	Struck of charge	M5D Dagger B		
I-001	1F/1A		1972-09-05	Destroyed 30/03/79	Mirage IIIDA		Crashed at Pilar (Buenos Aires province) 100% destroyed. Pilots Vicecommodore Viola and Captain Jorge L. Huck ejected

ARGENTINE AIR FORCE MIRAGE IIIEA/DA, DAGGER A/ DAGGER B/FINGER AND MIRAGE 5P/A MARA

SERIAL	S/N	built	in service	status	original a/c	converted	
I-002	2F/2A	Mayo-72	1973-02-05	Struck of charge	Mirage IIIDA		
I-003	1F/1D	1972-07-20	1972-09-23	Struck of charge	Mirage IIIEA		
I-004	2F/2D	1972-06-18	1972-11-01	Struck of charge	Mirage IIIEA		
I-005	3F/3D	1972-09-27	1972-12-01	Struck of charge	Mirage IIIEA		
I-006	4F/4D	1972-11-10	1973-03-18	Struck of charge	Mirage IIIEA		Received special paint scheme for the Mirage IIIEA 25th Anniversary in Argentine AF service (see photo)
I-007	5F/5D	1973-02-07	1973-04-13	Struck of charge	Mirage IIIEA		
I-008	6F/6D	1973-03-19	1973-05-05	Struck of charge	Mirage IIIEA		
I-009	7F/7D		20/5/73	Destroyed 23/03/76	Mirage IIIEA		Crashed. Pilot 1st. Lt. Jorge A. García ejected safely
I-010	8F/8D	1973-04-18	29/6/73	Struck of charge	Mirage IIIEA		Gate guardian at the Aerospace Surveillance & Control Directorate (Merlo, Buenos Aires province)
I-011	9F/9D	1973-06-19	1973-07-17	Struck of charge	Mirage IIIEA		
I-012	10F/10D	1973-07-12	1973-07-27	status	Mirage IIIEA		
I-013	11F/1HD	1979-10-30	10/79	Struck of charge	Mirage IIIEA		
I-014	12F/2HD		10/79	Destroyed 25/08/87	Mirage IIIEA		Crashed at Entre Ríos. Pilot Major Juan C. Franchini killed
I-015	13F/3HD		10/79	Lost 01/05/82	Mirage IIIEA		Shot down by an AIM-9L fired by Flt.Lt. P. Barton in Sea Harrier FRS XZ423. Pilot, 1st. Lt. Carlos E. Perona ejected
I-016	14F/4HD		11/79	Accident 08/10/83	Mirage IIIEA		Crash landed during take-off from Río Gallegos, pilot Ricardo Gonzáles safe. Aicraft struck of charge
I-017	15F/5HD	1980-03-27	12/79	Struck of charge	Mirage IIIEA		
I-018	16F/6HD	1980-04-18	01/80	Struck of charge	Mirage IIIEA		
I-019	17F/7HD		01/80	Lost 01/05/82	Mirage IIIEA		Shot down near Puerto Argentino/Port Stanley by own AA, after being damaged by an AIM-9L fired by an 801 NAS Sea Harrier, while trying to make an emergency Lansing at the airfield. Pilot Gustavo A. García Cuerva killed
I-020	msn 271		04/82	Destroyed 06/05/94	Mirage IIIBE	Mirage IIIDA	Destroyed in accident. Pilots 1st Lt Marcelo Del Punta and Captain Sergio A. Niclis ejected safely
I-021	msn 272	1982-12-12	07/82	Struck of charge	Mirage IIIBE	Mirage IIIDA	
C-603	?/102	1969-05-17	1982-06-04	Struck of charge	Mirage 5P	M5A Mara	
C-604	?/104	1975-11-03	1982-06-04	Destroyed 11/06/98	Mirage 5P	M5A Mara	Destroyed at Tandil, after the left main landing gear did not retract. Pilot Major Luis A. Briatore ejected
C-607	?/105		1982-06-04	Destroyed 13/03/89	Mirage 5P		Crashed at 150 km from Río Gallegos, totally destroyed, after an Enghien failure. Pilot, Lt José Romero ejected
C-609	7/188	1976-06-23	1982-06-04	Destroyed 08/08/00	Mirage 5P	M5A Mara	Crashed at 13:59 hrs in a quarry at Cerro Federación, atfer an Enghien stoppage, totally destroyed. The Italian pilot, Major Vincenzo Sicuso ejected
C-610	?/106	1976-04-14	1982-06-04	Struck of charge	Mirage 5P	M5A Mara	Gate guardian in Luis Piedrabuena city, Santa Cruz province
C-619	?/103	1975-09-01	1982-06-04	Struck of charge	Mirage 5P	M5A Mara	
C-628	?/107	1975-10-31	1982-06-04	Struck of charge	Mirage 5P	M5A Mara	
C-630	2/183	1968-07-22	1982-06-04	Struck of charge	Mirage 5P	M5A Mara	
C-633	4/185	1969-05-23	1982-06-04	Struck of charge	Mirage 5P	M5A Mara	
C-636	5/186	1969-06-02	1982-06-04	Struck of charge	Mirage 5P	M5A Mara	

MIRAGE IIIB/C IN THE ARGENTINE AIR FORCE

A/C	S/N	Transfer to Argentina	Transfer to Río IV	In service with the unit	Struck of charge	Notes
C-701	CJ2	18/12/82	21/12/82	27/3/85	3/94	Stored in the IV Air Brigade, last flight of 14/12/88. Built in 3/62, 2803.5 flight hours. Fully dismantled.
C-702	CJ4	18/12/82	26/12/82	Esc. X 16/3/84 Esc. 55 7/11/86	3/94	Gate guardian in a square in the city of San lorenzo, Santa Fé province. Last flight 2/2/90. Built in 6/61. 2917 flight hours
C-703	CJ12	18/12/82	23/12/82	Esc. X 16/3/84 Esc. 55 7/11/86	3/94	Stored in the IV Air Brigade, part of the unit's museum. Operated with X Air Brigade. Built in 7/62
C-704	CJ14	1/2/83	4/2/83	Esc. X 16/3/84 Esc.55 7/11/86	3/94	Stored in IV Air Brigade with a Mirage 5P nose. On strengh of X Air Brigade, last flight 30/6/89. Built in 4/62. 2672,45 flight hours. Was used for Kfir development trials.
C-705	CJ20	18/12/82	26/12/82	1986	27/6/89	Crashed near San Juan, pilot 1st Lt Bellini killed. Built in 4/62.
C-706	CJ22	1/2/83	4/2/83	Esc. X 16/3/84 Esc. 55 7/11/86		Stored in Area Material Quilmes, early in 2002, displayed as a gate guardian at Av. Cruz y Larrazabal, in the city of Buenos Aires. Only flew with X Air Brigade. Built in 2/62.
C-707	CJ29	1/2/83	9/2/83	Esc. X 16/3/84	25/10/85	Creashed on 29/4/85 at Río Gallegos. Pilot Major A. Kahiara ejected, Only flew with X Air Brigade. Built in 10/62. 2256,15 flight hours.
C-708	CJ31	18/12/82	23/12/82	17/10/85	3/94	Gate guardian in Tres Arroyos, province of Buenos Aire, last flight 12/8/86. Built in 10/62. 2243,55 flight hours.
C-709	CJ32	1/2/83	7/2/83	28/1/85	1991	At the Air Force NCO school as learning tool. Built in 12/62.
C-710	CJ33	29/3/83	8/4/83	17/10/85		Stored in IV Brigada Aérea. Built in 12/62.
C-711	CJ34	29/3/83	7/4/83	1985	1991	Gate guradinat VI Air Brigade, the only original Mirage IIIRJ in Argentina.
C-712	CJ40	29/3/83	6/4/83	Esc. X 1/8/85 Esc. 55 7/11/86	19/6/89	In the National Aviation Museum since 13/11/92. Operated with X Air Brigade, replacing C-707, last flight on 12/6/89. 2409 flight hours: 1949 hs in Israel and 460 hs in Argentina. Built in 8/63.
C-713	CJ42	1/2/83	9/2/83	1985	3/94	In Israel since 2003. Last flight 13/12/90. Built in 2/62. 2620,02 flight hours. On 21/8/85 due to a throttle malfunction took the crash barricade. Sold to Israel in June 1997 to be exhibited at the Hatzerim AB Museum. In IDFAF service shot dow twelve Arab aircraft and an AS-5 cruise missile.
C-714	CJ47	29/3/83	8/4/83	1985	3/94	Gate guardian in the city of Villa Carlos Paz, Córdoba. Built in 4/63.
C-715	CJ59	21/10/83	21/3/83	1984		At the Aerospace High Shool Funes, Santa Fé, as a gate guardian. Built in 10/63.
C-716	CJ64	20/3/83	6/4/83	1985	3/94	Gate guardian at the IV Air Brigade entrance since 1/5/03, last flight on 10/5/90. Built in 4/64, 2093,05 flight hours.
C-717	CJ65	1/2/83	7/2/83	21/11/85	3/05	Struck of charge at Centro de Ensayo de Armamentos y Sistemas Operativos (CEASO) in Río IV. Built in 4/62.
C-718	CJ66	29/3/83	7/4/83	1986	3/94	Last flight on 28/11/90. Built in 4/63. 2057,15 flight hours. Exhibited at "Santa Romana." Museum. "
C-719	CJ67	29/3/83	7/4/83	1986	3/94	Stored in IV Air Brigade Brigad, last flight 4/12/90. Built in 4/63. 2188,55 flight hours.
C-720	BJ1	18/12/82	23/12/82	18/1/85	29/7/88	Crashed on 29/7/88 some 15 km. South of Area de Material Río IV, pilot killed and passenger ejected. 2167,3 flight hours. Built in 2/66.
C-721	BJ2	1/2/83	7/2/83	17/10/84	1998	At the Area de Material Río IV Museum. Built in 3/66. Transferred to "Santa Romana" Museum.
C-722	BJ4	18/12/82	21/12/83	28/11/84	1998	Stored in Area de Material Río IV. Built in 1/68.

Deployment at Rio Gallegos, a few months after concluding the Falklands conflict.

Mirage performed a low level pass over the facilities and to give joy to ground staff letting them know that everything had gone well. Of course this deployment was no exception, no one wanted to lose it and enjoy. Barely they saw on the horizon began emotions and shouts exploded seconds after seeing them go crazy over their heads and see the "red" engine exhaust on with the afterburner. Pure adrenaline!

After coming down of the machines, the pilots returned very excited. Viewing from the air so many people that had gathered in the cities where they had made farewell passes made everything had a special dimension. As also to explore unique landscapes and mythical ones as the Cerro Fitz Roy or the Beagle Channel ... many feelings. Feelings to see the beloved and what was the meaning "Mirage" for citizenship; to understand that this is an icon representing the Air Force then reaching the end of its career; to be protagonists of this historical moment in Fighter Group 6, for staying until the end of the story going through difficult and uncertain about what comes now after the retirement.

At 11:23 September 11 the Mirage took off from Rio Gallegos bound for Tandil. All staff of the Technical Steps and many people in the BAM approached the runway to say good bye. Tears, watery eyes and hugs multiplied, becoming aware that they and Patagonia would not see any more on its skies the Mirage, those steel birds for more than four decades defended with blood and fire the airspace and Argentina's sovereignty.

Two Mirage IIICJs overflying the Andes. [Vcom Maggi]

Squadron 55 pilotos in Mendoza with a Mirage IIICJ.

Fuerza Aérea Argentina Mirages

The Argentine Air Force received during a ten-year period, 1972-1982, a total of 92 Mirage deltas of the following following variants: IIIEA/DA/BA, Dagger A/T, 5P and IIICJ/BJ.

The last were phased out of service in November 2015, and now thanks to the apathy of successive governments, this great South American country does not have any air defence, if we exclude the few operacional A-4AR Fightninghawks armed with "all-aspect" IR-guided AIM-9L Sidewinder air-to-air missiles.

Argentina's farewell to the Mirage

After 43 years of glorious service, despite there's no replacement decided yet, the Argentine Air Force Mirage fleet finally reached the end of their career. On a fully emotive and impressive ceremony and airshow, the Mirages said goodbye on 29 November 2015.

More than forty-three years have passed since on 23 September 1072 the first Mirage IIIEA from a batch of twelve aircraft (ten single seaters and two two-seaters) arrived in Argentina, starting a long and successful career at the

Mara close-up, the RWRs can be appreciated on the nose. [JC Cicalesi]

The four planes that performed the final demonstration, being prepared for the airshow.

VIII Brigada Aérea at Mariano Moreno, Buenos Aires. In 1978 the fleet was augmented by 26 IAI M5 Neshers (Mirage 5s assembled in Israel, including two two-seaters) which entered service at the VI Brigada Aérea in Tandil, Buenos Aires, called IAI M5 Daggers, while seven extra Mirage IIIEAs were purchased. Two extra Mirage IIIDA followed and thirteen extra Daggers (also including two two-seaters).

During the 1982 war with the UK over the Malvinas/ Falkland Islands, the Mirage IIIEAs performed air patrols, with two examples lost on the 1st of May and one pilot killed, while the Daggers flew air patrols and also attacked British ships, damaging eleven ships (of which the HMS Ardent was later sunk by Navy Skyhawks), while they lost eleven planes and five pilots. In the middle of the war, on 4 June, Peru delivered

The Dagger C-426 performing a roll. This is the last Dagger two seater operational from four received from Israel.

ten Mirage VP to cover the Dagger losses, as the main help received by any country during the war. Despite the planes were not sent to fight, as the war finished before they were readied for combat, they remained in service at the VI Brigada Aérea.

In 1983 the fleet was augmented by the last time, with 19 Mirage IIIC and three Mirage IIIB purchased to Israel, of which five were sent to the X Brigada Aérea in Río Gallegos, Santa Cruz, and the others to the IV Brigada Aérea, at Mendoza. In 1986 the Mirage VPs replaced the Mirage IIIC at the X Brigada Aérea, and in 1988 the VIII Brigada Aérea was closed and the Mirage IIIEA/DA were sent to Tandil. In the meantime, the Daggers were modernized to IAI M5 Finger standard, with avionics similar to the Kfir C2, while the Mirage VP were modernized to Mirage 5A Mara standard, with improved avionics.

The Mirage IIIC/B were in poor conditions and flew until 1991, when their unit was disbanded, leaving only one for tests, which flew until 2002. Also, in 1997 the Mirage 5As were sent to Tandil, closing the X Brigada Aérea and leaving the VI Brigada Aérea as the sole Mirage unit.

Replacement plans were developed since the early eighties, first with the SAIA 90 project, which meant the development of an indigenous fighter, but budget cuts starting in 1983 led to the cancelation of the project and, instead, the Fuerza Aérea Argentina (FAA) asked the USA for permission to buy F-16s or, maybe, F/A-18s, but the US government rejected the requirement.

The Mirage 5A serialled C-630 during a roll over the base. Ten Mirage VPs were received from Peru on 4 June 1982 in the middle of the Malvinas / Falklands war.

The Finger serialled C-408 as was painted during the Flaklands/Malvinas war.

Approaching the tarmac for the end of the ceremony.

The Mirage IIIDA serialled I-002, which is the plane with the longest operational time in the FAA, officially delivered to the force in France on 5 February 1972. Received a special colour scheme with the Argentinian flag.

Offers for IAI Kfirs, Mirage 2000s and Mirage F.1s were received through the years, but the budget cuts and lack of political decision postponed a final decision. Also, plans to modernize the Mirage IIIEA fleet and install refuelling probes on them and the Fingers were also cancelled, leaving to a situation in the 2000's when the operational capabilities of the fleet was degraded considerably, as well as the quantity of planes in service.

Finally, the Air Force command decided to retire them anyway, despite the government didn't gave them the budget to buy a replacement, because the planes were obsolete and to keep them operational had almost no sense. After making their last deployment on September 2015, for the Ariete Exercise in Río Gallegos, on 28 November started the first part of the retirement, when the VI Brigada Aérea opened their doors to the public on what in fact was the rehearsal of the final ceremony.

In the end, on 29 November, an impressive but very emotive airshow took place to say goodbye to this old warrior. The stars were five planes of any of the last versions operational, with one Mirage IIIEA (serial I-011), one Mirage IIIDA (I-002), one Mirage 5A Mara (C-630), one IAI M5 Finger (C-408) and one IAI M5 Dagger

two-seater (C-426) performing an incredible presentation, all with special colours. The Finger was painted with the colours used by the Daggers in the 1982 war, the Mara was wearing the colours they had when they arrived from Peru, the Mirage IIIDA received a special scheme with the Argentine flag, while the other two were applied a special scheme on the tail. As the Dagger two seater lost part of it during the rehearsal on Saturday, for the final retirement was wearing a more simple artwork.

Four of them, except the Mirage IIIDA, performed an impressive demonstration, flying the way they became famous, very low. In the end, the Mirage IIIDA made a farewell pass escorted by two IA-63 Pampa 2, as four Pampas were sent to the VI Brigada Aérea to keep the training of the pilots until a replacement arrives.

The airshow also counted with the presence and demonstrations of most of the types of the Argentine Air Force, including also the Pampas, the IA-58 Pucarás, a C-SAR demonstration using a C-130 Hercules, a Bell 212 and two Hughes 500D and other exhibitions by Mi-171, Learjet, Bell 412, Fokker F-27, Saab 340, a Navy Sea King and an interesting static exhibition, with more Air Force aircraft and a newly received Huey 2 of the Gendarmería Nacional.

The final ceremony, held on the late afternoon of the 29th, after the five Mirages stopped their engines, was very moving, with many war veteran pilots and mechanics, including the commander of the Argentine Air Force, Brigadier Mario Callejo, who was a Dagger pilot during the war.

Now the planes were retired and with a new government in Argentina, it's expected a final replacement will be decided soon.

Israeli Shahak and Nesher Aces

The IDF/AF delta pilots were credited with nearly 400 air victories from 1966 to 1979. All shotdowns were achieved during the Six-Day War in June 1967, the War of Attrition from 1969 to 1969 and the of Yom Kippur War in October 1973.

But also they occurred during the numerous border clashes before, between and after those wars. Less than 300 victories were credited to the pilots of Mirage IIIs between 1966 and 1974, the IAI Nesher (Vulture) jockeys received confirmation for more than 100 between 1973 and 1974, and a lone kill was credited to an IAI Kfir (Puppy Leon) pilot in 1979.

The first delta ace

Eleven aerial victories were credited to nine Mirage pilots before the Six-Day War. Five of these nine became aces but won only three full category aces in the Mirage fighter. But none of those pilots was the first Israeli Mirage III as with, at least officially. Israel started the Six-Day War with a successful preemptive strike which reduced the level of the expected Arab air activity, yet the Israeli pilots were engaged in combat with enemy aircraft and initially received accreditation for downing 43 Arab aircraft during this conflict; 28 pilots shared the same.

According to the official Israeli history Giora Rom, 119 Squadron pilot, got five kills between 5 and 7 June 1967, becoming the first Israeli delta ace. Rom shooting down two MiG-21s over the Abu Sueir air base in Egypt on the morning of June 5.

During the afternoon of the same day he got his third victory, also a MiG-21 in a dogfight over the T-4 air base in Syria. Two days later Rom earned his ace status when he downed two Egyptian MiG-17s over Sinai.

On 15 July 1967 Ran Ronen, 119 Squadron C.O. made history when he shot down an Egyptian MiG-21 with a Rafael Shafrir air-to-air missile (AAM). It was the first downing with an AAM in the history of the air war in the Middle East, nor that it was of an infrared missile as

Pilot	Total AA kills	Shahak & Nesher kills	Notes
Epstein Giora	17	17	
Salmon Avraham	14,5	14,5	
Snir Asher	13,5	12	
Baharav Israel	12	12	
Koren Yehuda	10,5	10,5	
Richter Yaakov	10,5	10,5	
Levy Shlomo	10	10	
Karmi Eitan	9	9	Including an AS-5 missile
Harish Dror	9	9	
Marom Oded	8,5	8,5	
Spector Yiftach	12	8	
Gonen Ilan	8	8	perhaps a not officially awared kill
Gil Uri	7,5	7,5	
Ronen Ran	7	7	
Amir Amos	7	7	
Zuk Michael	7	7	
Hertz Moshe	6,5	6,5	
Bar Amos	7	6	
Keidar Yermiyahu	7	6	
Sharon Menachem	6	6	
Even-Nir Uri	6	6	
Menachem Eliyahu	6	6	perhaps a not officially awared kill
Livni Gidon	5,5	5,5	
Rom Giora	5	5	initially he was credited with four kills
Navot Shlomo	5	5	
Shmul Menahem	5	5	
Neuner Ithamar	5	5	
Rozen Reuven	5	5	
Geva Yoram	5	5	
Dror Gideon	5	5	
Gilad Avraham	5	5	
Cohen Ariel	5	5	
Ben-Nun Assaf	5	4	
Dotan Ezra	5	3	
Agmon Yoram	6	2	

The Israeli delta fighter with more shotdowns was the Mirage IIICJ 59, a true creator of aces; eight pilots obtained victories aboard 59, they managed to reach aces or already they already were in 59, at the end of his career it was renumbered 159, being sold in 1982 to Argentina as C-713 and when it was withdrawn from use was sold for a symbolic price for the Israeli aviation museum at Hatzerim. [File Shlomo Aloni]

on 5 June an Egyptian MiG-21 downed an Israel Mirage III (Shahak for the IDF/AF) with an AA-2 Atoll. However it was the first in a long list of victories ccredited to the Rafael family of infrared guided missiles and was the beginning of a revolution in the air war; slowly but gradually the infrared missile supplanted the cannon as the air-to-air main weapon during the last three decades of the last century. After doubling this achievement, Ronen became the second Israeli delta ace. Asher Snir, also of 119 Squadron, followed closely after Ronen, becoming the third ace later the same day, by downing two Egyptian MiG-17.

Pilots of the other two squadrons of IDF/AF Mirage III finally managed to get the title adur-ing the first month of 1970. The first Mirage III kill of 1970 resulted in fourth Israeli delta ace Oded Marom, 101 Squadron C.O. earned his fifth victory on 4 January. Four days later, a pilot from 117 Squadron, Shlomo Navot, shot down a Syrian MiG-21, reaching the "magic" number five. The following four Mirage III pilots became aces aces during the War of Attrition in 1969-1970, these were: Giora Epstein of 101 Squadron on 25 March 1970; Israel Baharav also of 101 Squadron on 27 Marc 1970; Amos Amir, C.O. of 119 Squadron on 2 April 1970 and Avraham Psalm, from the same squadron on the same day. Likewise 117 Squadron added two new aces to his staff on the same day-15 May 1970- totaling the number of delta aces at 11. Yehuda Koren tells us:

"We were on patrol when the GCI controller joined us Sith a a pairo f jets from 119 led by Salmon. They went ahead and we were flying back.

Two frames from the gun camera showing the last moments of a Jordanian Hunter shot down by Ron Ronen, C.O of 119 Squadron on 13 November 1966. Officially Ron Ronen is the second pilot of the IDF/AF to obtain the ace title in the delta fighter on 15 July 1967. He scored seven victories. [Via Shlomo Aloni]

101 Squadron pilots gathered in the alert room during the War of Attrition. Seated left to right: Giora Epstein (17 kills), Yair Sela, Shlomo Levy (10 kills) and Yigal Shochat. Standing left to right: Eitan Ben-Eliyahu, Oded Marom (8.5 sacks) and Israel Baharav (12 kills). [Via Shlomo Aloni]

When we turned southbound I was as a leader and there was a MiG-21, which in my opinion, had not seen me. We were quite into Inchas and Bilbeis areas of Egypt Egypt. I launched the missile from quite a distance, possibly 2,000 meters and usually when you were shooting from an adequate distance missile rocket engine was still running when it slammed into the plane. In this case the propellant was exhausted and thought I had failed, but then came the explosion."

The last Israeli pilot to reach the ace status during the War of Attrition was Yiftach Spector of 101 Squadron, on 10 July 1970, being the twelfth ace.

Yom Kippur delta aces

Almost half of the total victories credited to the Shahaks and Neshers were credited to the four squadrons who flew these delta fighters during the Yom Kippur War of October 193. In

A pilot relaxing besides a QRA Nesher during the Yom Kippur War. Sitting in the cramped cockpit during alamras was not easy and the lucky pilots took off immediately. The less fortunate spent hours in the cockpit and when finally were ordered to scramble, another hour and a half was added n combat air patrol. [File Shlomo Aloni]

The risks of engaging in combat with enemy aircraft over the front line can be seen in the image through the gunsight of a Nesher. Flying low over hostile territory while looking for a samll target exposed the delta fighters to numerous threats: small arms fire, deadly ZSU-23x4 anti-aircraft guns, SA-7 MANPADS and mobile SAM Systems: SA-6, SA-2 and SA-3. [Via Shlomo Aloni]

a space of 19 days, from 6 to 24 October 1973, seventeen other fighter pilots got to be aces.

On the first day of the war, Menachem Shmul, IAI test pilot and reservist posted to 144 Squadron, was the thirteenth delta ace and the first to get that status Turing this conflict, as he tells us:

"My first mission in the Yom Kippur War was actually the first act of war. Patrollin the Sinai when we detect Egyptian aircraft crossing the Suez Canal (to attack Israeli targets in Sinai) and we intercepted them. I knocked down a Su-7 with a Nesher who IAI had delivered a few days before to the squadron. It was not a new Nesher, it was a machine that had been returned to IAI for some kind of work or modification. After it were returned to the squadron they did not have time to boresight the gunsight. I launched ana air-to-air missile and it fell to the ground, the other did not give me a clearlock-on tone, so I had to bring him down with guns. I closed, put the "Pipper" on the Su-7, opened fire and failed. I quickly realized what had happened, because by delivering the jet a few days before and since the procederes for acceptance took several days probably had not calibrated the gunshight. I tried again, this time by eye (the "Fitter" was very close), and got him down."

Three other reservists Delta pilots became aces: Dror Haris, 101 Squadron on 9 October; Ithamar Neuner, 117 Squadron on 12 October and Reuven Rozen, 113 Squadron on 13 October. They were followed by two regular pilots, Menachem Sharon, C.O. of 144 Squadron on 14

Nesher tail number 561 with twelve kills, was the top scorer, eight of them credited to Giora Epstein, the main Israeli ace, during the Yom Kippur War. [Via Shlomo Aloni]

On 8 October 1973 when it was known that Libyan Mirages were operating from Egypt, Israeli delta fighters were painted with yellow triangles framed in black for identification purposes, although the first combat between Israeli and Libyan Mirages did not take place until ten days later. [Via Shlomo Aloni]

October, while Shlomo Levy, Deputy Head of 113 Squadron on October 16, who just recently told us:

"We were on patrol over IDF the corridor, with enormous amount of vehicles which could be distinguished. Just when I thought anyEgiptian attack aircraft, with just opening fire would hit some, the contrller ordered us "Elite, intercept, 270, MiG-17", there were eight MiG-17s in two formations of four at low altitude, We dropped our fuel tanks and we turned right onto the MiG-17. It was amazing how slow flying, perhaps 250 knots. The maneuverability of the MiG-17 at low altitude is fantastic and did not have in it cockpit a "G" indicator, only a warning light that lit at 12 "G" but this does not mean that this is the limit of the plane. Simply that the pilot was able to stay conscious when reaching 12 "G"!.

I stood behind a couple and both separated, so I chased one of them, flying about heading northwest. I opened fire and hit the jet,which began to leave a trail of smoke and just before it slammed into the ground my wingman shouted "Lead behind you!". I looked and saw two MiG-17s in tight formation shooting at me. I was flying at 180 knots and within 300 feet of altitude above the ground. As the MiG turned better my only option was to descend and accelerate, since they did not have air-to-air missiles. I continued turning until getting into a southeast heading, and accelerated, but I felt I was getting too low and could crash. The MiG-17 had an interesting detail, their guns were tilted slightly upward. Usually when an aircraft opened fire and you looked back distinguished the fighter's belly but with the MiG-17you saw the top surfaces due to deflection of the guns. I looked back and saw flashing lights, then saw the explosions of shells in the sand dunes. I looked through the rearview mirror and see a big explosion. I accelerated to 400 knots and began a left turn back to the combat zone, but saw no aircraft, only smoke columns. When I goy closer I could discern on the ground two marks of crashed aircraft, and at the end of each the remains of a MiG-17. It could be that their pilots did no pay attention and crash or as a result of the guns deflection the guns, having descended too when they began to shoot at me."

Michael Zuk, a 101 Squadron pilot won the ace category on 17 October, becoming the nineteenth Israeli delta ace. During the final phase of the war the Arab air activity on the Egyptian front intensified considerably, which was good news for pilots of Israeli Shahaks and NeshersMirage and Nesher Israeli exploited to the maximum the increased oportunidadades to fight enemy aircraft. Ten delta pilots got the ace status during last six days of the war.

The last Israeli delta ace

The average between sorties and effective combat by the delta pilots during the Yom Kippur War was slightly higher than ten to one, and a pilot who had made fifty missions may have participated in five combats. Pilots who were successful were found in the right place at the right time to exploit its opportunities to the fullest. More than a third of the Israeli pilots who participated in the Yom Kippur War were aces, which attests to the high level of training and professionalism.

Combat with fighters reaching Mach 2 following tactics basically inherited from the Second World War would from then this arto f war

Ace Yoram Geva received credit for the first Nesher victory on 8 January 1973, flying Nesher 16. Although both photos show that this machine is armed with Shafrir 2 air-to-air missiles, Geva got his kill with an AIM-9D Sidewinder. [Via Shlomo Aloni]

The entry into service of Shafrir 2 had resulted in a dramatic change in the relationship between gun-missile shotdowns in the missile favour. The only drawback in the operational career of Shafir 2 took place in 1972 when the Mirage managed to bring down Syrian Su-7, while other Mirages succeeded with the AIM-9D. It was concluded that the homing head of Shafrir 2 was optimized to find the heat signature of the MiG-21. The problem was solved and many Shukois were among the victims of Shafrir 2 during the Yom Kippur War. [Via Shlomo Aloni]

Mirage 83 shows a kill mark of victory after the first shotdown by a Shafrir on 15 July 1967 missile, which made Ran Ronen an ace. [Via Shlomo Aloni]

Scramble!. Future ace Giora Epstein climbing up Mirage 52 Mirage armed with a Matra R.530 missile and two 500-litre drop tanks in 1967. (via Shlomo Aloni]

On October 12, 1973 Shlomo Levy, at the controls of Nesher 21 shot down three Syrian Sukhois, two with Shafrir missiles. Six of the ten kills obtained by Lavi were with the Israeli missile, which told us: " I don´t know absolutely nothing about success rates and average firing/hits, I only know that I fired six Shafrir 2 AAMs and got six victories.

would extinguish. The last four Israeli Nesher and Shahak kills Nesher were obtained in April 1974, during border clashes with Syria over control of Mount Hermon. Gidon Livni of 101 Squadron was the last Israeli pilot to obtain the ace title in the Delta fighter, on 29 april 1974, when he shot down a Syrian MiG-21:

"A pilot better remember his mistakes and not the successes. At that dogfight I could have shot down three aircraft but had no luck and brought down only one. Wewere in a long patrol and had almost run out of fuel when we were ordered to perform an interception at high altitude. We did not have enough time to accelerate, dropped our empty external tanks and arrived in the area not too fast. We saw above the MiGs with more advantage than us, so along with my section leader pulled up to reach them, but it was clear that we did not have enough energy (to com-

Detail photo showing Shahak 1(59) kill marks.

plete the maneuver). Then I saw another four MiG flying very fast at higher altitudes. I chased them, about 1,000 meters behind, but flying slower than them. I launched an air-to-air missile but nothing happened. The MiG was on my"Pipper" but the missile had not n detached from its pylon. Immediately after that they disappeared. They were recce MiGs and the others who were in the area were the escort. I went down and saw two planes veering right, but I could not see if they were enemies, so I closed to guns only distance as my missiles did not work. I chased the MiG wingam in trail; after a burst of my 30 mm cannon the Fishbed caught fire, but the pilot ejected and soon after that crashed into the ground. "

Ala No. 11, the Mirage III era

In the late sixties, it became urgent replacement of the already outdated F-86F Sabre, despite years earlier had been modified to carry two air-to-air missiles Sidewinder infrared guided.

So and beginning the policy of diversification in sources of supply of arms, a contract with Avions Marcel Dassault for the purchase of 36 Mirage was signed, comprising 30 IIIEE six IIIDE. In the last week of February 1970, coinciding with the withdrawal of the F 86F, a total of eight experienced pilots and forty special-

Serial 1 (59) was the higher scoring Shahak in the IDF/AF, before being sold to the Fuerza Aérea Argentina in June in order to cover the Falklads War losses (together with 21 more MIrage IIICJ/BJs); fortunately it has been preserved and is back in Israel. It can be seen that it has been reengined with the Snecma Atar 09C.

Mirage IIIEE/DE flight line, 111 Squadron, August 1992.

ists traveled to France, staying in Dijon Longvic making the period of instruction with Escadron de Chasse 2/2 "Côte d'Or ". On April 15, in the same air base located in northeast Frrance, the official ceremony of the first Mirage IIIEE the Air Force took place.

By then the EEs (the second E was for España-Spain), derived directly from the previous Mirage IIIC, was one of the most advanced fighter aircraft; a system of completely integrated weapons, with a Thomson CSF Cyrano IIa multifunction radar, Marconi Elliot doppler navigation system, Thomson CSF97 gunshight, forerunner of actual HUDs) Matra R 530 medium-range air-air missiles (first in Spain, with the possibility to carry electromagnetic or infrared guided homing. Anyway it was a real hall weather fighter, able to act as interceptor even with a SEPR 844 rocket engine to provide greater acceleration and as attack aircraft, bombs of various types, rockets, missiles and special weapons (including the AN 52 tactical nuclear bomb). Moreover, the "Dual Espagne" was a tow seater suitable for operational transformation, lacking the radar and doppler, losing some of their operational capacity, however, still kept its two DEFA 552 30mm

Two Ala 11Mirage IIIEEs in 1983, when they received badges and insignias undersized to make them less conspicuous.

CE.11 and C.11 during a training flight in the fall of 1978.

Mirage IIIEE 112-6 with its original color scheme.

guns with 125 rounds each and the possibility of bringing a pair of Sidewinder missiles.

On June 12, 1970 was a day written with golden letters in the history of Spanish military aviation, the first C.11 eight (the two-seater would be CE.11) landed in Manises Air Base at the controls were the pilots who had made the course in Dijon: Rodriguez, Gallarza, Palacín, Juberías, Guil, Parés, Guallar and Negron. Four departed from the region famous for its mustard and remaining Luxeuil. These brand-new appliances carrying the indication of 101 Squadron, continuing deliveries until 10 October 1972. Just two months after his arrival at Manises, the Mirage started practicisn air-to-ground missions at the Caudé weapons range, while a little later took part in their first "Redeye" air defence exercise.. In late 1970 there are already a dozen machines available, activating the ephemeral and little known 103 Squadron.

For budgetary reasons, the purchase was reduced to 24 single and six two-seaters, although one of the latter (CE.11 16) was lost in accident on December 16, 1970 and replaced by another of the same model, delivered on July 25, 1973. Also cancelled was a flight Simulator, while early in 1973 the recce Mirage IIIR, which also was not purchased, because by then the decision had been made to purchase the Mirage F1, considered the second generation of the French fighter. In May 1971 Ala 11 was reactivated with 111 (replacing 101) and 112 (replacing 103) with the respective radio call signs of "Dollar" and "Ruble" instead of the previous "Gamo". Shortly after the emblems, the 111 is created, it consisted of a hyena with a gag on blue background, with the slogan (in Latin, of course) "Excrementa edit Lacet semel pro anno et Tamen Irridet". While the 112 also had a (more similar to the old emblema of 1st

Mirage IIIEE with a Matra R530 air-to-air missile at the central station.

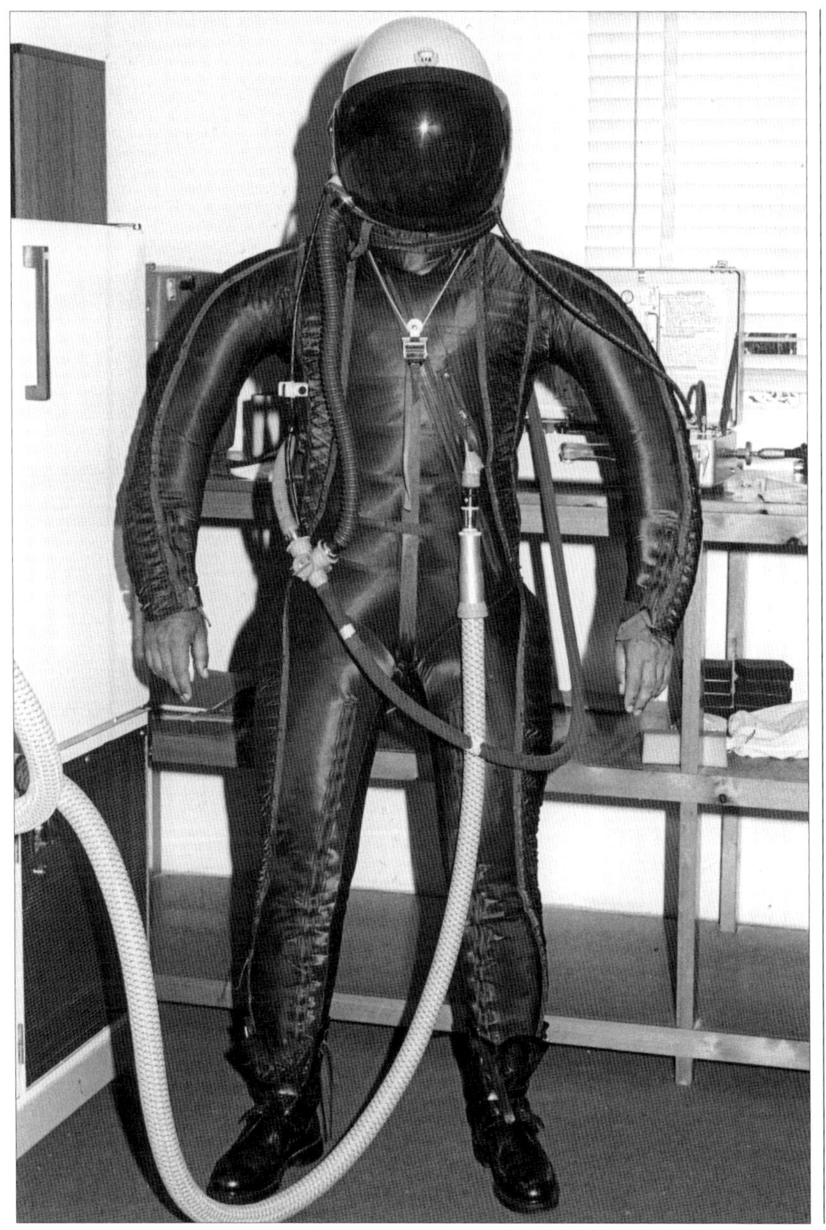

High altitudeflght equipment for the Mirage III pilot. This expensive suit, with the life support system was purchased with rocket engines, especially for high altitude interception using the Matra R530. Neither the suit nor the rocket were never used operationally.

Fighter Wing) muzzled hyena, on red background and the slogan "Do not worth". Previously the "Rubles" had created a logo which was not approved by the command and, on red background, showed a bat (this flying mamman is part of the shield of the city of Valencia), with a Matra R530 in its claws, taking in principle the slogan "Detect, Attack, Destroy", then move to "Do not worth" which would be included in the official.

The Mirage III was a major challenge for mechanics and other personnel specialist unit, while being an aircraft with all-weather capability, pilots should be califica¬dos night flight, performing the prescribed hours instructional plans and training, with the invaluable support of the approach radar (GCA) operators, with equipment from the fifties, have made countless night and in bad weather recoveries, earning the affection of all pilots who have passed through the unit. As the months passed, instructional plans were adapted to the required mission Ala 11, initially 70% of the missions were air to air, though not forgotten the attack, assessing in 1973 the Spanish made bombs by Expal, both low resistance (BR) as parachute retarded (BRP). Until December 31, 1989 11 Wing was part of the permanent QRA service, first with the Air Defense Command and later with the

Ala 11 pilots on January 8, 1992.

Air Combat Command. Two Mirage remained 24 hours a day, 365 days a year fully armed (guns and SideWinder missiles) with its pilots, mechanics and GCA operators ready in case of of "scramble" (for example, in 1982 there were a total of 15 "scrambles"), in half five and thiry minutes during daylight hours anda n hour by night, consisting its mission to identify aircraft that had violated Spanish airspace. Alarm shelters were located in the vicinity of the threshold of runway 30.

The closest was the Ala 11 of a war in the 22 years it operated the Mirage III, it was motivated by the crisis with Morocco because of the Western Sahara. For a week, and in coincidence with the "Green March", eight aircraft and twelve pilots were on alert for possible deployment to the area of operations, which did not occur. However, several months earlier, they had already tested rapid deployment, two Mirage III by each squadron were sent to Gando and El Aaiún airflieds, where they remained for several days.

In October 1982 they conducted the approval tests of the AIM-9P3 and upgrade of the AIM-9J, which in turn was a modernizad first-generation AIM-9B, with AIM 9P3 modernization 9J turn an AIM 9B with improvements in its guidance capability, range and proximity fuze. In October 1986 serveral Matra R530 missiles

111 Squadron pilotos besides C.11-17, on April 4, 1991.

C.11 instrument panel in the center is the radar display.

were fired (du to its inminente withdrawal from service) against reflective targets, launched fom an C212 Aviocar Light transport, and according to Jesús Romero, the CO of 111 Squadron one of the participants in these exercises, it was quite spectacular to watch as several seconds after pressing the trigger, the R530 appeared in front of the nose, leaving behind a huge trail of white smoke, as it sped toward its target, previously engaged by the radar Cyrano IIa.

End of an era

After the cancellation of the Mirage III upgrade programme (called C.11M), which would have meant a second youth for the French delta, mainly due to the bitter dissension between CASA and Ceslesa, despite the important investment already done, but also because of the severe budget cuts, both the Ministry of Defense and the Air Force decided not to spend a penny more on these aircraft, discarding the second

October 1, 1992, the Mirage F1 took over from the Mirage III at Ala 11.

general overhaul (GV 2) to be carried out in France, so that according to initial estimates, the Mirage III should have been removed on June 30, 1992, subsequently postponed to October 1. During those 22 years and four months, "the flat irons" (as affectionately was called in Manises the Mirage III by the shape of their planes) recorded some eighty thousand hours of flight, with a negative blanace eight aircraft destroyed in accidents and only two dead pilots. It was comparing to other users of this French fighter, which in certain areas of its flight envelope, was difficult, an extraordinary safety record. Moreover, the fleet availability was very good during their stay in Manises, with small bumps, as the end of the last decade, when spare parts were scarce, as had previously been stopped buying, calculating that the Mirage III would be discharged after the entry into service of the F-18 Hornet, another serious moment was related to fatigue problems with blades in one of the compressors of the turbojet SNECMA Atar 9C. Otherwise they were always in a creditable job for all kinds of exercises and maneuvers, including the latest Poopdeck with the Sixth Fleet of the US Navy, in June 1992, which for several aerial combat (simulated) put to embarrass several F-14B Tomcat aircraft from the carrier USS Saratoga, veterans of operation Desert Storm, it was a fitting climax to a brilliant career.

With the launch of the failed modernization and transfer of aircraft to Getafe, 112 Squadron passed away on December 31, 1989, it was a memorable day full of Jokes typical of Manises fighter, indeed, as in most of his colleagues across this planet. In those years, 75% of the missions of Ala 11 were air to surface, reflecting what will be the future with the modernized system, but when it was canceled and learned of the future mount 111 Squadron, missions changed toa ir-to-air in the same proportion. The last CO of the "Dollars" with the Mirage III was Major Javier Muñoz Castresana (2,500 flying hours in the C/CE.11), while Col. José Luis Martínez Esteban replaced Colonel Enrique Sacanell Apodaca as head of Ala 11 both had an outstanding and meritorious work in the concluding the Mirage III chapter. The last night flight took place on September 29, four aircraft plus two reserves, held mutual interceptions, using the radar, either independently or with the support of the Central Command Group and support, always under the eyes (electronic) "Pegasus". The next day was the last day of operational activity with the Mirage III, 111 Squadron had scheduled five sorties, most of bombing and shooting at the Caudé range. All aircraft worked perfectly without any discrepancy.

Farewell to a classic

On October 1, 1992 was the sad day that many will remember forever, that bright day of Valencia's warm autumn, the Mirage III and its pilots made an emotional farewell, participating eight Mirage III in a vibrant show, along with aircraft from other units and the first six Mirage F1s for the squadron. During this exhibition, which was chaired by General Chief of Air Command Levante, Lieutenant Colonel Joaquin Sanchez Diaz, head of the Oprations Group, he conducted a demonstration of virtuosity at the controls of his Mirage III. Both formations of 111 Squadron were formed by the following aircraft and pilots.

The final jets for Ala 11 aircraft, would be the Mirage F1EDA/DDAs bought to the Emirate of Qatar, the first arriving in August 2004, but in September 2008 when 11 Sqn had his full complement, Ala 11 was deactivated and Manises air base closed. However this historic unit would be reactivated at Morón air base, Sevilla, months later, initially equipped with F/A-18A Hornets, and in 2004 to begin receiving the advanced Eurofighter Typhoon.

ISMIR-NT-1495-1-AB91-S
ABRIL-1991

PERFIL TIPO: CAP / FS

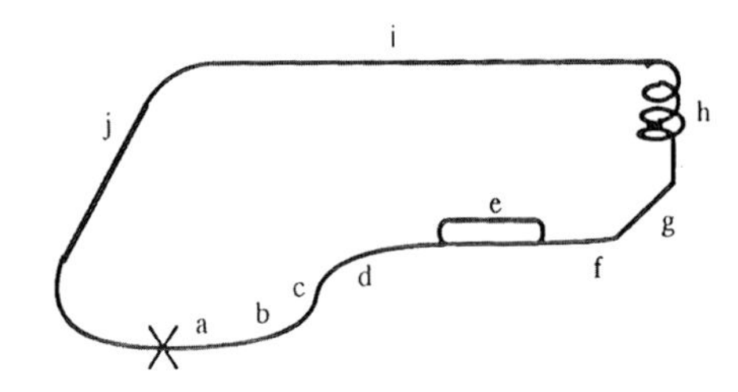

CONFIGURACION TIPO:

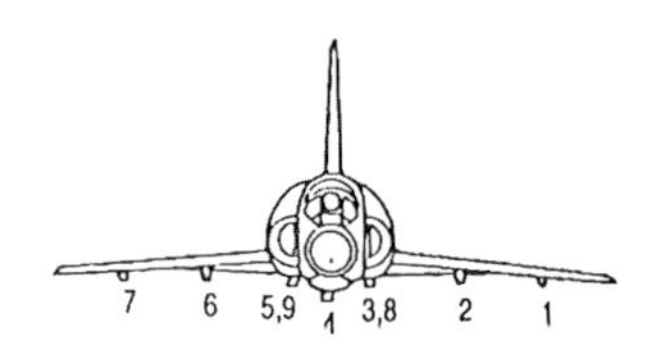

2 cañones DEFA de 30 mm. (250 cartuchos)

1 y 7: Misil Sidewinder AIM-9

6 y 2: Depósito de 500 litros.

CONFIGURACION DE REGRESO:

6 y 2: Depósito de 500 litros.

- A.11 -

<u>MIRAGE III</u>
C.11-18 Tcol Díaz (líder) "dólar 01"
C.11-8 Comdte Núñez,"dólar 02"
C.11-4 Cap Elices, "dólar 03"
C.11-10 Cap Quintana, "dólar 04"
CE.11-25 Cap Perelló/Ten Suevos, "dólar 05"
C.11-24 Ten Ruíz, "dólar 06"
CE.11-28 Comdte Moreno/Cap Sastre, "dólar 07"
CE.11-29 Comdte Lorenzo/Cap Pinilla, "dólar 08"
<u>MIRAGE F1</u>
C.14-34 Cap Albalat, "dólar 51"
C.14-01 Ten Haya, "dólar 52"
C.14-13 Ten Lardíes, "dólar 53"
C.14-50 Cap Bas, "dólar 54"
C.14-17 Cap Riego, "dólar 55"
C.14-22 Cap Serrano, "dólar 56"

After landing, the Mirage III and F1s formed two lines facing each other, except C.11-18 and C.14-34 parked between them. Pilots and mechanics of the "old" 111 formed on the side of 18 and the "new" at 34, the Colonel addressed a few words extolling the 22 years of service of Mirage III and welcoming to F1. Then three veterans placed a laurel wreath to C.11-18, along with the simple caption "Adiós Plancheta" they were Major Moreno (1.700 flight hours on the plane); Lieutenant Soret, GCA controller (12,000 approaches) and Second Lieutenant Idelfonso, a specialist with 21 years of service in Manises. Colonel Esteban then doused with champagne as a welcome and good luck symbol Mirage F1CE C.14-34 .

The 14 Mirage III remaining in Manises were transferred in flight to Getafe from 14 to 23 October 1992. About the "new" 111 Squadron, seven of its pilots were former Mirage III drivers.

The Mirage IIIs recorded a total of 80.512,25 flight hours in Manises in 75,172 sorties.

Failed upgrade

In July 1991, two years and eight months after the signing of the contract for the upgrade of eighteen Mirage IIIEs and five Mirage IIIDEs the programme was cancelled by the Ministry of Defence, when seven aircraft were more or less involved in the same and when it had been spent more than a quarter of the2 3,000 million pesetas budgeted. The cancellation was due, according to the Ministry, the inability and huge problems between the two awardees companies, CASA and CESELSA (who had formed a joint venture called ATTORN SA, not budget cuts. It could have been a very important experience for Spanish industry, as advance the modernization of Mirage F1 and the Air Force itself, although it must be remembered that if this programme had been commissioned to Dassault or Israel Aircraft Industries, the history of Wing No. 11 and Manises air base, would have been very different from what it was during the next seven years.

Despite this tremendous frustration, it is worth disaggregate what could have been but was not, the upgrade of the Mirage III in the "Super Plancheta". So the work as split into three main aspects:

Airframe:

Major inspection

-Deep airframe inspection.

-Removal and accesories inspection

-Alignment and calibration of equipment and instruments

-Scrape and painting

-Assembly and adjust equipment accessories and instruments (refuelling system including probes, single point ground pressure reflueling system, modification

/extension of the nose, four additional weapon stations -3, 5, 8 and 9

Life extension

-Repair and/or replacement of wing ribs ribs

-New location of drain holes

-Inspection the main spar of the plane

-Assembly with interference fit bushings

-Extension Life in 2,500 additional flying hours.

Avionics

- AN/AYK-14 mission computer (from the F-18A)

- Inertial Navigator

-Converter Central Inertial Navigation data

-ALR-300 radar warning receiver

-AN/ALE-40 radar and IR decoy

-ECM radar jammer

-Weapons Management System

-AN/APQ-159 multipurpose radar

-IFF/SIF

-VHF/UHF radios

-HUD – (Head-up-Display)

-UFC (Up Front Control)

ISMIR-NT-1495-1-AB91-S
ABRIL-1991

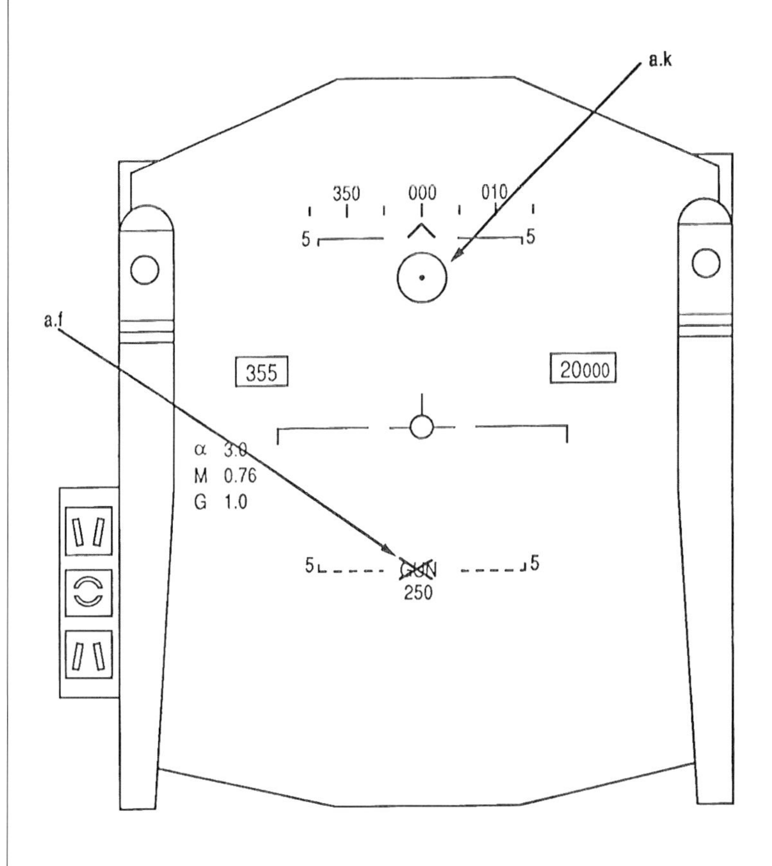

FIGURA 5.2.5

PAGINA CAÑON SIN SEGUIMIENTO RADAR

- 5.39 -

-Two multifunction displays

-New instrumentation

-HOTAS Control system

-Equipment integration with digital bus MILSTD 1553B.

Armament

Increased capacity and diversity of stores carried:

-AIM-9L/AIM-9JULI SidewinderAAM

-AGM-65G Maverick AGM

-AGM-88 HARM

-Paveway laser-guided bombs

-Laser designating pod

-ECM pod

MIRAGE III E SNA

Fig. 29 — VISOR
CABEZA DEL VISOR CON REGISTRADOR DE PUNTERIA

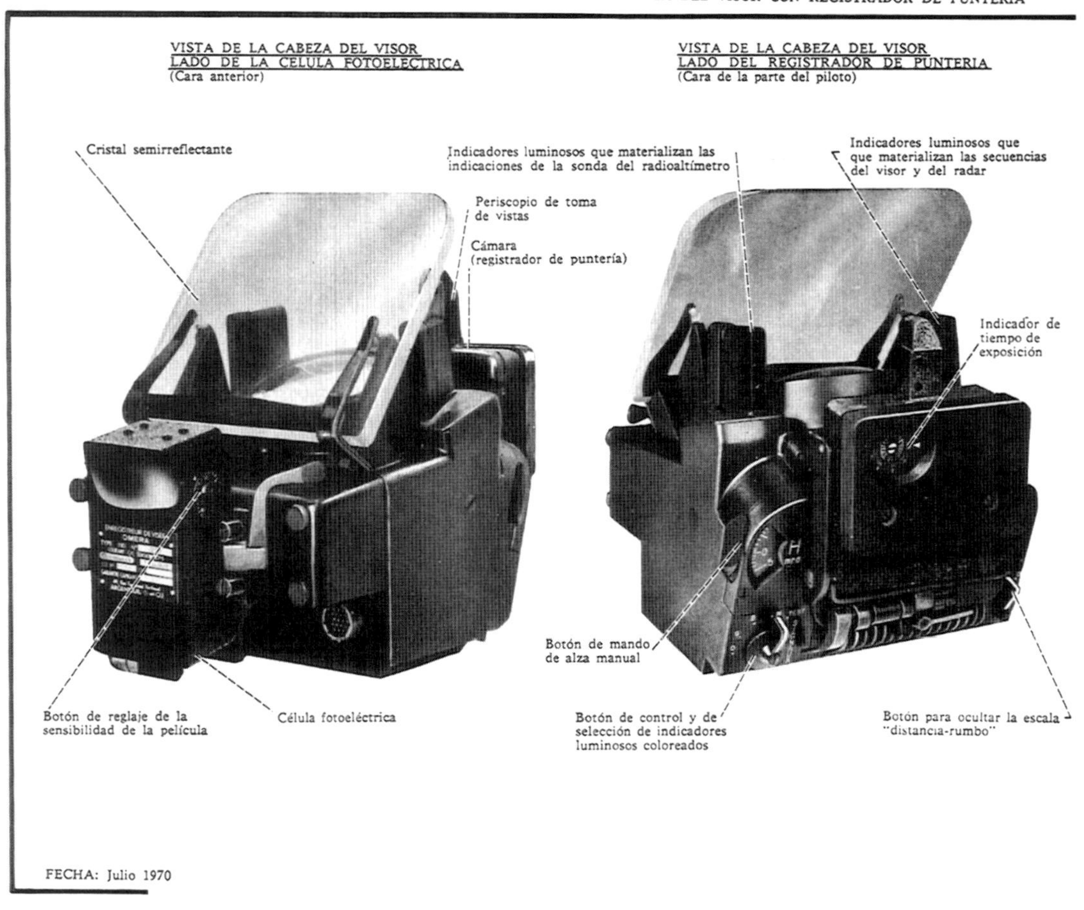

FECHA: Julio 1970

MIRAGE III BE

MISILE SIDE WINDER

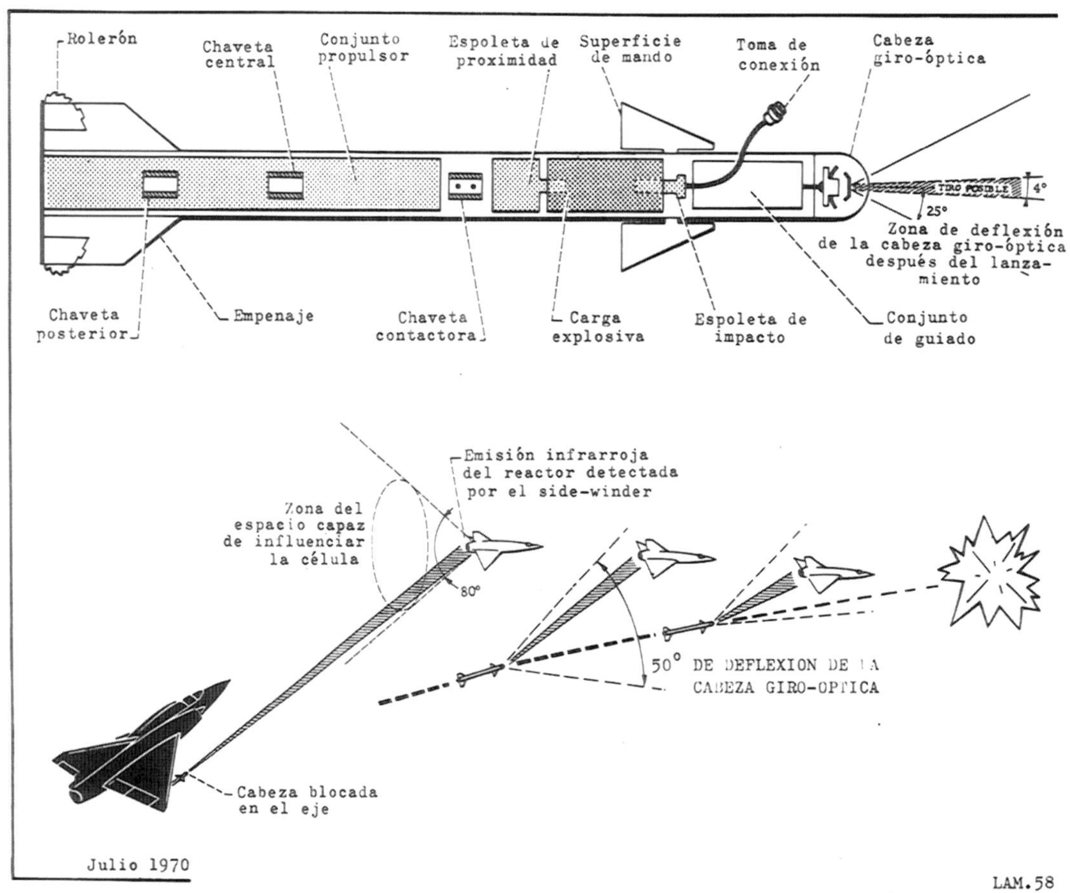

Julio 1970

LAM.58

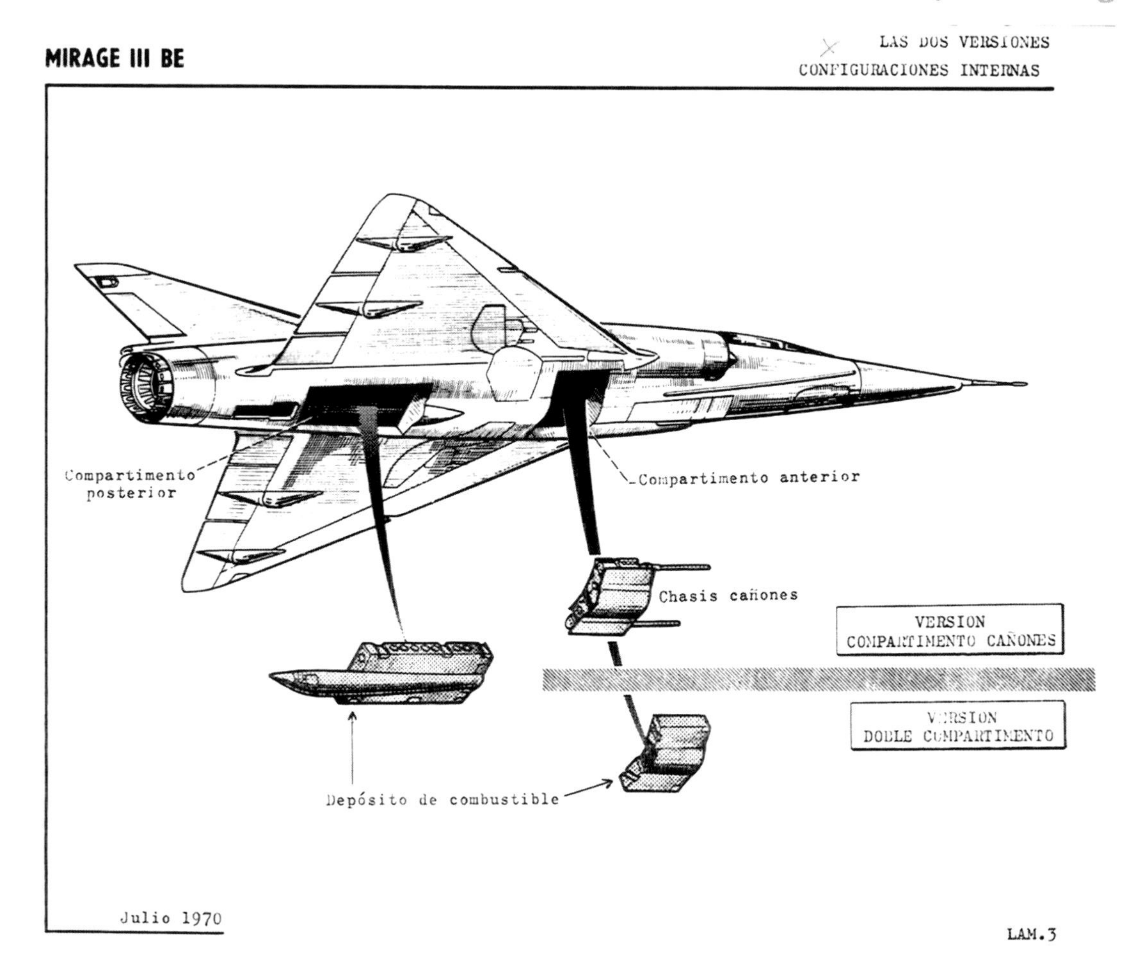
MIRAGE III BE
LAS DOS VERSIONES
CONFIGURACIONES INTERNAS
Compartimento posterior
Compartimento anterior
Chasis cañones
VERSION COMPARTIMENTO CAÑONES
VERSION DOBLE COMPARTIMENTO
Depósito de combustible
Julio 1970
LAM.3

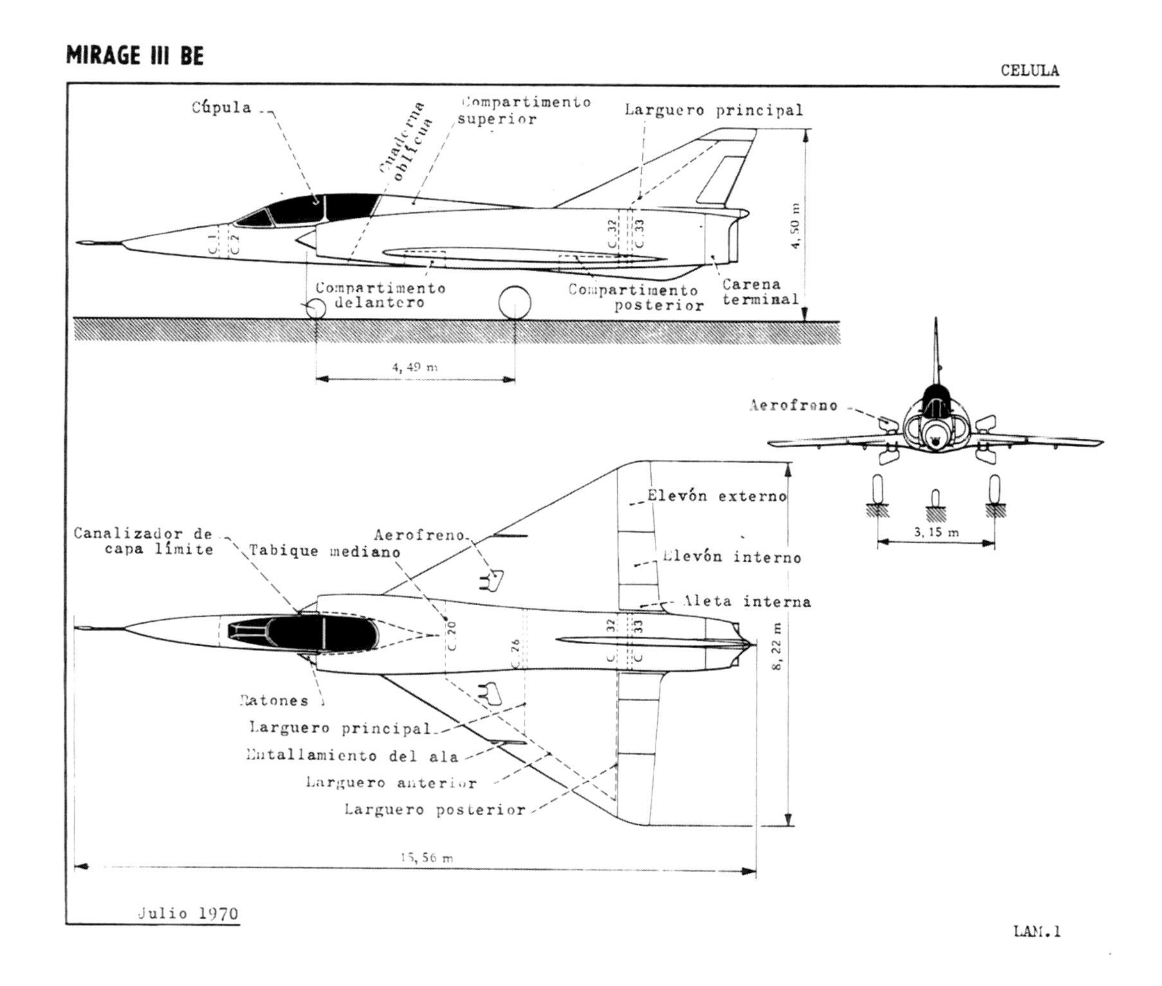
MIRAGE III BE
CELULA
Cúpula
Cuaderna oblicua
Compartimento superior
Larguero principal
4,50 m
Compartimento delantero
Compartimento posterior
Carena terminal
4,49 m
Aerofreno
3,15 m
Elevón externo
Canalizador de capa límite
Tabique mediano
Aerofreno
Elevón interno
Aleta interna
8,22 m
Ratones
Larguero principal
Entallamiento del ala
Larguero anterior
Larguero posterior
15,56 m
Julio 1970
LAM.1

MIRAGE III BE

LAS CARGAS EXTERIORES
CONFIGURACIONES EXTERNAS

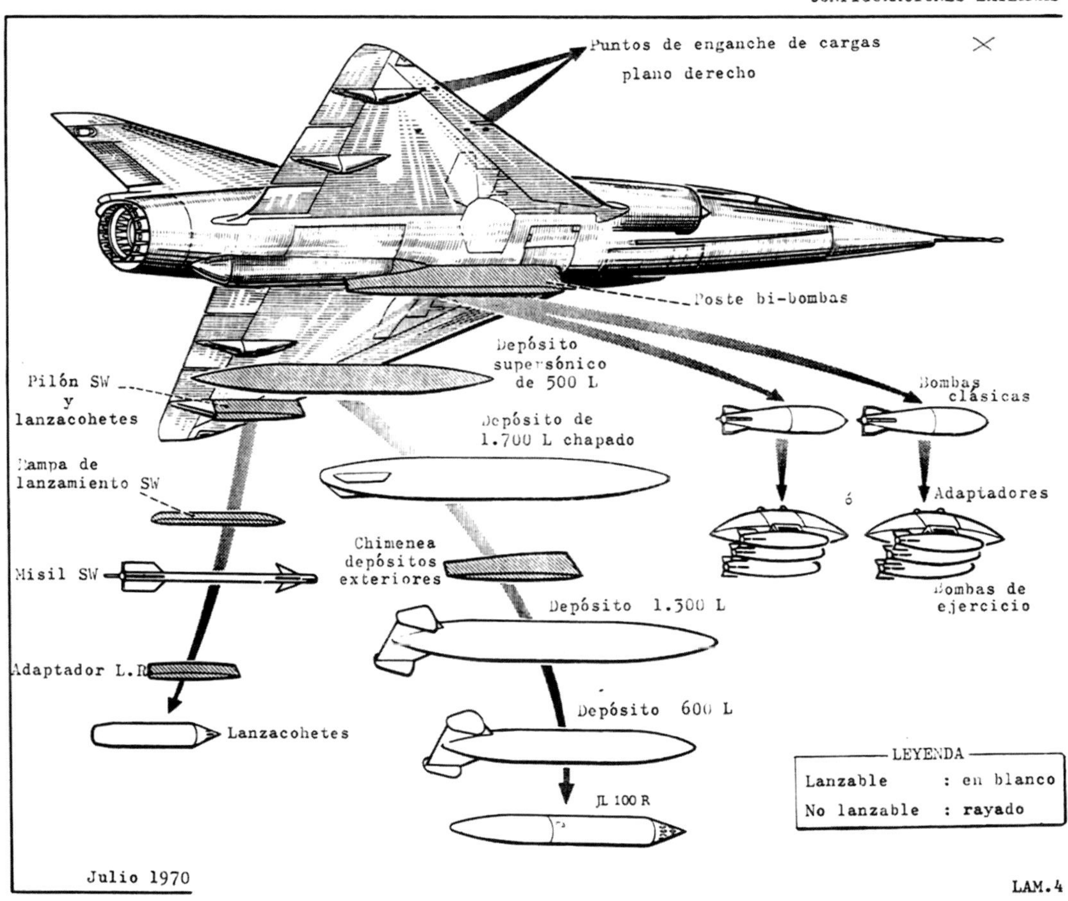

MIRAGE III BE

TABLERO DE A BORDO POSTERIOR

Reloj
Pulsador comproba ción incidencia
Indicador de ruta
Indicador fuego PC
Anemomachmetro
Indicador fuego reactor
Indicador aerofrenos
Altímetro
Variómetro
Indicador tren no fuera
Mando desembrague emergencia A/C (automando)
Tablero control tren
Pulsad. lanzam. cargas: Dep.Ext. / Ala / Fuselaje
Horizonte tonó
Horizonte
*Ajuste del palonier
Caja de conmutación radio

Indicador de incidencia
Indicador ratones
Indicador límite avión
Perfora-dinghy
Acelerómetro
Señalador rumbo marcación
Indicador guiador
Indicador 600 l
*Pulsador cese avisador sonoro
Contador combustible
Tacómetro
Tablero de averías
Indicador inyección PC
Indicador funcionamiento PC
Selector presiones hidráulicas
Manómetro presiones hidráulicas
Totalizador
Indicador temperatura tobera
Indicador de trasvase
Cuchillo rompe-cúpula

Julio 1970

*Instrumentos exclusivos de esta cabina

LAM.11

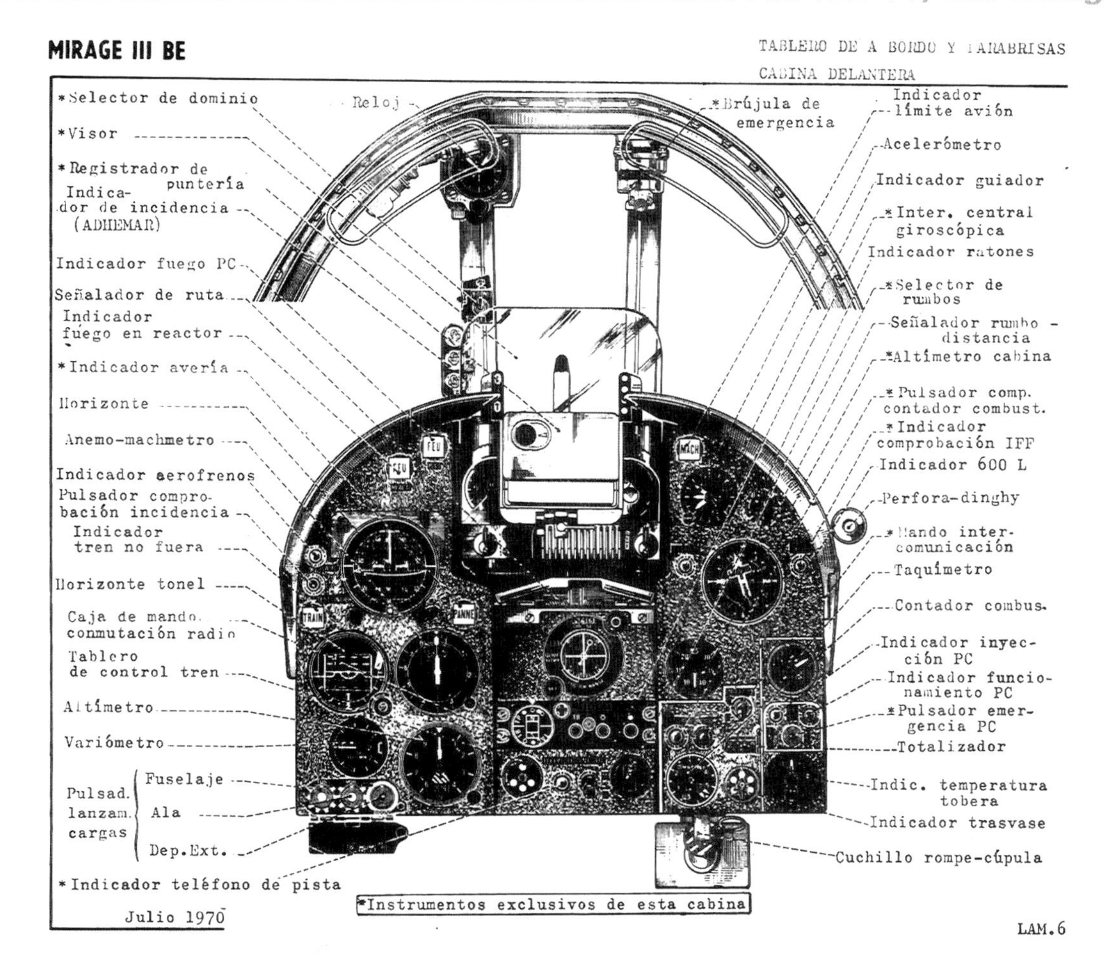
MIRAGE III BE
TABLERO DE A BORDO Y PARABRISAS
CABINA DELANTERA
*Selector de dominio
*Visor
*Registrador de puntería
Indicador de incidencia (ADHEMAR)
Indicador fuego PC
Señalador de ruta
Indicador fuego en reactor
*Indicador avería
Horizonte
Anemo-machmetro
Indicador aerofrenos
Pulsador comprobación incidencia
Indicador tren no fuera
Horizonte tonel
Caja de mando conmutación radio
Tablero de control tren
Altímetro
Variómetro
Pulsad. lanzam. cargas
Fuselaje
Ala
Dep.Ext.
*Indicador teléfono de pista
Julio 1970
Reloj
*Brújula de emergencia
Indicador límite avión
Acelerómetro
Indicador guiador
*Inter. central giroscópica
Indicador ratones
*Selector de rumbos
Señalador rumbo - distancia
*Altímetro cabina
*Pulsador comp. contador combust.
*Indicador comprobación IFF
Indicador 600 L
Perfora-dinghy
*Mando intercomunicación
Taquímetro
Contador combus.
Indicador inyección PC
Indicador funcionamiento PC
*Pulsador emergencia PC
Totalizador
Indic. temperatura tobera
Indicador trasvase
Cuchillo rompe-cúpula
*Instrumentos exclusivos de esta cabina
LAM.6

The cancellation of the Spanish MIrage III upgrade programme si nified the end for theses sleek fighters in ala 11 service, and the jets were withdrawn from service on October 1, 1992. [S. Mafé]

The Spanish Mirage IIIEE/DE fleet was coded as C.11 for the fighter (C meaning Caza – Fighter) and CE.11 for the trainer (CE – Caza Escuela – Fighter Trainer). [S. Mafé]

At the end of its operational life the surviving Mirage IIIEE/DEs were integrated in 111 Escuadron, the flying component of ala 11, call sign "Dólar". Actually, 111 Escuadrón (as well as Ala 11) fly the Eurofighter Typhoon from Morón air base, near Seville, while Manises air base, closet o Valencia, closed down as a military airflied in 1999. [S. Mafé]

Painted by Bill Dady

Dassault Mirage IIICJ – 101 Squadron Israeli Defence Force 1967

Painted by Javier "Javo" Ruberto

Dassault Mirage III CJ "Shahak" 768. 119 Squadron "Ha'Atalef". Tel Nof Air Base - June 1967

Aboard "Shahak" 768, an Argentine naturalizad Israeli pilot, won two of his four victories in aerial combat on Egyptian opponents in the Six-Day War performing combat air patrols over the Sinai Peninsula.

Dassault Mirage III EE - s / n 631 - C.11-23. Ala 11, 111 Squadron "Dollar". Manises Air Base, Spain - 1976

Delivered in 1970, the first generation Mirages performed 22 years of valuable service in the *Ejército del Aire* providing protection to the Spanish skies.

Painted by Javier "Javo" Ruberto

IAI Nesher / Dagger - # 592. 101 Sqn "First Jet Squadron", IADFAF. Eitam base 1978

In the late-70s the Argentina Air Force acquired 39 Israeli IAI Neshers, which after upgrades and refurbishement became the Dagger. In the illustration we see one of the jets used for conversión flights for the Argentine pilotos at Eitan air base.

IAI Dagger A - (c / n S-38) C-420. Fighter Group 6 - Airmobile Squadron II (The Marinete) San Julian - May 1982

On 29 May, integrating Squadron "Puma" and piloted by First Lieutenant Mario Callejo, was to attack British positions. On Peblle Island, the leader of the formation sighted a Sea Harrier CAP that went to intercept and was was ordered to eject the stores and applying afterburner turn on the left to avoid the impact of missiles had been launched against them.

Painted by Javier "Javo" Ruberto

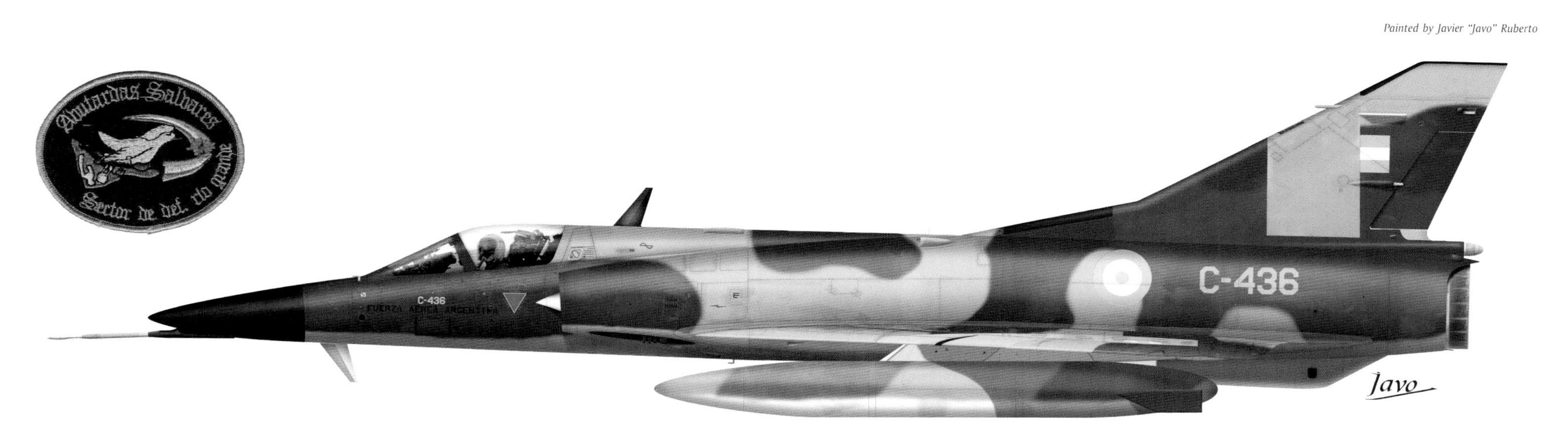

IAI Dagger A - (c / n S-29) C-436. Fighter Group 6 - I Airmobile Squadron (Wild Bustards) Rio Grande air base - May 1982.

One of the 39 IAI Dagger purchased from Israel in 1978, deployed south on April 6, being piloted this time by Captain Carlos "Talo" Moreno on 14 missions during the conflicto, and was the first pilot to fly over the Falkland Islands. On May 21, Lieutenant Juan Domingo "Pollo" Bernhardt piloting C-436 attacked the frigate HMS Ardent. On May 29, on this plane, Lieutenant Bernhardt would be shot down and killed by a Rapier missile while on a mission to attack naval targets in San Carlos Sound. Dagger C-436 performed seven missions during the Falklands War.

Dassault Mirage III CJ "Shahak" (c / n CJ14) C-704. Fighter Squadron X - X Air Brigade. Rio Gallegos 1985

Entered service with the Argentine Air Force after the Falklands War being deployed to Rio Gallegos Air Base where it flew until 1986. A Veteran of the Six-Day and Yom Kippur wars, is currently displayed with the camouflage scheme of an IAI Dagger in the city of Tres Arroyos as a tribute to First Lieutenant Volponi

Painted by Javier "Javo" Ruberto

Dassault Mirage III EA - (. C / n 4F / 4D) I-006. Squadron II Air Group 6 Game - Tandil, Buenos Aires -1997

For the 25th anniversary of the commissioning of the Mirage III EA, a colorful paint scheme in shades of blue was applied to I-006 with which would fly until receiving the gray air superiority applied to all aircraft of the Mirage family.